Network Security:
A Practical Approach

Jan L. Harrington

ELSEVIER

AMSTERDAM • BOSTON • HEIDELBERG • LONDON
NEW YORK • OXFORD • PARIS • SAN DIEGO
SAN FRANCISCO • SINGAPORE • SYDNEY • TOKYO
Morgan Kaufmann is an imprint of Elsevier

MORGAN KAUFMANN PUBLISHERS

Publishing Director	Diane Cerra
Acquisitions Editor	Rick Adams
Publishing Services Manager	Simon Crump
Project Manager	Sarah Hajduk
Assistant Editor	Mona Buehler
Design, Composition, and Illustration	Black Gryphon Ltd.
Copyeditor	Adrienne Rebello
Proofreader	Broccoli Information Management
Cover Design	Yvo Riezbos Design
Cover Image	Internet Security. Courtesy of Photodisc Green and Getty Images
Interior printer	The Maple-Vail Book Manufacturing Group
Cover printer	Phoenix Color

Morgan Kaufmann Publishers is an imprint of Elsevier.
500 Sansome Street, Suite 400, San Francisco, CA 94111

This book is printed on acid-free paper.

Library of Congress Cataloging-in-Publication Data
APPLICATION SUBMITTED

ISBN: 0-12-311633-3
For information on all Morgan Kaufmann publications,
visit our Web site at www.mkp.com or www.books.elsevier.com

Printed in the United States of America
05 04 03 02 01   5 4 3 2 1

Netw
A Pra

Contents

Preface

There is a funny saying that surfaces every once in a while: "Just because you're paranoid doesn't mean that they aren't out to get you!" If this describes the way you think about the security of the computers in your care and you're relatively new to computer security, then you're holding the right book.

Let's be honest: It seems like there are a million and two computer security books on bookstore shelves and listed at places like amazon.com. Why should you spend your hard-earned dollars (or your employer's hard-earned dollars, whichever the case may be) on this one? Well, maybe you should and maybe you shouldn't. Seem like a strange thing for an author to say? Not really, because not all security books are alike and not every book contains what you might need.

If you're looking for something that can double as a hacker's manual, then you've come to the wrong place. However, if you have a background in computer networking but are new to computer security and want a practical approach to how you can secure your network, then this book is for you. You will need a basic understanding of local area networks (LANs)(especially Ethernet), how LANs are connected to wide area networks, and how the Internet fits into an overall network architecture. You should be familiar with network interconnection hardware, such as routers and switches, and the types of transmission media that are used to create networks.

xii   Preface

This book is written in a casual style that's easy to read and understand—there are even cartoons on the first page of every chapter—but it isn't full of the fluff you might find in a magazine column. Instead of smart-aleck comments, you'll find a wealth of information about planning for security, managing security, the ways in which system crackers gain access to your network, and strategies for securing your network resources against attack.

Most people want concrete security information they can use. There are two features of this book that bring that right to you. First, all the chapters (except Chapter 1) end with a Hands On section that gives you specific techniques for implementing the concepts covered in the first part of the chapter. Second, you'll find little gray boxes scattered throughout the book, most of which start with "Reality Check." A reality check is a way of bringing the real world into focus, cutting through the platitudes and generalities that often appear in introductory security books.

How This Book Is Organized

So much of what we do in computing requires trade-offs, where a choice of one option limits what we can do somewhere else. For example, if you want to design a computer, the choices you make about the CPU determine the size of the system bus you can use and the amount of memory you can address. All those things are interconnected, and to do a good hardware design, you need to understand the impact of one decision on the other parts of the machine. Designing a secure network is the same: You need to understand the interaction of security measures and network usability. Choices you make for one can constrain the choices you have for the other.

So, where do you start? You can start at the bottom, working on securing each workstation on your network and then moving up to the servers and finally to your connection to the Internet. However, in most cases this results in a hodgepodge of security measures that aren't effective, either in terms of providing an adequate security net for your network or in terms of cost. A top-down approach, where you plan security well, is almost always more effective.

Therefore, this book begins with a look at security policies and at auditing compliance to such policies. Chapter 1 also presents an overview of the major laws that may affect how you need to secure the data stored on organizational servers.

Chapter 2 covers basic network layout options for handling security. You'll be introduced to firewalls and DMZs as well as methods of providing basic security through operating system file and directory permissions.

Chapter 3 then turns to physical security, the process of protecting your hardware from unwanted access. You'll read about securing networks against theft and vandalism, protecting server consoles, and handling backup.

Chapters 4 through 7 cover techniques external system crackers use to gain unauthorized access to network resources, including information gathering (including social engineering attacks where system crackers pretend to be someone they aren't), network attacks that can give them root access to servers or workstations, spoofing (where system crackers forge messages to make them appear to come from a trusted source), and denial of service attacks (through which system crackers prevent legitimate users from accessing network resources). Each chapter describes typical attacks and includes methods for safeguarding your network against such attacks.

Chapter 8 looks at malware, those nasty viruses, worms, and other junk that seem to appear out of nowhere. The constantly escalating war between virus detection software developers and the malware writers gives none of us any rest.

In Chapter 9, you'll find information about password security. As much as we would like to think that we have better user identification techniques, the combination of a user name and password is still the major way of identifying a user to a network. And once someone supplies a matching user name and password, the network gives the person access to all network resources associated with that user name.

Chapter 10 deals with remote users and covers additional ways of authenticating users beyond a simple user name and password. You'll also find discussions of VPNs (Virtual Private Networks) in Chapter 10.

Wireless networks are becoming more and more popular, especially as the speed of wireless transmissions increases. Unfortunately, wireless networks are also notoriously insecure. Chapter 11 therefore looks at the current state of wireless security and also discusses some forthcoming wireless security technologies.

Chapter 12 covers one of my favorite topics: encryption. Encryption makes it extremely difficult for anyone without the proper decryption key to understand the content of a message. And as computing power increases, so does the sophistication of the types of encryption we use. Along with encryption techniques, Chapter 12 also provides an overview of digital signatures and digital certificates that can certify message integrity and message authenticity.

The Software

There is a *lot* of security hardware and software out there, and it's always hard to decide what to cover in a book of this type. Wherever possible, I've tried to cover open source software solutions. Much of the open source software is very robust and very widely used. However, there are also some widely used commercial products about which you should be aware. A mention in this book isn't necessarily an endorsement of a particular commercial product, but it is an acknowledgement that the product is widely used.

The Platforms

I admit it—I'm a Macintosh fanatic, and have been since March of 1984. But that doesn't mean that I'm blind to what's really out there. This book therefore looks at the two major operating system environments: Windows and UNIX. (And, yes, Mac OS X is in there, too. It's UNIX, for heavens sake!) Let's be honest. If you don't want Windows, you can have UNIX, and if you don't want UNIX, you can have Windows.... There are other operating systems (for example, BeOS), but none except Windows and UNIX have wide enough distribution to be the target of system crackers.

Reality Check: If you're using something other than Windows or UNIX, then you don't have a lot to worry about in terms of most software attacks on your network. However, you should still be concerned about social engineering attacks, physical attacks, denial of service attacks, and spoofing. Having a less widely used operating system doesn't get you off the hook where security is concerned!

Acknowledgments

I'd like to thank the following people who made this book possible:

- ◆ Rick Adams and Mona Buehler, the editorial team at Morgan Kaufmann
- ◆ Sarah Hajduk, the production manager
- ◆ Adrienne Rebello, my favorite copy editor in the whole wide world
- ◆ James Jepson, who provided the Mac OS X Server screen shots
- ◆ The knowledgeable reviewers:
  - Brian D. Jaffe
  - Richard Newman
  - Rodney Pieper
  - John Rittinghouse

Thanks, everyone!

JLH

Chapter 1: In the Beginning ...

In This Chapter

- ♦ The internal and external views of network security
- ♦ Sources of external threats
- ♦ Sources of internal threats
- ♦ General defensive techniques
- ♦ Security policies
- ♦ Security audits and vulnerability testing
- ♦ Ongoing security activities

1.0 Introduction

If you were to talk with someone whose job it is to implement network security, you would hear a lot about buffer overflows, vendor patches, denial of service attacks, and so on. But network security is much broader than the details of attacks and defenses against them. A good network security scheme begins at the top of an organization, with extensive planning to determine where the organization should be concentrating its security efforts and money.

In this chapter, you will be introduced to many of the basic concepts behind a security strategy, including the general sources of security threats (to give you a framework for formulating a security policy) and the role of organizational security policies. The chapter concludes by looking at the concepts behind a security audit to check compliance with security policies as well as the actual security of the network.

1.1 Defining Security

Network security is a very broad term. In its fullest sense, it means protecting data that are stored on or that travel over a network against both accidental and intentional unauthorized disclosure or modification. The most often overlooked part of this definition is that it includes accidental occurrences, such as an inadequately debugged application program that damages data.

Another way to look at security is to consider the difference between security and privacy. *Privacy* is the need to restrict access to data, whether it be trade secrets or personal information that by law must be kept private. Security is what you do to ensure privacy.

Many people view network security as having three goals:

♦ Confidentiality: Ensuring that data that must be kept private, stay private.

♦ Integrity: Ensuring that data are accurate. For a security professional, this means that data must be protected from unauthorized modification and/or destruction.

♦ Availability: Ensuring that data are accessible whenever needed by the organization. This implies protecting the network from anything that would make it unavailable, including such events as power outages.

1.2 The Two Views of Network Security

The popular media would have you believe that the cause of most network security problems is the "hacker." However, if you ask people actually working in the field, they will tell you that nearly half the security breaches they encounter come from sources internal to an organization, and, in particular, employees. This means that it won't be sufficient to secure a network against external intrusion attempts; you must pay as much attention to what is occurring within your organization as you do to external threats.

1.2.1 Sources of External Threats

The Internet has been both a blessing and a curse to those who rely on computer networks to keep an organization in business. The global network has made it possible for potential customers, customers, and employees to reach an organization through its Web site. But with this new access have come the enormous problems caused by individuals and groups attempting illegal entry into computer networks and the computer systems they support.

Hackers and Crackers

External threats are initiated by people known in the hacking community as *crackers*. Initially, the term *hacker* referred to someone who could write an ingenious bit of software. In fact, the phrase "a good hack" meant a particularly clever piece of programming. Outside of the hacking community, however, anyone who attempts illegal access to a computer network is called a hacker.

Hacking often involves becoming intimate with the details of existing software to give the hacker the knowledge necessary to attempt an unauthorized system break-in. Nonetheless, those who adhere to the original definition of the term hacker wanted to differentiate themselves from those who perform illegal activities, thus the term cracker.

There are many ways to classify those who break into computer systems, depending on which source you are reading. However, most lists of the types of hackers include the following (although they may be given different names).

White Hat Hackers.

This group considers itself to be the "good guys." Although white hat hackers may crack a system, they do not do it for personal gain. When they find a vulnerability in a network, they report it to the network owner, hardware vendor, or software vendor, whichever is appropriate. They do not release information about the system vulnerability to the public until the vendor has had a chance to develop and release a fix for the problem. White hat hackers might also be hired by an organization to test a network's defenses.

White hat hackers are extremely knowledgeable about networking, programming, and existing vulnerabilities that have been found and fixed. They typically write their own cracking tools.

Script Kiddies.

The script kiddies are hacker "wannabes." They have little, if any, programming skill and therefore must rely on tools written by others. Psychological profiles of script kiddies indicate that they are generally male, young (under 30), and not socially well-adjusted. They are looked down upon by most other hackers.

Script kiddies do not target specific networks, but, instead, scan for any system that is vulnerable to attack. They might try to deface a Web site, delete files from a target system, flood network bandwidth with unauthorized packets, or in some other way commit what amounts to cyber vandalism. Script kiddies typically don't want to keep their exploits secret. In fact, many of those that are caught are trapped because they have been bragging about what they have done.

Cyberterrorists.

The cyberterrorists are hackers who are motivated by a political, religious, or philosophical agenda. They may propagate their beliefs by defacing Web sites that support opposing positions. Given the current global political climate, there is also some fear that cyberterrorists may attempt to disable networks that handle significant elements of a country's infrastructure, such as nuclear plants and water treatment facilities.

Black Hat Hackers. Black hat hackers are motivated by greed or a desire to cause harm. They target specific systems, write their own tools, and generally attempt to get in and out of a target system without being detected. Because they are very knowledgeable and their activities often undetectable, black hat hackers are among the most dangerous.

Types of Attacks

When a hacker targets your network, what might you expect? There are a number of broad categories of attacks.

Denial of service. A denial of service attack (DoS) attempts to prevent legitimate users from gaining access to network resurces. It can take the form of flooding a network or server with traffic so that legitimate messages can't get through or it can bring down a server. If you are monitoring traffic on your network, a DoS attack is fairly easy to detect. Unfortunately, it can be difficult to defend against and stop without disconnecting your network from the Internet.

Buffer overflows. A buffer overflow attack takes advantage of a programming error in an application or system program. The hacker can insert his or her own code into a program and, from there, take control of a target system. Because they are the result of a programming error, buffer overflow conditions are almost impossible for a network engineer to detect. They are usually detected by hackers or the software vendor. The most common defense is a patch provided by that vendor.

Malware. The term *malware* includes all types of malicious software, such as viruses, worms, and Trojan horses. The goal of a hacker in placing such software on a computer may be simple maliciousness or to provide access to the computer at a later date. Although there is a constantly escalating battle between those who write malware and those who write malware detection software, a good virus checker goes a long way to keeping network devices free from infection.

Social engineering.   A social engineering attack is an attempt to get system access information from employees using role-playing and misdirection. It is usually the prelude to an attempt to gain unauthorized access to the network. This isn't a technical attack at all, and therefore can't be stopped by technical means. It requires employee education to teach employees to recognize this type of attack and how to guard against it.

Brute force.   One way to gain access to a system is to run brute force login attempts. Assuming that a hacker knows one or more system login names, he can attempt to guess the passwords. By keeping and monitoring logs of who is attempting to log into a system, a network administrator can usually detect brute force break-in attacks.

> *Note: There is no gender discrimination intended with the use of the pronoun "he" when referring to hackers. The fact is that most hackers are male.*

You will learn a great deal more about all these types of attacks (and others)—including how they work, how to detect them, and how to defend against them—throughout this book.

The Steps in Cracking a Network

Script kiddies don't have much of a plan when it comes to cracking a network. They simply find some cracking software on the Internet and let it run against a range of IP addresses. However, other types of hackers are much more methodical in what they do. Cracking a network usually involves the following process:

1. Information gathering: During the information gathering phase, a hacker gets as much information as he can from public sources. The result often forms the basis of a social engineering attack.
2. Port scanning: Port scanning is an attempt to identify open TCP ports on a target system. This can not only tell the hacker where he can target an attack, but also can indicate which applications are running on your network.

3. Network enumeration: Once a hacker gains access through an open port, he will attempt to map the network, in particular looking to distinguish workstations from servers. He will attempt to discover which applications and operating systems are running on each host as well the layout of the network itself (how subnets, routers, switches, hardware firewalls, and other devices are interconnected).

4. Gaining and keeping root/administrator access: The previous three activities will give the knowledgeable hacker enough information to plan an attack. He will then do whatever is necessary to gain access to a user account. His ultimate goal is to escalate whatever access he gains to root/administrator status so that he has access to the entire system.

5. Using access and/or information gained: If he is looking for specific information or wants to make specific modifications to a compromised system, the hacker will either copy the desired information or make the modifications at this point.

6. Leaving a backdoor: A hacker may not take advantage of a system immediately after gaining control of it, or he may need to return at a later date. He may therefore leave software behind that will give him access at will.

7. Covering his tracks: Finally, the knowledgeable hacker will erase traces of his presence, including modifying system logs to remove records of whatever he has done.

If you haven't detected a hacker by the time he is attempting to gain root access, then it is probably too late. The job of a security professional therefore is to limit the amount of information a hacker gets from the first three steps in the process.

1.2.2 Sources of Internal Threats

Most internal threats come from two sources: employees and accidents. Employee threats may be intentional or accidental as well.

Employee Threats

In most cases, employees know more about a network and the computers on it than any outsider. At the very least, they have legitimate access to user accounts. IT personnel, of course, have various levels of increased access. Intentional employee security threats include the following:

◆ Personnel who employ hacking techniques to upgrade their legitimate access to root/administrator access, allowing them to divulge trade secrets, steal money, and so on for personal or political gain.

◆ Personnel who take advantage of legitimate access to divulge trade secrets, steal money, and so on for personal or political gain.

◆ Family members of employees who are visiting the office and have been given access to company computers to occupy them while waiting.

◆ Personnel who break into secure machine rooms to gain physical access to mainframe and other large system consoles.

◆ Former employees, especially those who did not leave the organization willingly, who are interested in revenge. Attacks may be physical, actually damaging equipment, or traditional hacking attacks.

As dangerous as the intentional employee security threat may be, employees can also cause a great deal of damage unintentionally, such as

◆ Becoming the victim of a social engineering attack, unknowingly helping a hacker gain unauthorized network access.

◆ Unintentionally revealing confidential information.

◆ Physically damaging equipment, resulting in data loss.

◆ Misusing a system, introducing inaccurate and/or damaged data, or accidentally deleting or modifying data.

Most unintentional employee threats theoretically can be handled through employee education. For example, it seems logical that instructing employees not to write passwords on sticky notes that are then affixed to monitors would help prevent compromised passwords. However, when you are dealing with human beings, even the best education can be forgotten in the stress of getting a job done on time.

Reality Check: Employee threats to security can come from the most unexpected places. For example, would you have a problem with an employee installing AOL software on his or her computer? If not, you should. Assuming that you allow employees to check and send private e-mail during working hours, why shouldn't someone be able to use an AOL account with AOL's easy-to-use software? Because AOL uses TCP ports in an unusual way—all traffic travels over ports 5910 through 5193—it therefore opens up an enormous security hole through any defenses you may have in place. Your employees can access AOL e-mail using a Web browser or any other e-mail client, without the AOL software. To enforce that solution, you need to be monitoring what software employees are installing on their own.

Accidents

Employees certainly can unintentionally damage a network. In addition, true accidents also occur. A security plan will need to guard against data damage and loss caused by

- ◆ Electrical power fluctuations
- ◆ Hardware failures
- ◆ Natural disasters such as fire and flood

Reality Check: If ever a disaster brought home the need for disaster planning, it was the terrorist attacks of 9/11/01. Among the buildings damaged was the Bank of New York's headquarters, which housed its main data center. The data center was rendered completely nonfunctional. Customers lost access to their funds for nearly two weeks while the bank reestablished its data processing at an alternate site. Although two weeks may seem like a very short time in which to set up and bring online a complete mainframe data center, it was a *very* long time for customers who couldn't deposit money, cash checks, or make or receive electronic funds transfers of any kind.

Guarding against accidental network damage includes power protection (for example, surge protectors and UPSs) and comprehensive backup schemes. When done well, backup takes significant planning and disaster recovery rehearsals.

1.3 The Organizational Security Process

How are you going to respond to the continual security threats aimed at your network? Where do you start? In the simplest sense, you start at the top: You must have top management support—both inside and out of IT—for the security effort. With management support in place, you can be proactive, developing security policies and procedures before they are needed.

1.3.1 Top Management Support

Implementing a security scheme for an organization costs money, whether it involves purchasing hardware and software, hiring personnel, training users, retraining IT staff, realigning IT staff responsibilities, or any combination of the preceding. Those expenditures have to be allocated by someone, and it's much easier to obtain the necessary funds if the top management in your organization is behind your security efforts.

In addition to obtaining the support you need, there is another important reason to ensure that top management is behind security policies and procedures: Top management personnel have access to the most sensitive information in the company, yet they are the least likely to pay attention to security. If you can make top managers stakeholders in the security process, they are much more likely to follow security procedures.

Finally, having top management support ensures that the corporate legal department is involved in security planning and implementation. This will make it much more likely that the organization's data security adheres to any relevant legal statutes.

How can you get top managers to share your concern for network security? There are several techniques you can employ, but no matter what you do, keep in mind that essentially you have to "sell" the need for security investment to those who control the money. Although no single technique can be assured to work in every situation, here are a few ideas that you can try:

◆ If you are a good speaker, use the tried-and-true method of making a presentation to management. Talk in terms that management understands: the amount of money that can be lost, or legal problems that will arise, if security is compromised.

♦ Hire some white hat hackers to perform an attack on your network. Present the result of that penetration test to management.

Caution: If you're considering hiring some white hat hackers, be sure that you have management approval first!

♦ Personal experience also can convince a manager that increased spending on security is needed. Install a software firewall on top management desktop computers and turn on the logging feature. Let the firewall run for a week or so. Then sit down with the managers and show them exactly how many attempts there have been to break into their computers.

♦ If top management at your organization is often convinced by outside documentation, search the Internet for Web sites that document the prevalence of security breaches. Also provide top management with relevant articles from computer trade weeklies such as *ComputerWorld*, *InfoWorld*, and *eWeek*. You can find additional, targeted articles at Web sites such as *Network Computing* (www.nwc.com) and *Network Magazine* (http://www.networkmagazine.com/).

Note: For an exhaustive list of online networking publications, check out http://www.hitmill.com/computers/networking.html#ezines.

In some cases, you may have no problem at all convincing top management that more security is needed in your organization. In fact, you may have the opposite problem: Top management may have read information that convinced them that the organization should undertake a massive security effort. In that case, your job is to slow down the overly enthusiastic managers so that you can engage in appropriate planning.

1.3.2 How Secure Can You Be?

Probably the most important thing to realize before you start developing a security scheme for an organization is that you can never be 100 percent secure. There will always be someone who can find a way into your system, either from the inside or outside. Therefore, instead of setting a goal of making the system totally uncrackable, you want to ensure that you make it as secure as you can for a reasonable amount of money.

The trick is to balance security risk with the amount of money you are going to spend. For example, let's say that you can make your network 80 percent secure for $125,000. To make it 90 percent secure, you must spend $200,000. Is the extra 10 percent security worth another $75,000 to your organization? The answer depends on the amount of risk that you are willing to tolerate. The point at which additional security becomes more expensive than it is worth can be determined only by each organization.

You also need to evaluate your security measures in a practical sense. From a security point of view, for example, it would be great to require 12-character passwords that were to be changed every day. But that simply isn't practical for users. They won't be able to remember their passwords and will either resort to writing them down (and leaving them in easily accessible places) or choosing passwords that are easy to guess. Therefore, such a rule isn't workable and shouldn't be part of your security plan. For each security measure that you adopt, you need to ask yourself whether it is practically feasible and whether, given a reasonable amount of training, technical staff and users will be able and likely to adhere to the requirements.

1.3.3 The Importance of a Security Policy

A *security policy* is a document that lays out the philosophy and structure of an organization's security efforts. It serves several purposes:

- ◆ A security policy is documentation of the commitment top management has made to security. A written security policy makes it easier for IT staff to justify security expenditures.

- ◆ A security policy provides a roadmap for IT staff who are planning network security implementation. It indicates what is to be secured and who is responsible for providing the security.

♦ A security policy identifies acceptable use of organizational computing resources. For example, it might indicate whether employees can use a corporate e-mail system for private e-mail and if so, to what extent.

♦ A security policy identifies who is to have access to what. This can be one of the most difficult parts of the policy to develop because access to information often connotes privilege in an organization.

♦ A security policy acts as a security contract with employees. They must adhere to the philosophy and behaviors included in the policy for continued employment.

♦ A security policy can be given to new employees before they begin work. In fact, some organizations require that new employees read the security policy and sign an affidavit indicating that they understand it and agree to abide by its provisions.

It takes a significant amount of effort to prepare and maintain a useful security policy. However, without one, an organization's security efforts are often disorganized, spotty, more costly than necessary, and ineffective.

Like a systems requirements document, a security policy needs to be a living document. It needs to be revisited at regular intervals to determine whether it requires updating. If you have kept implementation details out of the security policy, then updated technology will not necessarily require a change in the policy; only a fundamental paradigm shift—for example, a move from password/user ID pairs to biometric user identification—will affect the policy. However, changes in legal requirements or changes in business direction may require rewriting parts of the policy.

You will find an in-depth discussion of creating a security policy in the next major section of this chapter (Section 1.4 on page 25).

Reality Check: The idea of a security policy sounds great, but, like a formal systems analysis and design process, it can be very hard to implement. Why? Because no matter how good your intentions, there will be some people in an organization who find policy making a threat and oppose the effort, either actively or passively. They may be resistant to change, they may feel that a security policy will give the organization too much of an opportunity to monitor what they are doing, they may feel that the policy will interfere with their ability to do their jobs well, or they may simply be individuals who like to foment chaos by obstructing any new initiative. Probably the most difficult aspect of policy making is deciding who has access to what. The "I know something you don't know" syndrome gives some employees feelings of self-worth, and restricting their access can cause significant psychological turmoil.

1.3.4 Legal Issues

Many security plans are complicated by legal requirements for data privacy. If your organization stores any personal information about customers or clients, then those data are most likely subject to privacy regulations. The precise legal statues and regulations that affect an organization depend, of course, on the nature of the organization. This section discusses a selection of U.S. legislation that has wide applicability and is meant as an example only.

Children's Online Privacy Protection Act of 1998

Any organization in the U.S. operating a Web site, pen pal service, e-mail service, message board, or chat room that is accessible to children under 13 years of age is subject to the provisions of the Children's Online Privacy Protection Act of 1998. The purpose of this statute is to protect the safety of children on the Internet by controlling the way in which personal information is collected, stored, and disseminated.

The provisions of the law require that any operator of a computer installation that knowingly collects information from children under age 13 must state online what information is being collected and obtain parents' permission to do so. The operator must also disclose to parents—upon the parent's request—what information is being collected and under what circumstances it will be disclosed.

Under the provisions of this act, the only personal information about a child that can be collected without coming under the provisions of the bill are a first name and age. The last name, home address, e-mail address, telephone number, social security number, or any other information that specifically identifies an individual child is covered by the law. In addition, a Web site or online service may collect information that will not be stored to be used on a one-time basis. For example, a technical support Web site can collect information about the configuration of a child's computer system to answer a technical support question as long as the configuration information isn't stored once the technical support question has been answered.

The defining standard for what is permitted under this law is whether the information collected can be used to recontact the child in any way. The intent is therefore to protect children from predators who might find them using information gathered from an online source.

If you are operating within the U.S., it is your responsibility as a security professional to ensure that your operation stores personal information only about individuals over the age of 13 and that any interaction with children falls under the provisions of the law. You must have security in place to ensure that no one can illegally gain access to any legally gathered information about children.

Reality Check: Web sites that collect personal information to be stored on a server are responsible for ensuring that whoever fills out a form is 13 years or older. But how can a Web site verify that a user is of sufficient age? Most sites ask the user to check a box next to a statement such as "I am at least 13 years of age." Certainly any child who is computer literate enough to wander the Web will be smart enough to check the box, even if he or she is only 8 or 9 years old. The check box (or radio button, whichever it happens to be) may absolve the operator of the Web site of legal culpability, but it doesn't mean that the law is effective.

Note: For the full text of the Children's online Privacy Protection Act of 1998, see http://www.ci.gov/Documents/ CPPA_Act_1998.html.

The Gramm-Leach-Bliley Act

The Gramm-Leach-Bliley Financial Modernization Act of 1999 (GLB) governs the privacy of consumer financial information. Some of the privacy notices you now see on Web sites and the ability to prevent a business from sharing your private information with other businesses are a result of this law.

GLB applies to "financial institutions," a broad category defined to include not only banks and savings and loans, but also any company that provides financial services, such as stock brokerages, mortgage lenders, financial advisers, debt collectors, and accountants. Customers of financial institutions—people who have a long-term, ongoing relationship with a company—must be given a copy of the company's financial information privacy statement automatically. A consumer—someone who uses a financial institution's services but does not maintain an ongoing relationship with the company—must be given a privacy notice only if information will be shared with a third party.

GLB covers "nonpublic personal information," such as personal identifying information (name, address, social security number, and so on) and information generated when performing financial transactions.

If a financial institution intends to share nonpublic personal information with a third party, customers must receive an "opt-out" notice that describes a reasonable way to opt out of the information sharing. Customers must also be given reasonable time to opt out. Consumers need not be given the entire privacy policy, but must be given a reasonable way to obtain the full policy as well as an opt-out notice.

What does this mean for a computer security plan? It mean that nonpublic personal information must be safeguarded from unauthorized disclosure. Not only must it be protected from illegal access by hackers and employees, but you must also keep track of who has opted-out of permitted disclosure to third parties. Even if an organization doesn't come under the definition of a financial institution, it must still follow the provisions of the law for any information that will be reported to a financial institution.

> *Note: For the full text of the Gramm-Leach-Bliley Act, see*
> *http://www.ftc.gov/privacy/glbact/glbsub1.htm.*

Fair Credit Reporting Act

The Fair Credit Reporting Act (FCRA), originally enacted in 1970, is the U.S. law that gave those on whom credit data are kept by credit reporting agencies some control of the disclosure and content of that information. The law requires credit reporting agencies to obtain the consent of the person about whom information is kept before releasing that information to a third party. In addition, customers are entitled to copies of their credit reports and must be given a reasonable opportunity to correct errors.

Even if you aren't working for a credit reporting agency, this law has implications for how credit information is handled. Anything that will be reported to a credit report agency must be kept private and not released to anyone other than a credit reporting agency or the customer unless the customer gives consent.

> *Note: The full text of the Fair Credit Reporting Act can be found at http://www.ftc.gov/os/statutes/fcra.htm.*

Health Insurance Portability and Accountability Act of 1996

The Health Insurance Portability and Accountability Act of 1996 (HIPPAA) is designed to safeguard the privacy and security of medical information handled by doctors, hospitals, and insurance companies. If you are in charge of security for a healthcare organization, then this law has far-reaching implications for what data you keep and how it is secured.

HIPAA requires the consent of a patient or a patient's legal representative before confidential medical information is released. It also gives a patient the right to view his or her medical records (with the exception of some types of psychiatric notes), something that wasn't always possible before this law. (Doctors would routinely refuse to allow patients access to their medical files on the grounds that patients wouldn't understand what they read.)

Like financial information, medical information today is routinely sent over computer networks. For example, medical records go to insurance companies, lab results go to hospitals and doctors' offices, and so on. The security personnel in an organization that originates medical information are therefore responsible for the privacy and security of the data, not only when they are on local hard drives, but also when they are traveling over a network. In addition, the security plan needs to include provisions for verifying who is entitled to authorize the release of medical data for each patient.

Reality Check: HIPAA may be a positive step for many patients, but, in some cases, it has turned into a nightmare for hospitals. For example, before HIPAA, if a patient was incompetent and had no relatives to agree to medical treatment, a hospital would go to court and the court would appoint a legal guardian to act on the patient's behalf. Under HIPAA, however, it is now illegal to release the patient's information to the court without the patient's informed consent. But the patient is not capable of providing informed consent, thus the need for the court-appointed guardian. To get around this proverbial catch-22, hospitals have simply broken the law and released the necessary medical information to the courts to prove that the patient needed a legal medical guardian. This is an excellent example of how a well-intentioned law (policy) was written to be too restrictive. It interferes with the ability of people to do their work, and therefore people feel that they must circumvent the law.

Note: For in-depth information about HIPAA, see http://www.hipaadvisory.com.

1.3.5 Security Personnel

Once you have a security policy, who in your organization is going to be responsible for designing the implementation details and performing that implementation? Where is that person, or group of people, going to be placed in the organization? The answers, of course, depend on the size and nature of your organization and its network.

The Head of the Organization

In large organizations, the security function is headed by someone who might be called the Chief Security Officer, Chief information Security Officer, Vice President of Information Security, or Director of Information Security. Consider the following job description found at *http://www.csoonline.com/research/executive/description.html*:

"Reports directly to a senior functional executive (EVP, COO, CFO, CIO) or CEO. Most important criteria for the position is to be one or two removed from the CEO/COO. This position will require overseeing and coordinating efforts across the company, including Engineering, Network Infrastructure, HR, IT, Legal and other groups, to identify key corporate security initiatives and standards (for example, virus protection, security monitoring, intrusion detection, access control to facilities, and remote access policies). It will also involve working with outside consultants as appropriate for independent security audits.

The role of the security department is to safeguard the confidential information, assets and intellectual property that belongs to the company. The scope primarily involves computer security but also covers physical security as it relates to safeguarding of information and assets.

Responsibilities:

♦ Identify protection goals and objectives consistent with corporate strategic plan.

♦ Identify key security program elements.

♦ Manage development and implementation of global security policy, standards, guidelines and procedures to ensure ongoing maintenance of security.

♦ Assist with the investigation of security breaches and assist with disciplinary and legal matters associated with such breaches as necessary.

♦ Coordinate implementation plans, security product purchase proposals, and project schedules.

Qualifications:

♦ BA or BS in Computer Science, Information Management, or related field. Masters or PhD a plus.

♦ Eight to ten years of progressive experience in computing and security, including experience with Internet technology and security issues.

♦ Proven ability as a member of a management team and able to communicate technical and security-related concepts to a broad range of technical and non-technical staff.

♦ Ability to work and effectively prioritize in a highly dynamic work environment.

♦ Experience with disaster recovery planning, testing, auditing, risk analysis, business resumption planning, contingency planning; TCP/IP firewalls, VPNs and other security devices; as well as contract and vendor negotiation experience."

The preceding is a high-level executive position that may pay a six-figure salary (depending on the part of the country, the specific industry, and the individual's experience).

Middle Management

If your organization is too small for the executive-level position described in the preceding section, you may nonetheless have a security administrator's position such as the following job description found at *http://www.monster.com*:

"a. The development, documentation, and presentation of Information Security (IS) security education, awareness, and training activities for facility management, IS personnel, users, and others, as appropriate.

b. Establishes, documents, implements, and monitors the IS Security Program and related procedures for the facility and ensures facility compliance with requirements for IS.

c. Identifies and documents unique local threats/vulnerabilities to IS.

d. Coordinates the facility IS Security Program with other facility security programs.

e. Ensures that periodic self-inspections of the facility's IS Program are conducted as part of the overall facility self-inspection program and that corrective action is taken for all identified findings and vulnerabilities. Self-inspections are to ensure that the IS is operating as accredited and that accreditation conditions have not changed.

f. Ensures the development of facility procedures to:

(1) Govern marking, handling, controlling, removing, transporting, sanitizing, reusing, and destroying media and equipment containing classified information.

(2) Properly implement vendor supplied ... authentication (password, account names) features or security-relevant features.

(3) Report IS security incidents to [appropriate reporting destination]. Ensure proper protection or corrective measures have been taken when an incident/vulnerability has been discovered.

(4) Require that each IS user sign an acknowledgment of responsibility for the security of the IS.

(5) Implement security features for the detection of malicious code, viruses, and intruders (hackers), as appropriate.

g. Certifies to the [appropriate reporting destination], in writing, that each System Security Plan (SSP) has been implemented; that the specified security controls are in place and properly tested; and that the IS is functioning as described in the SSP.

h. Ensures notification of the [appropriate reporting destination] when an IS no longer processes classified information, or when changes occur that might affect accreditation.

i. Ensures that personnel are trained on the IS's prescribed security restrictions and safeguards before they are initially allowed to access a system.

j. Develops and implements general and remote maintenance procedures based on requirements provided by the [appropriate reporting destination].

Must have the following:

♦ Baccalaureate Degree & 2 yrs. experience in Information Technology

♦ Good writing skills

♦ IT versed in hardware and software

♦ Good communication skills

♦ Knowledgeable of a variety of operating systems

♦ Proficiency in M/S Office products

♦ Proficiency from a technical standpoint of a variety of computer application programs."

This position has no policy-making responsibilities, yet is not necessarily responsible for all hands-on security implementation. In fact, the job description indicates that the job holder will "ensure" implementation rather than perform it. This person is the direct manager of those who are implementing previously developed security solutions.

In a small or moderate-sized organization, this person may report to the CEO, a vice president, or the head of IT. Large organizations may split the responsibilities of this type of job into several pieces and hire multiple security administrators, all of whom report to the security executive.

The People in the Trenches

A quick check at *monster.com* reveals a wide range of job descriptions for people who will be implementing security plans. As examples, consider the following:

Network Security Analyst. "Candidates should have 4+ years experience in technical environments with the ability to identify technical and operational problems, then write-up the findings. Candidates will be expected to be able to identify false positives from the vulnerability scanners. Candidates with prior DC government experience are preferred.

The ideal candidate should have:

1. Experience performing quantitative and qualitative risk assessment and vulnerability assessments within the security environment.
2. Experience configuring, running, and analyzing commercial vulnerability scanners.
3. Strong background in networking, Windows and Unix environments."

Computer Security Systems Specialist.
"he following knowledge and skills are required for the Computer Security Systems Specialist position and relate to Sun Solaris 8, HP/UX, and Windows NT & 2000 operating system environments. Also, knowledge and skill in applying:

Remote Access skills—particularly Ciscos authentication server, 3xxx Series VPNs (CCNA and CCNP a plus).

Authentication skills, e.g. Certifications, smart cards, hard/soft tokens— Cisco VMS/CiscoSecure/Cisco ACS—TACACS and Radius.

Security Data Communications experience—particularly management and security Cisco 3xxx/7xxx Series routers and switches—SPF, BGP routing skills, and managing data comm logs.

Web development skills.

Intrusion Detection Systems (IDS)—particularly Dragon, Netscreen & Cisco PIX Firewall.

Unix—particularly Sun Solaris 8 & MAC OS 10."

Computer Systems Security Specialist.
"Roles & Responsibilities: Audit/Assessment (Gap Analysis, Risk Mitigation, Penetration & Vulnerability testing, Ethical Hacking), Design (Developing Policies & Procedures, Design for new Intrusion Detection Systems and PKI), Implementation (Install new Firewalls), Support & Maintenance, and Forensics.

To qualify for this role you must possess expert level TCP/IP, IDS, Snort, ISS Suite, Cisco, and Checkpoint running on Solaris and Nokia. You will be working on a team of four.

Position Requirements: A Bachelor's degree in Electrical Engineering, Information Science, Information Systems, Computer Science, Physics, Math, or other related discipline is desirable.

A minimum of eight years in defining computer security IT requirements for high level applications, evaluation of approved security product capabilities, and developing solutions to MLS problems."

How many hands-on security people will you need? Assuming that you want 24/7 security coverage, then you'll probably need at least three. Each works an eight-hour shift during the five-day work week and is on call over the weekend. To get live weekend monitoring, you'll need at least another two people. If your organization is large enough to require more than one person performing security monitoring, then double or triple the number of people needed.

1.3.6 Outsourcing Security

Most of the discussion in this book assumes that you are managing security in-house. But it would be shortsighted not to mention the option of outsourcing your security. When you outsource, you hire an outside organization to implement and monitor security for your network.

There are tangible benefits to outsourcing: you don't have to hire a security staff, and it often can cost less than managing security in-house. However, there are also significant risks: The security company you choose could go out of business, leaving your organization extremely vulnerable.

If you are going to outsource, then you may want to keep the management of your security policy in-house; you can outsource the implementation, such as security auditing/vulnerability testing and ongoing monitoring. You can even outsource mid-level management. But you need to remember that the ultimate responsibility and authority should remain internal to your organization. This gives you control over how your security is maintained and, if the worst should happen and the security company disappears, you won't be restarting from scratch: Your security requirements will be documented already, and you have the internal structures necessary to contract with a new firm without risking data security during the transition.

1.4 Preparing a Security Policy

A security policy needs to spell out guidelines for security activities in an organization. It should

- ◆ Justify both direct and indirect expenditures on security by stating the importance of network security to the organization.

- ◆ Indicate the scope of the security efforts, as well as any legal requirements.

- ◆ Specify security personnel, their job responsibilities, and organizational structure.

- ◆ Describe secure behaviors that all employees must use.

- ◆ Lay out procedures for reporting and handling security violations.

- ◆ Describe the organization's disaster recovery plan.

Notice that the preceding list doesn't include any details of how security will be implemented. The detailed implementation plan is left to the IT staff person in charge of security. Given that security technologies are constantly changing (and hopefully, being improved), it makes sense to keep implementation specifics—such as the name of a specific hardware or software product—out of a policy document.

A security policy should also avoid including the names of individuals so that you don't need to revise the policy whenever personnel change. Instead, refer to job titles (for example, CSO, or "Chief Security Officer") when describing human responsibilities.

Because developing a security policy is a difficult process, your organization may decide to purchase a set of templates (cost ≥ $600) or use free templates available at *http://www.sans.org/resources/policies/#template* rather than starting from scratch.

A security policy can be a lengthy document. Many organizations break their policy into a collection of smaller documents, each of which addresses a specific type of security. As an example, let's examine the password security policy from the SANS collection of templates.

The policy begins with a statement of the importance of password security to the organization:

> "Passwords are an important aspect of computer security. They are the front line of protection for user accounts. A poorly chosen password may result in the compromise of <Company Name>'s entire corporate network. As such, all <Company Name> employees (including contractors and venders with access to <Company Name> systems) are responsible for taking the appropriate steps, as outlined below, to select and secure their passwords."[1]

followed by the purpose of the policy:

> "The purpose of this policy is to establish a standard for creation of strong passwords, the protection of those passwords, and the frequency of change."

and its scope:

> "The scope of this policy includes all personnel who have or are responsible for an account (or any form of access that supports or requires a password) on any system that resides at any <Company Name> facility, has access to the <Company Name> network, or stores any non-public <Company Name> information."

The next section contains a statement of the elements of the policy:

> ♦ "All system-level passwords (e.g., root, enable, not admin, application administration accounts, etc.) must be changed on at least a quarterly basis.

---

1 The password protection policy is reprinted with permission of SANS (*http://www.sans.org*).

- ◆ All production system-level passwords must be part of the InfoSec administered global password management database.

- ◆ All user-level passwords (e.g., email, web, desktop computer, etc.) must be changed at least every six months. The recommended change interval is every four months.

- ◆ User accounts that have system-level privileges granted through group memberships or programs such as "suid" must have a unique password from all other accounts held by that user.

- ◆ Passwords must not be inserted into email messages or other forms of electronic communication.

- ◆ Where SNMP is used, the community strings must be defined as something other than the standard defaults of "public," "private" and "system" and must be different from the passwords used to log in interactively. A keyed hash must be used where available (e.g., SNMPv2).

- ◆ All user-level and system-level passwords must conform to the guidelines described below."

General policies are followed by specific guidelines to be used in implementing the policy. The first set describes guidelines for constructing passwords:

"Passwords are used for various purposes at <Company Name>. Some of the more common uses include: user level accounts, web accounts, email accounts, screen saver protection, voicemail password, and local router logins. Since very few systems have support for one-time tokens (i.e., dynamic passwords which are only used once), everyone should be aware of how to select strong passwords.

Poor, weak passwords have the following characteristics:

- ◆ The password contains less than eight characters.

- ◆ The password is a word found in a dictionary (English or foreign).

- ◆ The password is a common usage word such as:

- Names of family, pets, friends, co-workers, fantasy characters, etc.

- Computer terms and names, commands, sites, companies, hardware, software.

- The words "<Company Name>", "sanjse", "sanfran" or any derivation.

- Birthdays and other personal information such as addresses and phone numbers.

- Word or number patterns like aaabbb, qwerty, zyxwvuts, 123321, etc.

- Any of the above spelled backwards.

- Any of the above preceded or followed by a digit (e.g., secret1, 1secret).

Strong passwords have the following characteristics:

♦ Contain both upper and lower case characters (e.g., a-z, A-Z).

♦ Have digits and punctuation characters as well as letters e.g., 0-9, !@#$%^&*()_+|~-=\`{}[]:";'<>?,./).

♦ Are at least eight alphanumeric characters long.

♦ Are not a word in any language, slang, dialect, jargon, etc.

♦ Are not based on personal information, names of family, etc.

♦ Passwords should never be written down or stored on-line. Try to create passwords that can be easily remembered. One way to do this is create a password based on a song title, affirmation, or other phrase. For example, the phrase might be: "This May Be One Way To Remember" and the password could be: "TmB1w2R!" or "Tmb1W>r~" or some other variation.

    NOTE: Do not use either of these examples as passwords!"

It is then followed by behavioral guidelines for safeguarding passwords:

"Do not use the same password for <Company Name> accounts as for other non-<Company Name> access (e.g., personal ISP account, option trading, benefits, etc.). Where possible, don't use the same password for various <Company Name> access needs. For example, select one password for the Engineering systems and a separate password for IT systems. Also, select a separate password to be used for an NT account and a UNIX account.

Do not share <Company Name> passwords with anyone, including administrative assistants or secretaries. All passwords are to be treated as sensitive, Confidential <Company Name> information.

Here is a list of "don'ts":

◆ Don't reveal a password over the phone to ANYONE.

◆ Don't reveal a password in an email message.

◆ Don't reveal a password to the boss.

◆ Don't talk about a password in front of others.

◆ Don't hint at the format of a password (e.g., "my family name").

◆ Don't reveal a password on questionnaires or security forms.

◆ Don't share a password with family members.

◆ Don't reveal a password to co-workers while on vacation.

If someone demands a password, refer them to this document or have them call someone in the Information Security Department.

Do not use the "Remember Password" feature of applications (e.g., Eudora, OutLook, Netscape Messenger).

Again, do not write passwords down and store them anywhere in your office. Do not store passwords in a file on ANY computer system (including Palm Pilots or similar devices) without encryption.

Change passwords at least once every six months (except system-level passwords which must be changed quarterly). The recommended change interval is every four months.

If an account or password is suspected to have been compromised, report the incident to InfoSec and change all passwords.

Password cracking or guessing may be performed on a periodic or random basis by InfoSec or its delegates. If a password is guessed or cracked during one of these scans, the user will be required to change it."

The remaining guidelines cover application development:

"Application developers must ensure their programs contain the following security precautions. Applications:

♦ should support authentication of individual users, not groups.

♦ should not store passwords in clear text or in any easily reversible form.

♦ should provide for some sort of role management, such that one user can take over the functions of another without having to know the other's password.

♦ should support TACACS+ , RADIUS and/or X.509 with LDAP security retrieval, wherever possible."

remote access:

"Access to the <Company Name> Networks via remote access is to be controlled using either a one-time password authentication or a public/private key system with a strong passphrase."

and passphrases:

"Passphrases are generally used for public/private key authentication. A public/private key system defines a mathematical relationship between the public key that is known by all, and the private key, that is known only to the user. Without the passphrase to "unlock" the private key, the user cannot gain access.

Passphrases are not the same as passwords. A passphrase is a longer version of a password and is, therefore, more secure. A passphrase is typically composed of multiple words. Because of this, a passphrase is more secure against "dictionary attacks."

A good passphrase is relatively long and contains a combination of upper- and lowercase letters and numeric and punctuation characters. An example of a good passphrase:

"The*?#>*@TrafficonThe101Was*&#!#ThisMorning"

All of the rules above that apply to passwords apply to passphrases."

The policy concludes with a statement of what should occur if the password policy is violated:

"Any employee found to have violated this policy may be subject to disciplinary action, up to and including termination of employment."

As mentioned earlier, this policy does not dictate what software should be used to manage passwords. It does not state, for example, that password policies such as frequency of password changing should be enforced by an operating system. However, the people in charge of actually implementing the policy may choose technology that automates compliance to the policies.

1.5 Security Audits

The best security policy in the world isn't worth much unless it is implemented effectively. A *security audit* is a process that determines how well your network is protected against a variety of threats. Security audits usually include

◆ Risk assessment: A risk assessment is a high-level analysis of the security risks faced by the organization.

◆ Vulnerability testing: Vulnerability testing involves attempts to crack the network, looking for weak points in the security implementation.

◆ Examination of known vulnerabilities: This differs from vulnerability testing in that, rather than attempting to crack security, it checks the network for software and hardware vulnerabilities that have been reported to vendors. For example, this activity determines whether vendor patches have been applied to vulnerable software.

◆ Policy verification: policy verification involves the comparison of procedures with what is specified in an organization's security policy.

Just as you must consider security from both the inside and outside of an organization, a security audit must also examine external security (protection from attacks) and internal security (adherence to internal security policy by employees and any others with data access).

Who should perform an audit? Generally, the term "audit" implies an outside firm. Considering that it's quite difficult to perform an unbiased assessment of compliance to policies that you've developed yourself, you will probably want to hire an outside firm to perform the audit. This also will give the audit more credibility than if you had performed it yourself.

Assuming that you hire an outside firm to perform a security audit, what should you expect during the audit? A typical audit will include many of the following activities:

1. Pre-audit contact: Before coming on-site to perform the audit, the audit team will request a copy of the organization's security policy. In this way the team can be familiar with the environment it will be auditing and the organization's approach to security before the audit starts.

2. Initial meeting: During the first meeting between an audit team and an organization, the audit team meets with the organization's management, especially those employees involved with the administration of network security. The team and management discuss the scope and objectives of the audit. The team describes what it intends to do and requests the documentation it would like to examine.

3. Risk assessment: The audit team analyzes the network to identify what it considers to be points of vulnerability. Techniques that may be used include automated activities such as port scanning and manual activities such as reviewing network documentation. These vulnerable areas will be the target of much of the audit activity.

4. Physical security audit: The audit team looks at protections that involve physical computer security, such as locked doors and their access mechanisms.

5. Network configuration audit: The audit team compares documentation of the configuration of the network with the results of automated network discovery tools to determine if the organization really knows what devices are on the network.

6. Penetration testing: The audit team uses manual and automated methods in attempts to crack through the network's defenses and to gain access to both servers and workstations. This is often the most extensive portion of the audit and may involve social engineering attacks to test employee sophistication in detecting such efforts.

7. Backup recovery audit: The audit team either checks backup and recovery procedures manually or simulates a disaster so that employees can demonstrate backup and recovery procedures.

8. Employee audit: The audit team installs passive monitoring tools to capture what employees are doing with the network. This helps the team determine whether employees are complying with the organization's policies on acceptable computer use.

9. Preparation of audit report: The audit team prepares a written report detailing the findings of the audit.

10. Report to management: The audit team finishes its job by presenting its findings and the written audit report to the organization's management.

1.6 Summary

Network security is the ongoing process of maintaining the privacy of data that should remain private. Security threats are intentional and unintentional, and can come from outside or inside an organization. Employees, who typically have more knowledge of a network than external crackers, are responsible for more than half the security violations that trouble networks.

Although it is virtually impossible to make a network totally secure, an organization that wants to minimize its risk as much as is technologically and financially feasible will begin by creating a security policy. The policy contains the goals, objectives, and standards for security activities. Implementation details are left to network administrators, giving them the flexibility to upgrade security equipment and procedures without requiring changes to the policy.

The security of a network typically is verified by an audit performed by an outside firm. The audit uses the organization's security policy as a guide to determine what and how to test.

Chapter 2: Basic Security Architecture

In This Chapter

♦ The basic layout of a secure network
♦ Firewalls
♦ File and folder permissions

2.0 Introduction

Network security presents a classic "which came first" problem: Where should we start discussing the details of risks and solutions? To understand vulnerabilities, you need to know some of the solutions; to understand the solutions, you need to understand vulnerabilities. (All together now: sigh.)

This chapter therefore provides you with introductory information about configuring a network so that it will support secure transmissions. We'll look at the layout of a secure network and at some very fundamental techniques for providing security, including firewalls (and DMZs), and setting file and folder permissions.

2.1 Secure Network Layouts

If you weren't concerned about network security, you could design a network topology primarily with performance in mind. Unfortunately, the world isn't that kind to us, and we therefore need to think about security not only in terms of software and human behavior, but also in terms of network design. The luckiest security professional in the universe is someone who has input to the design of the network before it is built. And if you come in after the network is up and running, you must be prepared to argue for necessary changes to the topology needed to support security measures.

Reality Check: It is very likely that a security professional will be called in years after a network has been in place. Someone has cracked the network and management doesn't want it to happen again. This means that the security professional is likely to encounter a hodgepodge of disorganized security measures: a virus checker here, a firewall there .... Don't expect anything to be clean and simple when you are approaching a network without previous security planning.

A simple network—perhaps a home network or a network in a very small business—doesn't need much in the way of security architecture. As you can see in the generalized illustration in Figure 2.1, there is no specialized security hardware. The edge router, the router that acts as the gateway between the Internet and the network, runs firewall software and performs network address translation (NAT), using its built-in proxy-server to hide the internal IP addresses from the Internet. Other types of security software may run on one or more of the servers. However, it probably isn't worth the money for the owners of a very small network to invest in stand-alone network appliances.

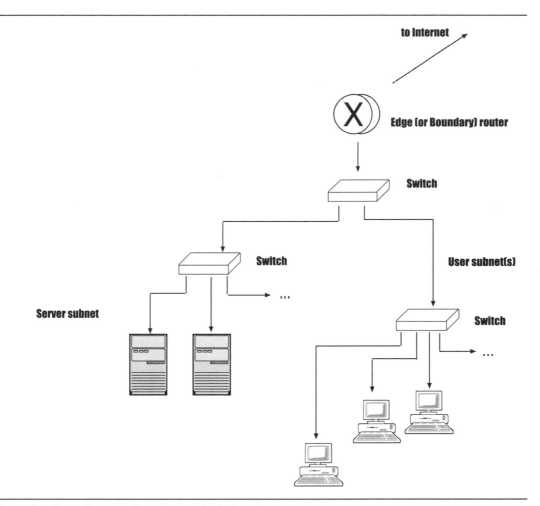

Figure 2.1 A small network with security in its edge router

Larger networks, or those that include extremely sensitive data, need a somewhat different architecture. In particular, the firewalls found in routers usually aren't sophisticated enough to be tailored to the needs of the organization. (They are generally *packet filtering* firewalls rather than *proxy* firewalls, both of which will be discussed shortly.) They also don't provide the performance needed by larger networks. Therefore, a stand-alone firewall appliance is particularly useful. The firewall appliance can not only provide better performance, but also will have the capabilities needed by a larger organization.

Assuming that the organization isn't hosting its own Web server, a generalized architecture might appear like Figure 2.2. Notice that the firewall appliance sits between the edge router and the remainder of the network.

> *Note: The network illustrations in this section use switches to illustrate network interconnectivity. However, very large networks often use routers at the upper levels. If that applies to your network, simply substitute a router for each switch.*

When a network includes shared resources that need to be exposed directly to the Internet, such as a Web server, then the network architecture usually includes a *DMZ*, a part of the network that isolates the exposed machine from the internal network. For example, the generalized topology in Figure 2.3 includes two firewall appliances. The Web server is connected in the DMZ, after the first firewall but before the second. The first firewall allows incoming Web traffic; the second does not. The only permitted access to the internal network is from application calls made by the Web server.

But why have the DMZ in the first place? Why not simply put the Web server outside a single firewall? Because you want to protect the Web server. The first firewall will stop unwanted traffic, but will let Web traffic through. Web servers are favorite targets of script kiddies and cyber activitsts—crackers who are interested in promoting a civic or political agenda by disrupting the Web sites of those who disagree with them—and therefore need as much protection as can be given to something that must be open to the Internet.

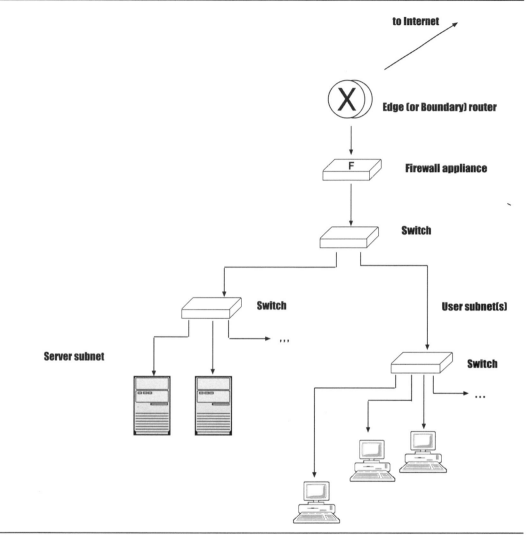

Figure 2.2 A larger network security architecture for a network that isn't hosting a Web site

2.2 Firewalls

A *firewall* is a network's first line of defense. It can block packets destined for specific software ports, filter traffic based on IP addresses, or

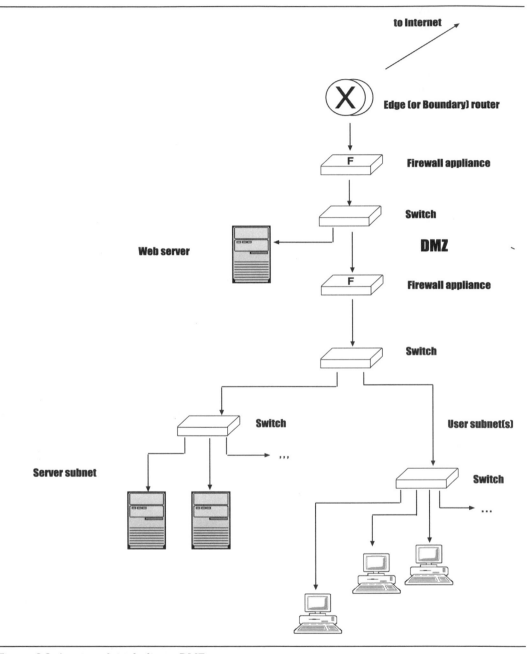

Figure 2.3 A network including a DMZ

even block packets destined for specific applications. Because firewalls are so important to network security, this section looks at the types of firewalls and how they work.

First and foremost, a firewall is software. It can run on a workstation, a server, a router, or a stand-alone piece of hardware (the aforementioned *firewall appliance*). The type of hardware on which a firewall is running is generally independent of the type of traffic filtering the firewall provides. The following discussion therefore focuses on the actions of firewall software rather than specific hardware.

In addition to blocking potentially dangerous traffic, firewalls usually log traffic, either all traffic or blocked traffic (depending on software configuration). Such logs contain the source IP address of the blocked packet, the destination address, the date and time the packet arrived at the firewall, the port for which the packet was destined, and the disposition of the packet (transmitted or blocked). Some firewalls also assign a threat level to each packet. Firewall logs therefore provide a valuable source of information about the traffic attempting to enter a network, and can provide substantial clues to system cracking attempts in progress. (You will find more about using firewall logs and other system logs throughout this book.)

2.2.1 Packet Filtering Firewalls

Packet filtering firewalls work at levels 3 and 4 of the TCP/IP protocol stack, filtering TCP and UCP packets based on any combination of source IP address, destination IP address, source port, or destination port. The simplest packet filtering firewalls filter only incoming packets and block those destined for ports that have been "closed." More sophisticated varieties allow an administrator to define rules that combine criteria. For example, a rule might allow Web traffic (port 80) onto the network only if packets have the destination IP address of the organization's Web server. Any other Web traffic would be blocked.

> *Note: If you are unfamiliar with the details of the TCP/IP protocol stack, see Appendix A.*

> *Note: For a listing of well-known TCP ports, see Appendix B.*

Packet filtering firewalls, especially those running on routers or on stand-alone appliances, also provide *network address translation* (NAT). An edge router presents a single IP address to the Internet (or internet or intranet). As packets arrive, the firewall examines the packet to determine the port to which the packet is directed. The firewall then uses an internal table to map the port to the internal IP address of the host on which the port is open. The internal IP addresses are usually nonrouteable addresses that are then hidden from the Internet.

Almost all personal firewalls, those designed to run on and protect a single workstation, are packet filtering firewalls. They differ only slightly from those that run on routers designed for home networks. Typically, personal firewalls have better logging capabilities than those found on home network routers, and, of course, don't provide NAT.

Tip: If you want to install a personal firewall on the workstations on your network, you don't necessarily have to spend money on one, at least if your computers are running Windows. Download the free version of ZoneAlarm from *www.zonelabs.com*. Its logging features are certainly not as complete or easy to use as the commercial version of the software, but the price is right.

2.2.2 Stateful Firewalls

There are two major limitations to packet filtering firewalls. First, they don't examine the payload of a packet, and second, they don't keep track of what happens to a packet once it gets through the firewall.

Does it matter what a packet does once it's been approved by the firewall? Indeed it does. Some system crackers can design packets that change the port to which they are destined after they pass through a firewall. For example, a packet might be addressed to port 80 so that it can pass through a firewall that has port 25 (SMTP) closed. Once the packet is onto the local network, it changes its port so that it can access the e-mail server and leave a virus or other malware behind.

A stateful firewall keeps track of the state of communications sessions. It monitors both the incoming and outgoing packets in each TCP connection. For example, when a packet originates within the local network, the firewall keeps track of the destination address and allows traffic from the destination addressed to the source back onto the local network. By the same token, a packet that appears to be a response to a request by an internal host but that doesn't correspond to an existing TCP session can be blocked. In addition, a stateful firewall monitors the port used by packets once they enter the local network, and blocks packets that attempt to change their ports.

Like packet filtering firewalls, stateful firewalls work at levels 3 and 4 of the TCP/IP protocol stack and are therefore relatively independent of the application to which packets are destined.

2.2.3 Application Proxy Firewalls

Application proxy firewalls take a different approach than the two preceding types. They work at the application layer of the TCP/IP protocol stack, providing proxy service for specific applications. Each application proxy sits between the internal network and the world outside. There is no direct communication between the internal computer and the other end of the conversation, as there is with packet filtering and stateful firewalls. Instead, packets travel between the external system and the proxy. The proxy examines the packets and determines which packets should be passed on to the application.

Application proxy firewalls provide a high degree of security and excellent logging features. However, the need to have a separate proxy for each application to be protected is a major limitation, especially if proxies aren't available for some of the software that you need to protect.

2.2.4 Comparing Types of Firewalls

As you would expect, each of the three types of firewalls has its pros and cons. You can find a summary of them in Table 2.1. Notice that there is increasing price and effectiveness as you move from packet filtering to application proxy firewalls.

However, before you rush out and purchase an application proxy firewall, don't forget that you must have a proxy program for each application you want to protect. The protection for each application that has a proxy is excellent, but those applications for which proxies aren't

	Packet Filtering	**Stateful**	**Application Proxy**
Price	Least expensive	Moderately expensive	Most expensive
Speed	Fast	Fast	Slower
Ease of configuration	Easy	Moderate	Moderate
Application independence	High	Moderate	Low. Must have a separate proxy program for each application for which traffic is to be filtered.
Amount of packet examined	Header information only	Header and contents	Header and contents
Sophistication of filtering rules	Low	Moderate	High
User authentication	None (uses IP addresses)	None (uses IP addresses)	High
Network exposure	Both ends of allowed communication connected directly through the firewall unless NAT is in effect	Both ends of allowed communication connected directly through the firewall unless NAT is in effect	Ends of conversation isolated from each other by application proxies
Packet types filtered	TCP and UDP	TCP and UDP	Generally TCP only (although a few do handle UDP)
Effectiveness	Lowest	Moderate	Highest

Table 2.1   Comparison of types of firewalls

available won't be protected; you'll still need some other type of firewall to handle them.

All three types of firewalls are effective at stopping a good portion of unwanted network traffic. Home network and small business network users will be well served by packet filtering firewalls, for example. Whatever you do, at least install a firewall where your network connects to the Internet. Nothing else will give you as much protection for the money.

Reality Check: When it comes to engineering design, many engineers refer to the "three ball theory," which talks about juggling three balls labeled Fast, Cheap, and Easy. You can have any two of them, but not three. This certainly applies to designing a network security architecture.

2.3 Hands On: Setting File and Directory Permissions

One of the most commonly overlooked basic security techniques is to adjust the user permissions of files and directories on servers and workstations. This is another simple—and virtually cost-free—step you can take to provide a large level of security on your system.

What should you secure? And from whom? To a large extent, those rules are set as part of security policy. Some of the answer is also common sense. For example, if you have sensitive information stored in a database, you don't want to leave the directory in which the database files are stored wide open for any user to copy. Typically, when a user copies a file into his or her own directories, the user becomes the owner of the file and has all rights to it.

You need to be very careful when deciding on file and directory permissions because the ability of a user to copy files and then own them can have often unforeseen consequences. For example, in the mid 1980s, I was administering a UNIX system for a computing research group. I wrote a shell script that extracted data from the log file that stored system login attempts (successful and unsuccessful). The script formatted the data, printed a report, and then cleaned out the log file to keep it from becoming too large. Because I wanted to share the script with others in the group, I set the permissions to the executable script file to allow reading —but not executing. A colleague copied the script and became the owner of his copy. Eager to see how the script operated, he made his copy executable and ran it. The result? Wiping out the log file, destroying all entries since the last time I ran the script.

How you set file and directory permissions varies from one operating system to another. In this Hands On section, we'll look at techniques for three major platforms.

2.3.1 Windows

One of the problems you will discover if you have computers running Windows on your network is that the default installation leaves many files and folders wide open. Everyone in the world can have access to files and folders that aren't part of the operating system itself, in particular when file sharing is enabled. If an end user is storing sensitive data on the computer, then this constitutes a major security vulnerability. You will therefore want to monitor and change permissions for many items.

The users and or groups of users that have access to a Windows file or directory are handled through file and folder property sheets. To set permissions:

1. Right-click on the file or folder for which you want to change permissions.
2. Choose Properties from the pop-up menu.
3. If necessary, click the Security tab. You will see a panel showing the current permissions assigned to the item (see Figure 2.4).
4. If the user or group to which permissions should be assigned does not appear in the Name box, click the Add button to the right of the Name box. A list of users and groups defined on the computer appears (see Figure 2.5).
5. Select the users or groups to which permissions will be assigned and click OK. The selected items will now appear in the Name box on the property panel.
6. Configure the permissions by clicking the Allow or Deny check boxes in the Permissions area of the panel.

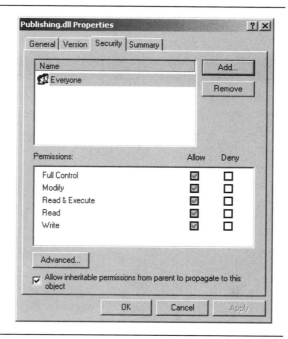

Figure 2.4 Windows security properties for a file

2.3.2 UNIX

Although the UNIX operating system has a reputation for not being secure, it nonetheless has a system for controlling access to files and directories. Each file and directory has three categories of access rights: for its owner (by default, the user that created the file or directory), for its group (by default, the group to which the owner belongs), and for the rest of the world (all users not the owner or members of the owner's group). Within each category, a user may be permitted to perform any combination of reading, writing, or executing the file or directory.

The permissions assigned to a file or directory are visible in the leftmost column when the -l argument is used with the ls command:

```
-rw-r--r--  1 jon    users   2408 Aug 30 14:30 saved_mail
-rwx------  1 jon    users    540 Jan 15 15:25 usage
```

Assuming that the characters in the leftmost column are numbered from the left, character 1 indicates whether the item is a directory (d) or a

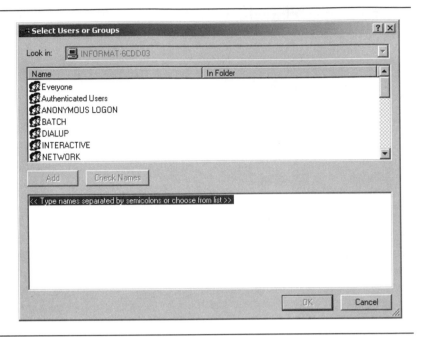

Figure 2.5 Choosing users and/or groups to which permissions should apply

regular file (-). The remaining nine characters are the access rights. Characters 2 through 4 refer to the owner, 5 through 7 to the group, and 8 through 10 to the rest of the world.

Within each group of three characters, the leftmost position contains an r if the user can read the file or directory. The center character contains a w if the user can write to the file or directory. The rightmost character contains an x if a file is executable by the user (it is a program that can be run); it contains an x for a directory if the user has permission to make that directory its working directory or to use the directory in a path name. A hyphen in any position (-) indicates the absence of an access right.

In the preceding example, the saved_mail file has the default permissions assigned to any file created by the user that owns the file. The owner is given the right to read and write the file; the owner's group and the rest of the world can read the file (including the right to copy it into their own directories), but cannot modify it.

The file usage is a shell script that was written by a system administrator to collect data for a report on all the people who have logged into the system. Because it cleans out a system file, destroying the information about who has logged in, it must be carefully protected. For that reason, only the owner has the right to read, write, or execute the file. Although the script itself is not proprietary, if any other user were to copy the file into his or her account, there would be nothing to prevent that user from running the script and destroying valuable information before the system administrator had run the report.

> *Note: Users and applications can gain temporary access to restricted files through commands such as sudo (superuser do) and suid (set user ID), both of which require an end user to enter a superuser password.*

Changing File and Directory Permissions

You can change file and directory permissions with the chmod command. A user can change the permissions only for those files and directories for which it is the owner. The one exception is the superuser (the root user), who can change permissions on any files and directories in the system.

The chmod command can be used either by supplying numbers for the new access rights or by using letters to represent the permissions. When numbers are used to assign access rights, each type of permission is given a value:

4	Read the file or directory
2	Write the file or directory
1	Execute the file or search (execute) the directory

The rights given to a user category are determined by adding the values for the individual permissions. For example, if the owner of a file is to have the right to read and write the file, then the owner's rights have the value of 6. However, if the file is also executable, then the owner's rights are 7.

The numbers are supplied as arguments to chmod in the following manner:

```
chmod <owner rights><group rights><<world rights> file_name
```

Therefore, if the owner of a file named `inventory` is to have read and write permissions, the owner's group read permission, and the rest of the world no permission, the command is written

```
chmod 640 inventory
```

When letters are used to assign permissions, each type of access right has a unique character:

r	Read
w	Write
x	Search or execute

If the permission is to be added, then it is preceded with a plus (+); if it is to be removed, then it is preceded with a hyphen (-). The user category to which a permission applies is also indicated by a letter:

u	User (the owner)
g	Group
o	Other (the rest of the world)

If used without a user category, the permission is applied to all three user categories. For example,

```
chmod +x usage
```

would have the unfortunate effect of making the `usage` file executable by not only its owner, but by all members of the owner's group, and everyone else on the system.

Instead, the command can be issued as

```
chmod o+x usage
```

The o restricts the execute access to just the owner of the file.

Changing File Owners and Groups

The owners and groups to which files and directories belong can be changed by either the file or directory owner or the superuser. Changing owners requires the `chown` command; changing groups requires the `chgrp` command. Both have a similar syntax:

```
chown <new owner name> file_name

chgrp <new group name> file_name
```

For example, the current owner of the usage file may wish to further restrict use of that file by changing its owner to the system's administration account, sysadm. To do so, the chown command is written

```
chown sysadm usage
```

2.3.3 Mac OS X

Mac OS X is a UNIX implementation and does provide command line access through its Terminal program. However, it is much easier to use the GUI to change file and directory permissions on single items or a small group of items. (If you want to use a wildcard to affect many files with a single command, then the command line is the way to go.)

To use the GUI:

1. Select the file or folder for which you want to set permissions.
2. Select File->Get Info or press Command-I. The Get Info window appears (see Figure 2.6).
3. If necessary, click the triangles next to Ownership & Permissions and Details to expose the pop-up menus.
4. Choose the permissions from the pop-up menus.
5. Close the Get Info window to save the changes.

If you select multiple files or directories, the operating system presents you with a slightly different Get Info window (see Figure 2.7). Notice that you can nonetheless set the same permissions for each of the selected files.

2.4 Summary

The most fundamental piece of security software is a firewall. Whether it runs on a workstation, a router, or a stand-alone appliance, it is a network's first line of defense against unwanted network traffic.

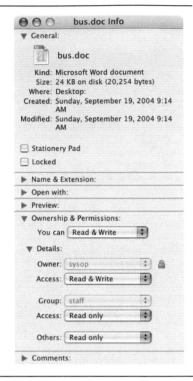

Figure 2.6 Using the Mac OS X GUI to change file or directory permissions

Small networks may have only a single firewall running on an edge router. Such firewalls, as well as firewalls that run on individual workstations, filter traffic by discarding packets that are addressed to TPC/UDP ports that have been "closed."

Stateful firewalls, which typically run on a dedicated firewall appliance located just behind a network's edge router, monitor what happens to packets after they pass through the firewall on to the internal network. They can prevent packets from changing port assignments once they have been cleared by a firewall. Stateful firewalls also monitor outgoing packets and allow response traffic to valid outgoing messages.

Application proxy firewalls, which also typically run on dedicated firewall appliances, isolate specific applications from external attacks. Although application proxy firewalls are generally considered to be the most secure, a network requires a separate proxy program for each application to be protected.

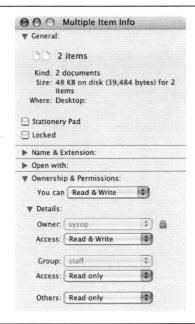

Figure 2.7 Changing permissions for multiple files using the Mac OS X GUI

When a network has resources, such as Web servers, that must be exposed to the Internet, the network architecture may include a DMZ, and area isolated from the internal network yet protected by a firewall. The DMZ is behind the first firewall; a second firewall behind the DMZ isolates the resources in the DMZ from the rest of the local network.

File and directory permissions provide another first line of defense in a security architecture.

Chapter 3: Physical Security

In This Chapter

♦ Dealing with theft and vandalism
♦ Securing the system console
♦ Handling system failure

3.0 Introduction

One of the most overlooked aspects of network security is the physical security of networking hardware and software and, in particular, your data center. In many instances, you can gain a significant amount of protection with a relatively small expenditure by paying attention to the physical environment of workstations, servers, and network interconnection hardware.

3.1 Dealing with Theft and Vandalism

For many years, the mental picture many people held of a security threat to a computer involved a disgruntled employee with an ax. Such an attack is rare today, but physical theft and vandalism can't be discounted. Laptops and other small devices are, as you would expect, particularly vulnerable.

Reality Check: So you think no one can steal your hardware? Think back to scenes from the first World Trade Center bombing (the truck bomb in the parking garage) where companies were given a short period of time to remove anything they needed from their offices. The television showed people wheeling large laundry carts full of PCs out of the building. Not only did the companies in question seem to be lacking a disaster recovery plan, but they had opened themselves to the theft of their equipment, and, perhaps more importantly, all the data on them.

There are a number of simple things you can do to thwart thieves and vandals:

♦ Use lockdown cables to secure desktop and laptop systems. (You can find details of specific types of lockdown systems in the Hands on section at the end of this chapter, beginning on page 72.) If desktop systems must be mobile—stored on wheeled carts, for example—lock the equipment to the carts.

♦ Secure your servers and wiring closets behind locked doors.

◆ Be stingy about to whom you give access to server rooms and wiring closets. Make sure that the individuals with access rights really need that access on a consistent basis. Those who need access on a temporary or irregular basis should be admitted by supervisors rather than given keys, access cards, combinations, or other access rights.

◆ Monitor the interior of server rooms and network interconnection hardware locations with video cameras. Connect the cameras to videotape recorders (in the case of analog cameras) or hard disks (in the case of digital cameras) to provide a permanent record of traffic in the monitored areas. If a breakin should occur, the recordings from the cameras may be able to provide significant information to law enforcement. How long should you retain the recordings? Check with your organization's legal department before making a final decision. Depending on the type of organization, recordings may be held as short a time as a week or as long as an entire auditing cycle. (Why an entire auditing cycle? Because it may take the results of an outside audit to uncover a security breach that wasn't detected by any other means.)

◆ Remove all signs identifying the rooms and closets in which servers, network interconnection hardware, and wiring are stored. You don't want to make it too easy for a potential thief or vandal to find your equipment.

◆ Require users to password both the boot and the screensaver on their laptops. In most cases, what is on a laptop is far more valuable than the laptop itself. Your insurance policy can replace the computer, but no money can make up for the exposure of confidential corporate information.

Reality Check: Passwording a laptop may or may not be effective in all cases. A knowledgeable thief will remove the computer's battery and let the capacitor that maintains the memory holding the passwords drain. At that point, the thief can replace the battery and boot the computer normally. Once the machine is up, the thief can remove the screensaver password. Fortunately, this trick doesn't work with all of today's laptops; with some laptops it can take weeks for the capacitor to drain, rather than just a few days.

The most difficult thief or vandal to guard against is the employee. Consider the following scenario: An employee calls the IT department early one morning, stating that his car was broken into during the night, and his laptop was stolen. A check of the police department shows that the break-in was reported and that the laptop was on the list of items taken. The IT department then reports the theft to the company's insurance carrier and the machine is replaced. The truth is, however, that the laptop was never in the car and the entire break-in was staged. The laptop is safely hidden away in the employee's possession, neatly stolen and ready for whatever the employee chooses to do with it.

> *Note: Not all corporate insurance policies cover equipment that is not located on company premises and/or in an unattended vehicle; you need to check your policy.*

Your first line of defense against internal theft is an accurate equipment inventory that is verified at least yearly. The inventory should indicate the location of every piece of hardware and who is responsible for it. Second, whenever someone is given the use of hardware designed to be moved frequently—a laptop or PDA, in most cases— he or she should be required to read and sign a statement of responsibility for that item. In other words, you make the employee responsible for the equipment entrusted in his or her care. It is up to the employee to obtain his or her own insurance for the company's equipment when it is not on company premises.

In addition to keeping track of your inventory and protecting mobile equipment as much as possible, you also need to be aware of who has access to equipment that is stored behind locked doors. If everyone in the company has access, then the locks are useful only for keeping out nonemployees who don't have friends working for the company.

The biggest hurdle isn't finding a good way to lock a room, but deciding who should have access and under what circumstances. For example, a server room needs to be cleaned frequently, and a janitor probably needs access outside normal working hours. Should that janitor be allowed into the server room alone, or should he or she be accompanied by a corporate security guard? Should the janitor have his or her own key or access code, or should the janitor be admitted by the security guard? The answers to questions of this type should be spelled out in the organization's security policy.

Note: Keep in mind that access to secure resources gives the person with access a feeling of power and prestige within the organization. Therefore, when you decide to deny someone access to a resource (be it a server room or some data in a database), you are taking away some of his or her self-perceived status in the organization. This can make decisions about who has access to what resources very, very difficult in an interpersonal sense.

Once you have decided who will have access to the locked room, then you need to decide how people will gain access. Will you give them keys? Keys are easily lost, stolen, and/or duplicated. What about something that can't be duplicated, such as a keypad? How will you manage the access codes? This type of decision isn't part of a security policy because it is an implementation detail. The technology for securing a room is going to continue to change, and your security staff should be free to upgrade that technology without revisions to the security policy. For specific ideas about securing rooms, see the Hands On section at the end of this chapter (page 72).

3.2 Protecting the System Console

The most vulnerable computers on a network are those that administer the network and the servers. Such machines—often called "system consoles" when they control a server of some type, in reference to the terminals used to administer mainframes—have highly privileged access because users working at those computers must be able to manage users, passwords, file and directory permissions, as well as configure interconnection devices. In addition, because they are used frequently, system consoles often are left logged in to the highly privileged account.

A knowledgeable person can walk up to a logged in system console and do anything the account lets a user do. In most cases, a hacker will use the system console to create a new account, giving that new account as much access to the system as possible. Then, the hacker will leave and access the new account from another location. This is particularly effective in situations where more than one network staff person creates new accounts. The unauthorized account is much less likely to be recognized as such.

To protect the system console, there are a few simple things you can do:

◆ Keep system consoles behind locked doors.

◆ Do not leave administrative accounts logged in when no one is at the keyboard. This behavioral change may be hard to implement, as many system operators find it convenient to leave their accounts logged in, especially when in a locked "glass house."

◆ Place only one person in charge of creating new accounts. This will make it much more difficult for an unauthorized account to go unnoticed.

To take console security one step further, you can place all system consoles in a room with either a video surveillance system or a staff member who is physically present in the room at all times.

3.3 Managing System Failure

Of all the things you can do to protect your network, accurate, up-to-date system backup is one of the most important. If your backups are managed properly, you will always have a fall-back position, regardless of what disaster may befall your system.

3.3.1 Backup Solutions

Backup used to be easy: you copied your data files to floppy disk and put the disks in a drawer. Times have changed considerably. To put it more precisely, storage capacities have increased. When we have hard disks that are hundred of gigabytes in size, we need equally large backup devices. And the proverbial desk drawer just isn't a very safe place for backup copies to reside!

The Backup Plan

Backup policies should be part of an organization's security policy. When formulating that policy, you need to answer a number of questions. First, what needs to be backed up? Just your data files, or data files and applications? In many cases, applications can be restored from their original distribution media. Although it takes longer to recover when you have to reinstall your applications, backups will be faster and take up less storage space.

How much should you back up? If you need to back up everything, then you will be doing a *full backup*. Full backups ensure that the contents of the backup media are complete. Because the backup contains the most recent copy of each file, restoring from a full backup is also faster than any other type of restore. On the other hand, copying every file to backup media is the slowest type of backup. You therefore might want an *incremental backup*, during which you copy only those files that have been changed since the last backup (archival or incremental). Because an incremental backup involves only a subset of the files, it can be performed much faster than a full backup. However, restoring from incremental backups is more difficult because you must find the most recent copy of each file before restoring it.

As files age and sit unused, you may decide that you no longer need them online. If you nonetheless need to retain the files (for legal or other reasons), then you will want to create an *archival backup*, during which you copy the files to some type of removable media and then delete them from online storage. The backup media are then stored in a safe place where they can be accessed if ever needed.

Reality Check: Be careful about relying on single copies of media such as CD-ROMs and DVDs for archival backups. They can become damaged more easily than you might think. Having lost the files to several of my books that way, I would suggest that if you are archiving to optical media, make at least three archival copies. If one becomes damaged, immediately create another copy from one of the remaining undamaged ones.

Reality Check: How long should you keep archival backups? There is no single, easy answer to that question. Consider, for example, the important role that historical e-mails have played in court cases in the past few years, such as those in the Microsoft anti-trust case. Check with your legal department to help determine how long e-mails and other materials should be kept. Check with your users to see what types of data they have need for occasionally.

How often should a backup be made? Perhaps you need a complete archival backup daily (or even more frequently), or perhaps you need an archival backup once a week, with incremental backups done daily. Given that it takes longer to recover from a set of incremental backups than from a single archival backup, but that making a complete archival backup takes longer than an incremental backup, what is the best mix of archiving and incremental backups for your organization? How quickly do you need to be back up and running after a system failure? How volatile are your files (how quickly do they change?)? How much modified data are you willing to lose?

Can you make backups while the network and/or servers are in use? Are there any application programs that must be shut down to make backups of the data files they use? If you must bring some machines and/or applications off-line, when can you do so with minimal impact on your users?

Who will perform the backups? Usually making backups is the responsibility of system operators, but you need to ensure that the backups are actually being performed.

Reality Check: Even if you designate the responsibility for making backups to a specific job description, you still must pay attention to what is (or isn't) occurring. I once had an outpatient psychiatry clinic of a major hospital as a consulting client. The receptionist was supposed to run a backup tape each evening before she left. However, in her hurry to leave each evening—she was scheduled to leave an hour later than most other staff—she was just turning off her workstation without signing out. The temporary icons left by the software on her hard disk alerted me that something was amiss and a hunch, followed by a check of the backup tapes, revealed that not only wasn't she shutting down properly, but she wasn't making the backups either. Unfortunately, it took a month before this came to light, during which time the clinic was extremely vulnerable.

How many "generations" of backups will you keep? Conventional wisdom states that you should keep three sets of backups, each one backup period older than the preceding. When time comes to create a fourth backup copy, you reuse the media from the oldest of the three existing backup copies. The idea is that if the first backup is damaged, you have two more to fall back to.

The three generation backup is good in theory, but beware: In some cases you can end up with all three backup copies being damaged. This is particularly true if a system has been infected by a virus or worm that isn't detected immediately, or if a file is corrupted by being written to a bad disk sector or some other similar problem. (You won't detect the latter until someone attempts to read the file, by which time it may be too late to recover a clean copy of the file.)

Where will you store the backups? It's convenient to have the backups close at hand—somewhere on site—but if your physical facility is damaged, your backup media possibly will be damaged as well. Therefore, you probably want to keep at least one backup copy off-site. Which site will you use? Do you want to pay simply for off-site storage, or do you want a true "hot site," where you can run your software until your facility is restored? A good storage site will be secure from environmental extremes (heat, cold, fire, and water) and will be easily and readily accessible. You will need 24/7 access to your off-site backups, in all kinds of weather. A mountain-top cave may be cool and dry and safe from flooding, but it could be too hard to reach in the winter.

Backup Media

During the period when your files were so small they would fit on a single floppy disk, choosing backup media was easy. Floppies were cheap, easy to store, and provided random access for quick file restores. However, to accommodate today's large file sizes we have a variety of different options.

Tape.   The first medium used for large system backup was magnetic tape. Initially running on reel-to-reel tape drives, tape provided the capacity necessary to hold large files for mainframe systems. Although not particularly fast, tape backups can often be run in the background with other processing and therefore may have minimal impact on system performance.

Even today, tape provides the highest backup capacity for the lowest cost. However, tape is a sequential access medium; to reach a specific file you must read past all preceding files on the tape. To make matters even more inconvenient, many tape drives can't read backwards. That means that if you need a file that precedes the tape's current location, the tape must be rewound and read again from the beginning.

Nonetheless, if you are backing up large files, then tape may be your only feasible option. The other media described in this section probably will be too costly or won't have enough storage capacity. Keep in mind, however, that hard disk storage sizes often outstrip tape capacities and that backing up extremely large files may still require more than one tape.

Large installations, whose data storage capacities run in the multiple terabyte range, turn to high density cartridges for backup. For example, in Figure 3.1 you can see IBM's 1 terabyte data cartridge compared to the 1500 CDs you would need to use to obtain comparable storage capacity. Such cartridges are read and written by tape drives in a variety of sizes, varying primarily by the number of tapes they can handle at one time (see Figure 3.2). In some cases, tape storage systems are managed by robots under software control. The robots pull cartridges from storage shelves, load them into the tape drive, and, when cartridges are full, remove them from the drive and return them to their places on the storage shelves.

Tape cartridges for desktop systems come in a wide range of formats, ranging in capacity up to about 160 gigabytes. This is considerably smaller than many of today's hard drive storage. You may therefore need to allocate more than one tape for each archival backup.

Despite their limitations, the high storage capacity of tape cartridges makes tape the backup media of choice for the majority of large networks. There just isn't anything else that can handle the archival storage of gigabytes (and even terabytes) of files.

CD and DVD.   As soon as CD burners became affordable, many computer users looked at them as a replacement for floppy disk or tape backup. Certainly the media are more durable—a CD stores hundreds of times more than a floppy disk—and provides random access to the contents of the disc. However, hard disk capacities have rapidly outstripped the less than 700 Mb capacity of a CD, making them ill-suited for server backup.

For a time, DVDs looked to be the best alternative, but even when double-layer, double-sided recordable DVDs are available, the maximum capacity will be only around 14 Gb. This clearly isn't enough to back up today's hard disks without a lot of media swapping.

Figure 3.1   Comparing a 1 terabyte tape cartridge to CD storage

DVD blanks are much cheaper than tape cartridges. They are also easier to store and longer lasting. Coupled with their random access capabilities, they are limited primarily by their low storage capacity. Nonetheless, CD and DVD may be a reasonable backup choice for individual desktop or laptop computers.

Hard Disk.   The highest capacity device available for use as a backup medium is a hard disk. This isn't a particularly low cost solution, but it has several advantages:

- ◆ A hard disk provides fast, random access recovery of individual files.
- ◆ If an entire hard disk becomes unreadable, the backup disk can replace the damaged primary disk almost immediately.

Figure 3.2   Four tape storage systems

♦ RAID software or hardware can be used to control writing to
the backup drive each time something is written to the primary drive (*disk mirroring*). This alternative ensures that an
up-to-date backup copy is always available, although it does
slow down writing to the disks.

Which costs more, tape or hard disk? The answer is that it depends on your overall backup scheme. As an example, consider the trade-off for a desktop network server: If you are keeping three generations of back-ups, then you will need three backup hard drives. Assuming that your backup drive is large enough to store all files that need backing up, three hard drives (for example, external FireWire drives) will cost about the same as a high-capacity cartridge tape drive. Add in the cost of tape cartridges, and the initial investment in the tape drive is more than the three backup hard disks.

The tape drive, however, is not limited in capacity. If you upgrade the size of the hard disk in the server, you don't necessarily need to replace the tape drive; you just need to get more cartridges. Unfortunately, the backup hard drives may no longer be large enough to be useful, and will need to be replaced. In the long run, tape therefore can be much cheaper.

There are situations in which the cost of using a hard disk as a backup medium isn't an overriding factor. If you need a system that is always available, and you can't afford to have any lost data, then your best choice is another hard disk. You should consider setting up disk mirroring, or even setting up a *shadow computer*, a machine that is identical to your primary server that can become the primary server if the current primary goes down for any reason.

The Internet.   Some organizations have decided to use servers connected to the Internet to store backup copies. The organization uses the Internet to transfer files that should be backed up, usually employing FTP transfers. The biggest benefit to this solution is that the organization doesn't have to maintain its own backup facilities; it doesn't have to purchase backup hardware or software, or worry about upgrading the platform as storage needs increase.

However, there are several drawbacks. First, the Internet isn't terribly fast or reliable for the transfer of extremely large files. Second, the organization is placing all its backup copies in the hands of another company. If that company goes out of business, the backup copies will be inaccessible and the security of the data they contain will be suspect. Third, backing up over the Internet may not be cost-effective.

In-House Backup

Another major question you need to answer about backup is where you will perform and store the backups. Most organizations continue to make and retain their own. If you are going to do so, then you need to answer the following two questions, in addition to those discussed earlier in this chapter:

◆ Who will be responsible for ensuring that backups are being made as scheduled? Typically, computer operators or network administrators make the backups. There should be, however, a supervisor who monitors compliance with backup policy and procedures.

◆ How will you secure the backup copies? Assuming that you are keeping three generations, where will each one be stored? At least one copy should be in some type of fireproof and waterproof storage, such as a fireproof filing cabinet. You should also seriously consider off-site storage. (For more information on off-site storage, see the section on Hot Sites that follows shortly.)

Outsourced Backup

An alternative to handling your own backup is to contract with an outside firm to perform the backups. The company you hire generally will access your servers either over the Internet or using a dedicated leased line. It will make the backup copies and store them on its own premises. The difference between this solution and the use of the Internet discussed earlier in the section on backup media is that the organization whose data are being backed up is not actually performing the backup. If you outsource, the company you hire does all the work. You provide the access to your servers and step aside.

Outsourcing completely frees an organization from having to deal with backup. However, it is subject to the same drawbacks as using an Internet server as a backup medium. In addition, you must also give the company you hire access to your servers.

Hot Sites

An organization of almost any size should seriously consider keeping a backup copy off-site. Fires, flood, earthquakes—all manner of natural and unnatural disasters—can render your data processing facility unusable. Many organizations use *hot sites*, companies in the business of providing off-site storage for backup copies. Hot sites also keep hardware on which you can load your backups and run your business should your hardware become unavailable.

One of the best-known hot sites is Iron Mountain (*www.ironmountain.com*). Originally located in a worked-out iron mine in upstate New York, Iron Mountain now provides secure storage throughout the United States. The services provided by this company are typical of what you can expect from a hot site:

- ◆ Storage for records in any format, including paper files.

- ◆ Secure document shredding.

- ◆ Off-site storage for backup copies, including the pickup and delivery of media on a regularly scheduled basis. You make the backups and Iron Mountain stores them.

- ◆ Outsourced backup. Iron Mountain makes and stores the backups.

- ◆ Outsourced archival storage for all types of electronic records, such as e-mail and images.

- ◆ Hardware on which you can run your business should your hardware become unusable.

3.3.2 Power Protection

An often overlooked aspect of physical data protection is electrical power. Unregulated power is often subject to voltage spikes (surges), brownouts, and blackouts. At the very least, power problems can result in data loss; in the most severe cases, equipment can be seriously damaged or destroyed.

Surge Protection

A surge protector (for example, Figure 3.3) absorbs sudden increases in line voltage—caused perhaps by a lightning strike or problem with the power grid—protecting equipment from damage. At the low end, a surge protector is inexpensive and works—at least once. In this situation, you get what you pay for. Look for surge protectors that have indicator lights that show they are still working.

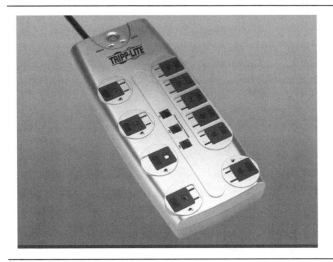

Figure 3.3   A surge protector with indicator lights to let the user know that surge protection is in effect

Reality Check: There is power running through landline (wired) telephones. Power surges therefore can jump from electrical lines to telephone lines and damage anything attached (telephones, fax machines, and modems). Therefore, it is a good idea to run your telephone lines through a surge protector (or other power protection device) as well as electrical connections. Most power protection equipment today includes jacks to protect telephone lines, as in the middle of the surge protector in Figure 3.3. If the telephone line protection is available, for heavens sake, use it!

Line Conditioners

Surge protectors are fine as far as they go, but they can't do anything to handle low voltage conditions that can occur when an electrical system is overloaded (a brownout condition) or a piece of high-voltage equipment starts up. (Think this doesn't happen to you? Think again. do the lights dim when the air conditioner starts up?)

Line conditioners combine surge protection with brownout protection. They contain capacitors that store a small amount of electricity that is discharged when the line per voltage drops. A line conditioner therefore provides a more constant voltage than unconditioned line voltage. This can help lengthen the life of your equipment as well as avoid data damage.

Line conditioners, such as that in Figure 3.4, tend to be more expensive than surge protectors, but are less expensive than uninterruptable power supplies.

Figure 3.4   A line conditioner

Uninterruptable Power Supplies

An uninterruptable power supply (UPS) provides a battery that will run a computer system for a short period of time after the loss of line power. Many UPSs also provide surge protection and line conditioning. Small UPSs look much like overgrown surge protectors; those for larger systems, such as that in Figure 3.5, can be rack-mounted.

UPSs come in two varieties. The first charges its battery from the line and passes line current through to equipment connected to it. When line

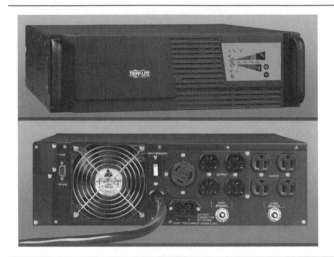

Figure 3.5   A rack mountable UPS

power is interrupted, the UPS switches quickly to its battery. The second type always runs the computer from its battery. There is no cutover when line power is interrupted.

The second type of UPS is considerably more expensive than the type that cuts over to battery power, but it does provide continuous, conditioned power. The time gap for the cutover from line power to battery power was also once an issue. However, the cutover is so fast today that most UPSs use this method.

3.4 Hands On: Providing Physical Security

We've come a long way since we used skeleton keys to provide security. Physical security devices range from commonplace access cards to the stuff of science fiction (retina scans, face scans, and so on). This final section of this chapter will introduce you to some specific physical security solutions. Keep in mind, however, that this technology is always improving and that you should research your solutions carefully before buying.

This section also looks at some of the specifics of conducting a disaster recovery drill, something that should be performed at regular intervals to ensure that disaster recovery plans actually work.

3.4.1 Physical Solutions

There are three basic ways to provide physical security: secure equipment with locks of one type of another, enforce strict personal identification for admittance to locked areas, and monitor what occurs in secure areas with cameras. The first two solutions can be closely related today, in that secure area locks use a variety of personal identification schemes.

Individual Computer Locks

Not all hardware that needs to be secured is located in server rooms or wiring closets: many PCs and printers are installed in environments such as offices, workshops, warehouses, or factory floors. If your facility is unoccupied at night and on weekends or if there are many nonemployees visiting your facility, then you may want to consider locking down portable equipment with lockdown systems.

Room Locks and "Keys"

The first type of computer room security involved simple locks with keys. A lock with a key is better than no lock at all, but keys are so easily lost, stolen, and/or duplicated that most secure locations rely on something more difficult to obtain and counterfeit.

Combination Locks.   A combination lock provides a better alternative to a physical key because the key lies within a person's head. Although it can be forgotten, it can't be lost or stolen.

> *Note: One of the big problems with any key that has to be remembered—be it a lock combination or password—is that human beings have a tendency to write it down. If the written key falls into unauthorized hands, the key is compromised. You can read more about this issue in Chapter 8.*

The type of combination locks used on school lockers are often hard to use. Once opened, they can also be removed from a latch. Therefore, many secure facilities have opted for combination locks that can be permanently affixed to a door. The simplest of these locks are mechanical and set with a single combination. However, electronic push-button combination locks can be programmed with a different combination for each person who should have access. High-end electronic "smart locks" store which combinations were used, as well as when they were used, for downloading to a handheld device (and ultimately, to a PC), can restrict access based on date and time, and can lock out individual users or groups of users.

Tokens.   If you want to avoid the issues surrounding the security of remembered keys, then you can require users to present a physical token for access. The most commonly used token today is a credit card-sized card with a magnetic stripe. The user swipes the card through a magnetic stripe reader to gain access.

Cards with magnetic stripes can be lost, stolen, or counterfeited, just like metal keys. However, they are more flexible than keys because the magnetic stripes can be programmed with a variety of information, including the specific locks to which a user has access and days/times when that access is allowed.

If you need to store more information about a user than you can store on a magnetic stripe, then there are tokens—such as the iButton from Dallas Technologies in Figure 3.6—that can store a PIN or biometric identification (for example, fingerprint or retina scan). The token, which is small enough to embed in a ring or hang on a key ring, can then be combined with a second type of identification (for example, a password). If such a token is lost or stolen, it is useless because the finder or thief can't use it without the secondary identification.

Biometrics.   Biometrics—the use of biological features for identification—may sound like futuristic technology. However, biometrics are feasible and currently in use. The simplest are fingerprint devices. The security system stores a digitized fingerprint for each user. To gain access to a secure facility, the user places his or her finger on a reader, which then takes a digital picture, compares it to the stored fingerprint, and grants access if a match is made.

Figure 3.6 Using an iButton to unlock a door by placing the token against a sensor

Other biometric devices include voice recognition, hand scanners, retina scanners, iris scanners, and face geometry scanners. All provide positive identification of an individual. For additional security, biometric identification can be combined with a PIN.

In the minds of many people, biometric devices are still the stuff of science fiction. That is not always the case, however. For example, fingerprint readers, such as the Fellowes mouse in Figure 3.7, are small, portable, and cost less than $100.

Monitoring with Cameras

Using remote cameras to monitor traffic into and out of secure areas is not a new concept. It can be a very effective security technique under specific circumstances:

- ◆ If access to secure areas is restricted during specific hours, any person a camera picks up during those hours is probably attempting unauthorized access.

- ◆ If everyone who is authorized to access a secure location is known by sight to security personnel, any unknown person seen by a camera is probably attempting unauthorized access.

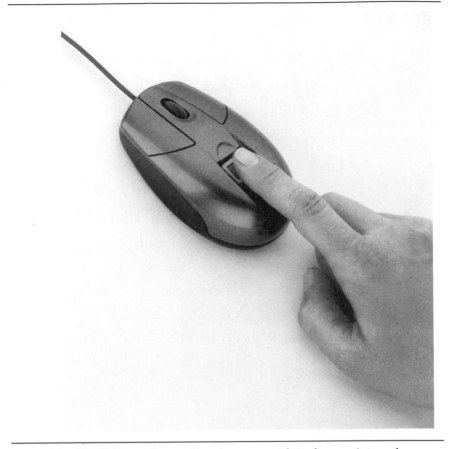

Figure 3.7   The Fellowes Secure Touch mouse with its fingerprint reader

Cameras can also show unusual activity outside a secure area, such as someone being coerced to use a key, token, or biometric device, or a physical attempt to break into the secure area.

3.4.2 Disaster Recovery Drills

Having a good disaster recovery plan is essential to any security policy, but that plan is useful only if it works. Just like a school holds a fire drill, you need to conduct a disaster recovery drill to ensure that you really can get your network back up and running after a disaster.

Your disaster recovery drill can be announced or unannounced. The latter will provide a better test of your disaster recovery planning, but may be much more difficult to organize. In either case, you will simulate as many types of network disasters as feasible and observe how the IT staff recovers. If all goes well, you'll know that your planning was sufficient. It is more likely, however, that at least part of the written plan won't operate as expected, and you will therefore be able to identify things that either need modification in the disaster recovery plan or modification in the implementation of that plan.

The first step in a disaster recovery drill is the planning of the drill itself. Questions you need to answer in the planning stage include:

- What will be tested?
- How will the failures be simulated?
- How long will the drill run?
- How will the results of the drill be recorded?
- Will the IT staff be aware that a drill is in progress, or will they be led to believe that the disaster is real?

An organization that is serious about disaster recovery will have two sets of contingency plans: one to use when recovery using internal resources is feasible and one to use when it is necessary to use data and/or equipment stored at a hot site.

The internal tests should include simulations of the following:

- Power failure: External storage isn't damaged, although any work in progress is lost. This may not seem like a major type of failure because disks remain intact. Consider, however, the effect of a sudden shutdown on a disk file system. Most modern operating systems are vulnerable to file system corruption if the operating system does not perform its shutdown routines. Therefore, bringing a system that goes down from a power failure back to a trustworthy, working state can be a major challenge.

- Media failure: Losing one or more disk drives is a nightmare that haunts many system administrators. If such a disaster should occur and mirrored drives are not available, system operators will need to find alternative media and restore the system from the most current backup.

♦ Backup failure: Another major point of failure is the loss of backup copies. This can occur when one or more generations of backup have become corrupt or when a disaster (such as flood or fire) destroys in-house backups. Simulating a backup failure can be used to trigger an external disaster recovery drill.

External testing requires the assumption that neither your internal hardware nor software is functional. It should also assume that there are no available backup copies in-house. The typical external test involves determining how long it takes to get your information systems up and running on your hot site's equipment, using backup copies stored off-site.

3.5 Summary

One of the most overlooked aspects of network security is the physical security of computing equipment and the software used by that equipment. In this chapter, you have read about strategies for dealing with theft and vandalism, including locking down equipment, securing the facilities in which equipment is kept, and protecting mobile devices such as laptop computers.

We have also considered the vulnerabilities associated with "system consoles," the terminals or PCs used to administer large computers and/or networks. General strategies for securing a system console include physically restricting access to the console and ensuring that privileged accounts are not left logged in when not in use.

The most important physical protection your system can have is a good backup scheme. This chapter reviewed options for backup media, strategies for managing backup copies, and the importance of disaster recovery drills.

Computers can also be protected physically by specialized locks (including biometrics and tokens). In addition, some installations may want to consider monitoring facilities with cameras.

Chapter 4: Information Gathering

In This Chapter

- ◆ Social engineering
- ◆ Using published information
- ◆ Port scanning
- ◆ Network mapping

4.0 Introduction

An attack on a computer network doesn't necessarily begin with technology. In fact, some system violations are made possible through information gathered directly from employees and other public sources, most of which is available legally.

In addition, simple electronic tools can give a system cracker information about the layout of a network, what operating system is in use, and what TCP/IP ports are open. All this information goes into assembling a profile of a network that can then be used to identify specific parts of the network that are vulnerable to attack.

In this chapter we'll start by looking at a form of information gathering that involves scamming users out of information such as user names and passwords. Known as *social engineering*, it usually involves role-playing by the person attempting to gain unauthorized system access. There is also an electronic version of social engineering—phishing—that involves tricking people by sending them misleading e-mails.

We'll then turn to published information available on the Web through Internet registration databases. Finally, we'll examine some tools that are useful for troubleshooting a network, but that can also yield information that you probably don't want a cracker to know.

4.1 Social Engineering

To understand social engineering, think "Mission Impossible" (the TV series) on a small scale. The person trying to obtain system access typically engages in a simple role play that tricks someone out of supposedly confidential information. Here's how such an escapade might play out:

CEO's secretary answers telephone: "Big Corporation. How may I help you?"

Cracker: "Good morning. This is John Doe from Standard Software. We're the people who supply your accounting software. Your IT department has purchased a software upgrade that needs to be installed on your computer. I can do it over the Internet, without even coming into your office and disrupting your work."

Secretary: "Say, that sounds terrific. Is there anything I need to do?"

Cracker: "All I need is your user name and password. Then I'll upload the new files."

Secretary: "Sure, no problem. My user name is Jane Notsmart; my password is Jane."

Cracker: "Thanks, Jane. The files will be on their way in just a couple of minutes."

The cracker then does exactly what he said he would do: He uploads files to Jane's machine. But the files certainly aren't an upgrade to the accounting software. Instead, they give the cracker root access to the secretary's computer. The cracker can come back later, log in to her machine, and cruise through the entire corporate network.

Could it really have been that easy? Are users really that gullible? Oh, yes, indeed. We humans tend to be very trusting and need to be taught to be suspicious. And it's just not the technologically unsophisticated who fall for such social engineering scams. Our tendency to trust anyone who says he or she is in a position of authority provides an opening for clever crackers to trick just about anyone.

> *Note: If you don't believe that humans trust most things said to them by someone who seems to be in a position of authority, check out http://www.age-of-the-sage.org/psychology/milgram_obedience_experiment.html. This Web page documents a classic psychological experiment conducted by Stanley Milgram in 1974 that revealed a very disturbing aspect of human behavior.*

There is really only one defense against social engineering: good user education. You will need to warn users about the types of social engineering attacks that can occur and include instructions about how users should report such attempts. Such types of employee training sessions often include role-plays that try to ensnare the participants with examples of social engineering.

Reality Check: In many cases, it isn't enough to give users broad guidelines such as "don't give out your user name and password." They need specific behavioral rules. For example, to prevent the installation of unauthorized software you might establish the following rules:

1. Software is to be installed only by an IT staff person.

2. IT staff people will present photo ID cards.

3. IT staff people will never ask for your user name and password.

It's tough to be completely proactive when it comes to social engineering because you can't anticipate every type of scam that a cracker might devise, so all you can do is use your best guesses to anticipate situations that might arise. And in some instances, you'll need to create new rules after an incident has occurred.

4.1.1 Electronic Social Engineering: Phishing

Social engineering can be done via e-mail as well as in person or over the telephone. The intent is to trick the person into revealing information such as account names and passwords, bank account numbers, or credit card numbers.

One of the oldest types of phishing involves convincing a victim that he or she has been selected to help transfer millions of unclaimed dollars from an African bank and, as payment, will receive a significant percentage of the funds. In Figure 4.1 you can find a typical e-mail that is intended to scam bank account information from its victim. (This e-mail appears exactly as it was received, grammatical errors and all.) Like an in-person or telephone social engineering attempt, it plays on the victim's gullibility and, in this case, greed. Even though these scams are well known, people fall for them repeatedly, sometimes losing hundreds of thousands of dollars when the scammer empties a victim's bank account.

The other typical phishing expedition involves fooling the e-mail recipient into thinking he or she has received a legitimate e-mail from a trusted source, such as eBay, PayPal, or the recipient's ISP. The e-mail (for example, Figure 4.2) directs the recipient to a Web site (see Figure 4.3)

FROM THE DESK OF, MR PETER NWA. EC BANK OF AFFRICA PLC. SEND YOUR REPLY TO
THIS EMAIL IF YOU ARE INTERESTED. nwa-peter@caramail.cm ATTN:MY FRIEND, I am
the manager of bill and exchange at the foreign remittance department of the EC
BANK OF AFRICA LAGOS, NIGERIA. I am writing following the impressive information
about you. I have the assurance that you are capable and reliable enough to
champion an impending transaction. In my department, we discovered an abandoned
sum of US$28.5m (twenty eight million and five hundred thousand US dollars), in
an account that belonged to one of our former customers who died along with his
entire family in a plane crash, in November, 1997. Since we received the
information about his death, we have expected his next of kin to come forward
and claim his money, as enshrined in our banking laws and regulations. So far
nobody has come forward, and we cannot release the funds unless someone applies
as the next of kin as stipulated in our guidelines.Unfortunately, we have
discovered that all his supposed next of kin or relations died alongside with
him in the plane crash, and effectively leaving nobody behind for the claim. It
is consequent upon this discovery that other officials and I in my department
decided to make this business proposal to you and release the money to you as
the next of kin or relation of the deceased person, for safety and subsequent
disbursement, since nobody is coming forward for it, and the mnoey is not reverted
into the bank's treasury as unclaimed. The bank's regulation stipulates that if
after five years, such money remains unclaimed; the money will be reverted to
the bank's treasury as unclaimed fund. The request for a foreigner as the next
of kin in this transaction is predicated upon the fact that the said customer
was a foreign national, and no citizen of this country can claim to be the next
of kin of a foreigner. We agree that 30% of the total sum we be given to you for
your assistance in facilitating this transaction. My colleagues and I are going
to retain 60% of the total sum, and 10% will be set aside for the expenses that
we may incur in facilitating the remittance. To enable us effect this remittance,
you must first apply as the next of kin of the deceased. Your application will
include your bank coordinates, that is, your bank name, bank address and telex,
your bank account. You will include your private telephone no. and fax no., for
easy and effective communication during this process. My colleagues and I will
visit your country for disbursement according to the agreed ratio, when this
transaction is concluded. Upon the receipt of your response, I will send to you
by fax,the text of the application. I must not fail to bring to your notice the
fact that this transaction is hitch free, and that you should not entertain fear
as you are adequately protected from any form of embarrassment Do respond to this
letter today through my email address(nwa-peter@caramail.com) to enable us
proceed with the transaction. Yours sincerely, MR PETER NWA. EC BANK OF AFRICA.

Figure 4.1   A typical money-stealing e-mail

where—in this case—the user is asked to enter everything but his or her
driver's license number! When you click the Continue button at the bottom of the Web page, you receive an error message (see Figure 4.4). You
can bet, however, that all the text entered on the preceding page was
stored somewhere where the thief could retrieve it.

Note: The Web page in Figure 4.3 has been broken up into three parts so that it could be reproduced in this book in a size that you could read. However, when viewed on the Web, it was a single page.

As with "live" social engineering attempts, the best defense against phishing is good user education. It can be difficult for users who aren't technologically savvy to look at the routing information of an e-mail or the URL of a Web and determine whether the addresses are legitimate. Therefore it is often more effective to stick with behavioral rules, such as "Never give your user ID and password to anyone," and "Never follow links in e-mails."

Reality Check: Is phishing really a big problem? According to the Anti-Phishing Working Group (APWG at *http://www.antiphishing.org*), it's a very big problem and it's getting worse. Consider the following: APWG found that five in 100 people respond to phishing e-mails, while only one person in 100 responds to spam e-mail. Add that to its data for 2004, which shows a steady increase in the number of phishing sites from 192 in January to 407 in December. The result is a serious challenge to end-user confidence in the e-mails they receive. Some observers believe that users will become so afraid of e-mails from commercial sites that e-commerce will be seriously crippled. Although such a prediction may well be too extreme, it does highlight the seriousness of phishing attempts that prey on human fears, such as having an account cancelled.

4.2 Using Published Information

Often the information on which a cracker bases a social engineering attack comes from legal, publicly available sources. Two of the most "useful" sources are corporate Web sites and domain name registration databases.

What can you get from a Web site? Names, positions in the organization, and contact points. For example, consider the Web page in Figure 4.5. Although the names of employees don't appear directly, take a look at the e-mail addresses: You can easily discern the first initial and last name of most people, along with their job responsibilities.

```
Dear eBay member ,

 Since the number of fraudulent eBay account take-overs has
increased with 100% in the last 4 weeks , eBay Inc. has decided to
verify all eBay account owners and their personal information in
order to clarify all accounts status .
This is to prevent unauthorized external access to eBay accounts
and personal information .
This is the only time you will receive a message from eBay security
team , and you are to complete all required fields shown in the
page displayed from the link below .

Click the following link and complete all required fields in order
for a better account verification :

http://update-secure-ebay.com

 Account confirmation is a due ; if you refuse to cooperate  you
dont leave us any choice but to shut-down your eBay account .

 Thank you for your cooperation
```

Figure 4.2   A user ID/password stealing e-mail

Domain name registration databases contain information about the organization (or individual) that owns a domain name. In addition, they may expose the IP addresses of servers (in particular, domain name servers) with static IP addresses. The software that performs the domain name database searches may be supplied as part of an operating system (for command-line operation) or it may be part of a GUI-based network management utility.

To find out who owns a domain name and the domain names of their DNS servers, you use the whois command. As you can see in Figure 4.6, the information includes the name of the person or company who registered the domain name, their mailing address, an administrative contact (along with address and phone number), a technical contact (also with address and phone number), as well as the DNS servers in use.

It is possible to restrict the information that appears as the result of a whois search by changing settings with your domain name registrar. (The exact details vary, of course, from one registrar to another.) For more information, see the Hands On section that begins on page 97.

Another double-edged utility (one that can be used to help administer a network or to engage in information gathering) is nslookup. Running

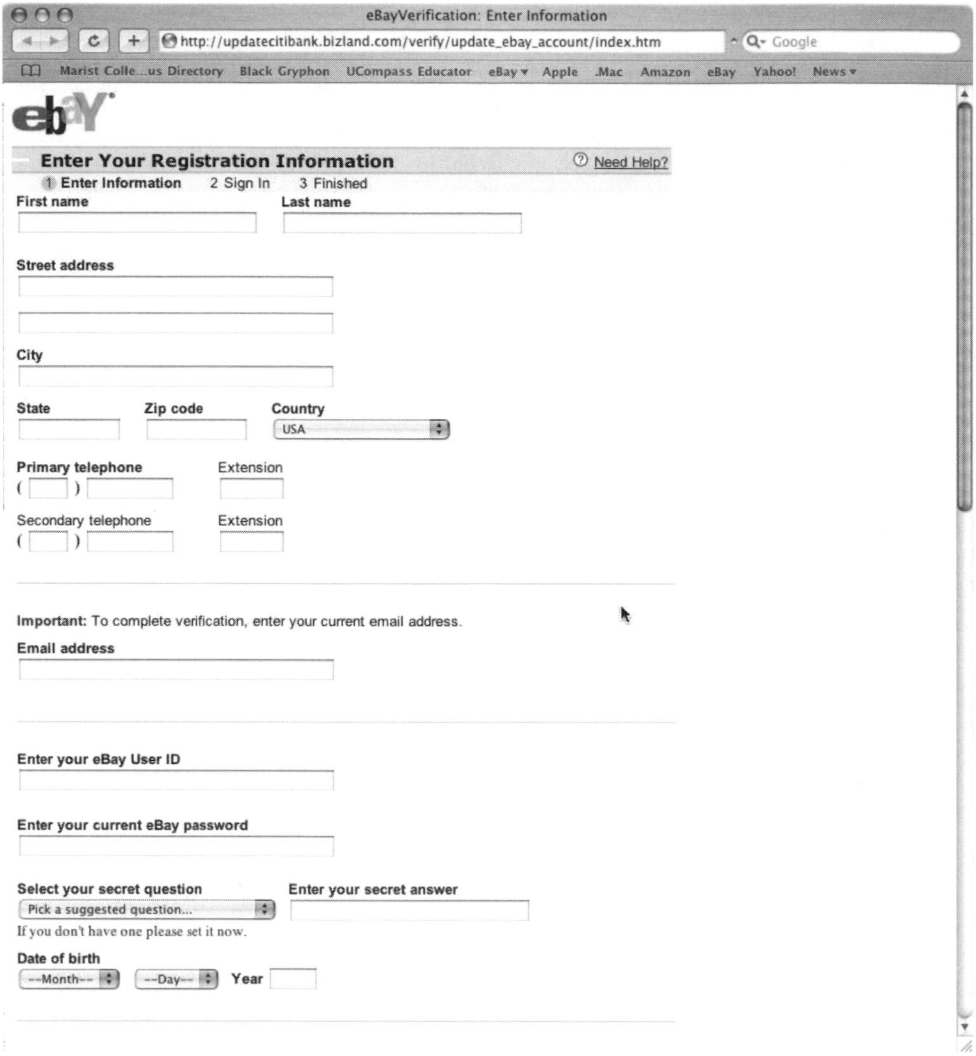

Figure 4.3   A fake Web page designed to collect user IDs and passwords (continues)

the utility against a domain name provides the IP addresses of domain name servers (see Figure 4.7). In its full implementation, `nslkup` provides an interactive mode that can list all reachable hosts on a network. However, some UNIX implementations have deprecated `nslookup` in deference to the `dig` and `host` commands.

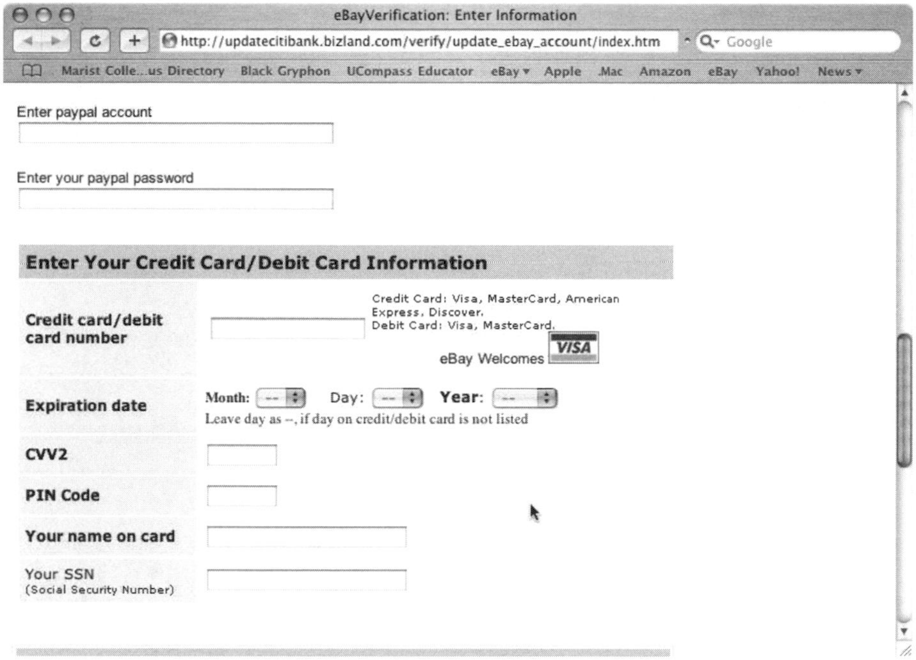

Figure 4.3 (continued)   A fake Web page designed to collect user IDs and passwords

The dig (*domain information groper*) command, like most UNIX commands, takes many options. However, in its simplest form, the command is issued

```
dig @server name type
```

where @server is a domain name or IP address, name is the DNS resource record you want to find, and type is the type of query. Only the domain name or IP address is required, however.

As an example, consider the dig output in Figure 4.8. (The command appears at the top line of the output.) Notice at the bottom of the output that you can see the IP addresses of servers that are exposed to the Internet. It is not illegal to use dig to find these addresses, and if the command is issued only a few times, it is almost impossible to detect that it has occurred. The cracker then can use the IP addresses gathered as targets for further information gathering or as the targets of actual attacks.

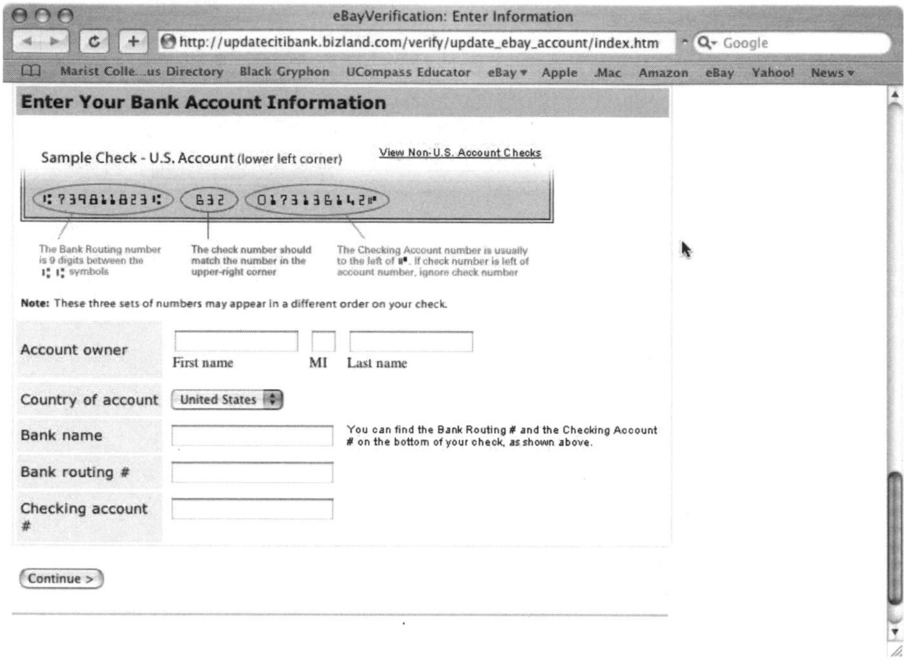

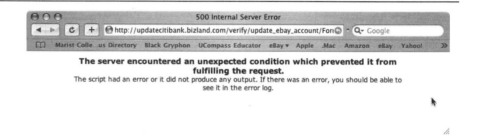

Figure 4.3 (continued)   A fake Web page design used to collect user IDs and passwords

Figure 4.4   The result of entering information on the fake Web page

The host command is also a DNS lookup utility. You issue the command followed by the domain name or IP address you want to query, as in

```
host verizon.net
```

The result is the IP address associated with the domain name:

```
verizon.net has address 206.46.230.37
```

Figure 4.5   A Web page containing information identifying employees, their positions, and methods of contact

Note: Most of the discussion in this chapter has assumed that information gathering is being performed by crackers who are not employees. Why? Because employees don't need to resort to trickery to gather such information; in most cases, it's available to them already.

```
Registrant:
The Traincellar (TRAINCELLAR-DM)
    2120 Hwy 35
    Oakhurst, NJ 07755
    US

    Domain Name: TRAINCELLAR.COM

    Administrative Contact:
        Hirschman, Jeff  (JH12466)                    jeffh@IHRSE.COM
        The Train Cellar
        2120 Hwy 35
        Oakhurst,, NJ 07755
        US
        (732) 493-3400 fax: (732) 493-3401

    Technical Contact:
        Hunnewell, Rem  (RH850)            remh@IHRSE.COM
        Iron Horse BBS
        RT 35
        OAKHURST, NJ 07755
        US
        (732) 493-3400

    Record expires on 28-Apr-2008.
    Record created on 28-Apr-1998.
    Database last updated on 6-Jun-2004 16:47:53 EDT.

    Domain servers in listed order:

    NS1.GRAFIX-NET.COM              12.106.157.16
    NS2.GRAFIX-NET.COM              12.106.157.17
```

Figure 4.6   The result of a whois search

```
Server:            151.202.0.85
Address:           151.202.0.85#53

Name:              www.verizon.net
Address:           206.46.189.10
```

Figure 4.7   Information returned by nslookup

```
; <<>> DiG 9.2.2 <<>> www.verizon.net any
;; global options:  printcmd
;; Got answer:
;; ->>HEADER<<- pcode: QUERY, status: NERRR, id: 41755
;; flags: qr aa rd ra; QUERY: 1, ANSWER: 1, AUTHORITY: 4, ADDITIONAL: 4

;; QUESTION SECTION:
;www.verizon.net.                    IN      ANY

;; ANSWER SECTION:
www.verizon.net.         3600     IN      A       206.46.189.10

;; AUTHORITY SECTION:
verizon.net.                      86400    IN       NS  ns2.verizon.net.
verizon.net.                      86400    IN       NS  ns2.bellatlantic.net.
verizon.net.                      86400    IN       NS  ns4.verizon.net.
verizon.net.                      86400    IN       NS  ns1.bellatlantic.net.

;; ADDITIONAL SECTION:
ns1.bellatlantic.net.    32951    IN       A        199.45.32.40
ns2.verizon.net.         86400    IN       A        151.203.0.86
ns2.bellatlantic.net.    157627   IN       A        199.45.32.41
ns4.verizon.net.         86400    IN       A        151.203.0.87
```

Figure 4.8   Additional information returned by dig

Reality Check: If your Web site is a potential source of information for a system cracker, consider your employee directory! What information could a cracker obtain if he or she had a copy of a printed or online listing that contains names, office numbers, phone numbers, and perhaps e-mail addresses? There are numerous such sources of information that initially don't seem related to an organization's network that a cracker can use (ever heard of "dumpster diving"?).

4.3 Port Scanning

In TCP/IP terminology, a *port* is a software identifier that corresponds to a specific application or protocol running on a host. For example, by default HTTP uses port 80. An edge router typically provides the only IP address for an internal network. All packets for hosts on the internal network are addressed to the router's WAN IP address. Therefore, the router determines where to deliver a packet on its local network in part by looking at the port requested by the packet and then sending the packet to the host running the corresponding application. (It's actually a little more complicated than this because more than one computer may be using the same protocol or application, in which case the router needs to examine the destination host name as well.)

An *open port* is any port for which packets will be accepted. Packets for closed ports are dropped. Because packets for open ports are passed through the edge router not an internal network, they provide an access tunnel through any defenses the router might have. If a cracker can determine which ports are open through an edge router, he or she has identified potential avenues for system attacks.

The port numbers used by protocols and applications are generally not kept secret. In fact, those ports that are used by TCP/IP are called *well-known ports*. You can find a listing of common well-known ports in Appendix C.

An Aside: It is possible, and sometimes desirable, to use a port other than the well-known port for a protocol. For example, if you have multiple Web servers on a network (and they are not clones of one another), then you want only one of those servers to use port 80. The others need to use a different port—which you can code into its IP address—so that each Web server can receive the correct packets. If you see an IP address in the form X.X.X.X:9999, where the 9s are replaced with a number, then you know you're seeing a redirection from a standard port. For example, http://192.168.1.101:8080 indicates that HTTP traffic is intended for port 8080 on the host with IP address 192.168.1.101. (Don't try this address; as you probably recognize, it's an internal, nonrouteable address used just for this example.)

As a first example of a port scan, take a look at Figure 4.9, which contains the result of a port scan on a host that has open ports for the most common TCP/IP protocols. The scan result shows the port numbers along with the protocols or applications that are listening for traffic on each port.

Today, network administrators know better than to leave unused ports open. A port scan on an edge router, such as that in Figure 4.10, is likely to show very few open ports. This particular router allows Web traffic through, but little else.

```
Port Scanning host: 192.168.1.100

        open Port:                    21          ftp
        open Port:                    22          ssh
        open Port:                    80          http
        open Port:                    139         netbis-ssn
        open Port:                    427         svrlc
        open Port:                    515         printer
        open Port:                    548         afpvertcp
        open Port:                    631         ipp
        open Port:                    3031        eppc
Port Scan has cmpleted ...
```

Figure 4.9   A port scan of a wide open host

```
Port Scanning host: 192.168.1.1

        open Port:                    80          http
        open Port:                    2468        qip-msgd
        open Port:                    5678        rrac
        open Port:                    6688
Port Scan has cmpleted ...
```

Figure 4.10   The result of a port scan on an edge router

One of the ironies of computer security work is that the tools that crackers use to perform port scans and other information gathering activities are also useful for troubleshooting networks and performing penetration testing. Therefore, the tools are widely and legally available, and, in some cases, are actually supplied with an operating system.

This means that to defend against a port scan, you need to be very proactive. First, on all hosts close all ports that will not be used. To do so, you shut down the services (the applications or operating system daemons) that run on those ports. Also block traffic for all unnecessary ports using a firewall on your edge router. (For details, see the Hands on section of this chapter that begins on page 97.)

Reality Check: If you have a good, well-configured firewall on your edge router or as a stand-alone firewall appliance, do you need firewalls on the hosts on your internal network? Probably not. However, home users that are connected directly to the Internet without going through a firewall-equipped router do need their own firewalls. Even a dial-up connection isn't safe from port scans. The ranges of IP addresses used by major ISPs are well known at this point, and script kiddies run software that attempts port scans through the entire range of addresses automatically.

4.4 Network Mapping

One of the goals of information gathering is to determine what hosts are running what software at what IP address. Port scanning tells the cracker which applications are running somewhere on the network, but not which hosts are running them or if the machines are actually on the network at any given time. This is where *network mapping* comes in.

Network mapping is the process of discovering the IP addresses of computers that are actually functioning and, if possible, the OS they are running.

> *Note: If you are a network administrator, you can use specialized network mapping software to help locate problems on your network. You know which servers, printers, and other shared hosts should be available. If your software doesn't see them, then you have a problem. Network mapping and discovery software, like many network utilities, can be used for both legitimate and illegitimate purposes. (More on this software in a bit.)*

The network mapper's basic tool is the `ping` utility. It sends an ICMP packet to a designated host, requesting a packet in reply. As you can see in Figure 4.11, as long as you know the domain name of a host, you can send a ping, see the IP address, and—if packets are returned—determine that the host is up and running.

```
Ping has started ...

PING www.verizon.net (206.46.189.10): 56 data bytes
64 bytes from 206.46.189.10: icmp_seq=0 ttl=245 time=69.052 ms
64 bytes from 206.46.189.10: icmp_seq=1 ttl=245 time=60.268 ms
64 bytes from 206.46.189.10: icmp_seq=2 ttl=245 time=86.209 ms
64 bytes from 206.46.189.10: icmp_seq=3 ttl=245 time=80.798 ms
64 bytes from 206.46.189.10: icmp_seq=4 ttl=245 time=69.675 ms
64 bytes from 206.46.189.10: icmp_seq=5 ttl=245 time=75.434 ms
64 bytes from 206.46.189.10: icmp_seq=6 ttl=245 time=84.186 ms
64 bytes from 206.46.189.10: icmp_seq=7 ttl=245 time=57.906 ms
64 bytes from 206.46.189.10: icmp_seq=8 ttl=245 time=79.214 ms
64 bytes from 206.46.189.10: icmp_seq=9 ttl=245 time=71.564 ms

--- www.verizon.net ping statistics ---
10 packets transmitted, 10 packets received, 0% packet loss
round-trip min/avg/max = 57.906/73.43/86.209 ms
```

Figure 4.11   The result of a ping that sent 10 packets

An Aside: ICMP stands for *Internet Control Message Protocol.* It is an extension to IP (*Internet Protocol*) that defines packets for carrying error, control, and information messages. ICMP is used to broadcast network errors such as a host or network becoming unreachable. It can also help regulate traffic. For example, if a router becomes overwhelmed with more packets than it can handle, ICMP *source quench* messages are sent to hosts requesting that the rate of packet transmission be slowed. (Of course, too many source quench packets would add even more packets to an already overloaded network, so such packets are not sent often.) ICMP's *echo* function sends a message between any two hosts. (Ping is based on this capability.) ICMP also announces a *timeout* that occurs when a packet's TTL (*time to live*) expires. (TTL is really a maximum number of router hops that a packet can make, rather than a time interval. Each time a packet goes through a router, its TTL is decremented.) In fact, the *traceroute* utility program that reports the path a packet takes over the Internet works by sending packets with short TTLs and watching the return path of the ICMP timeout messages.

In Case You're Interested: The ping utility was named after the sound made by sonar. To learn about the history behind the utility, see *http://ftp.arl.mil/~mike/ ping.html*, which was written by the utility's author.

The ping output doesn't tell the cracker what applications a host might be running, or even differentiate between a server and an end-user's computer. However, with a little cleverness, the cracker can figure that out. If he or she sends the pings in the middle of the night, machines that answer are probably servers. Then, the cracker can perform a port scan to determine whether he or she has identified a Web server, an e-mail server, or something else.

Network mapping and discovery software provides significantly more information about a network, and displays it in a graphic format. For example, consider the network map in Figure 4.12. It shows the physical layout of the network, the architecture of interconnection devices (hubs, switches, routers), the network name(s) of the devices, and the IP addresses of network interfaces on connected devices.

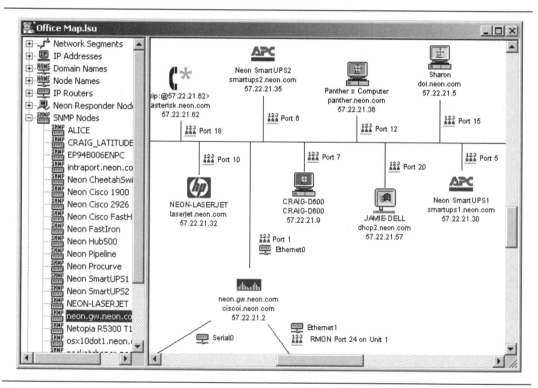

Figure 4.12   A network map produced by network mapping and discovery software (LAN Surveyor by Neon Software)

Reality Check: As fancy as network mapping and detection software may be, and as handy a network management tool as it may be, it still relies primarily on `ping` to do its job. Most network mapping software also uses SNMP to obtain information from interconnection devices; devices that cannot respond to SNMP requests often can't be identified.

From an external cracker's point of view, the major limitation of network mapping and discovery software is that you need to be connected to the local network to use it. This is not, however, much of an impediment to an employee who has been given network access. In fact, the biggest impediment facing an employee who wants to use such software is cost. Network mapping and discovery software is expensive, and if the organization hasn't paid for it, it can take a big bite out of an individual's wallet.

> *Note: Keep in mind that a user doesn't need to be physically within an organization's building to be connected to the local network. Remote access, perhaps through a dialup connection or a VPN, can allow a remote user to connect to the network and use all network resources to which he or she has been given access (or, in the case of a system cracker, has gained access).*

To prevent network mapping, you need to block the response to `ping`. You can either block all ICMP traffic, or simply turn off ECHO RESPONSES. In most cases, you'll want to perform this configuration on your router. (The specifics of *how* you do it depend on the router.)

4.5 Hands On

The most prudent defense against social engineering is good user education. However, when you want to limit published information and block port scans, the defenses are technical. In this section we'll look at some techniques you can use to protect your network against these latter types of information gathering.

4.5.1 Limiting Published Information

Limiting the information that is published about an organization and its domain name is a combination of technology and common sense. The common sense part means that when you choose e-mail addresses for a Web site, you ensure that they don't reveal employee names and titles. You also need policies for the security of printed documents that divulge corporate information. For example, as trivial as it might seem, you need to ensure that employee directories are handled as confidential information.

The information that appears as the result of a whois search is controlled through your domain name registrar. For example, in Figure 4.13 you can see a Web page that can be used to specify what information should appear about a domain name's administrative contact. (Exactly what you see will vary, of course, from one registrar to another.) If you restrict all information in your DNS entry, a whois query will return something like Figure 4.14.

4.5.2 Disabling Unnecessary Services and Closing Ports

When you start up a computer, the operating system launches a collection of services, those programs that primarily run in the background to manage many operating system functions and provide additional system capabilities (for example, data communications). Each service that can be reached over a communications network listens to one or more specific ports. Therefore, one way to close those ports and prevent anyone from using potentially dangerous services is to stop the services from running. Exactly how you do this depends on your operating system.

One of the problems with current versions of Windows is that dangerous services are enabled by default. In other words, when you install the OS, the system is configured to start most available services. This means that you should disable many of them before connecting the computer to a network. How big a problem is this? Consider the list of services in Figure 4.15, which shows the services that should be disabled for a typical Windows XP installation.

> *Note: Not all unnecessary services present security risks. However, they do consume main memory and CPU time. It therefore makes sense to turn them off, even if they aren't dangerous.*

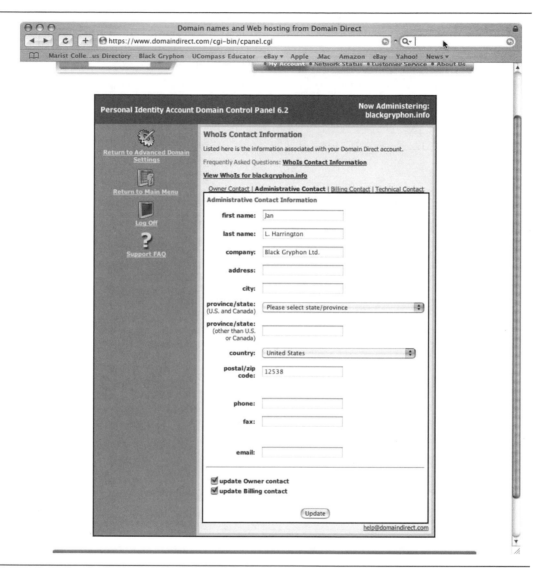

Figure 4.13   Restricting information that will appear in a whois search result

How do you turn them off? Although you can chase down each service individually, probably the easiest way is to use the Services tool:

1.   Starting at the Windows XP desktop, navigate your way through My Computer->Control Panel->Administrative Tools.

```
Domain Name: VERIZON.NET
Registrar: EMARKMONITOR INC. DBA MARKMONITOR
Whois Server: whois.markmonitor.com
Referral URL: http://www.markmonitor.com
Name Server: NS2.BELLATLANTIC.NET
Name Server: NS1.BELLATLANTIC.NET
Name Server: NS2.VERIZON.NET
Name Server: NS4.VERIZON.NET
Status: REGISTRAR-LOCK
Updated Date: 24-sep-2003
Creation Date: 06-jul-1999
Expiration Date: 06-jul-2004
```

Figure 4.14   The result of using `whois` on a restricted DNS database entry

2. Launch the Services tool. As you can see in Figure 4.16, the right side of the window lists all running services.

3. Double-click on a service to open its Properties sheet.

4. Click the Stop button (see Figure 4.17).

Not all Windows XP services can be disabled. For example, in Figure 4.18 you'll notice that the Stop button is not active for the Plug and Play service, which is essential to the operating system's functioning and therefore should never be disabled.

If you are running Linux (or some other flavor of UNIX), then you may want to disable some or all of the services in Figure 4.19. Disabling services can be done from the command line, using the `/sbin/chkconfig` command:

```
/sbin/chkconfig -level 0123456 service_name ff
```

This will prevent the service from starting the next time you reboot the computer. To stop a service immediately, use

```
/sbin/service service_name stop
```

> *Note: You must be running as the superuser to use the preceding two commands.*

The problem, of course, is that you need to know the names of the services that are running. To find out, you need to use a two-step process. First, the command

```
netstat -an
```

- Alerter
- Application Layer Gateway Services
- Automatic Updates (*Leave running if you want to use Microsoft's Automatic Update facility.*)
- Background Intelligent Transfer Service
- ClipBook
- Computer Browser (*Leave running if the computer is part of a Windows NT/2000 Domain.*)
- Distributed Link Tracking Client
- Error Reporting Service
- Fast User Switching Compatibility
- Fax
- IIS Admin (*The only reason for having this service is to support the personal version of IIS. As far as security is concerned, running a Web server on a multipurpose machine isn't a good idea because it allows unknown traffic onto an internal network.*)
- IMAPI CD-Burning CM Service (*Leave running if you have a CD burner.*)
- Indexing Service
- Infrared Monitor (*Leave running if the computer has, and uses, an IR port.*)
- Internet Connection Firewall (ICF) / Internet Connection Sharing (ICS) (*Leave running if computer uses either of these services.*)
- Messenger
- MS Software Shadow Copy Provider
- NetMeeting Remote Desktop Sharing (*Leave running if computer uses Desktop Sharing in NetMeeting.*)
- Portable Media Serial Number (*Leave running if you use an MP3 player that you connect directly to the computer.*)
- QS RSVP
- Remote Desktop Help Session Manager (*Leave running if the computer is supported through Remote Assistance.*)
- Remote Registry
- Removable Storage
- Routing and Remote Access
- Smart Card
- Smart Card Helper
- SSDP Discovery Service (*Leave running if there are Universal PnP devices on the network.*)
- System Restore Service (*Leave running if you use the System Restore feature.*)
- Telnet
- Terminal Services, *including:*
  - * Remote Desktop
  - * Remote Assistance
  - * Fast User Switching

Figure 4.15   Windows XP services that should be disabled

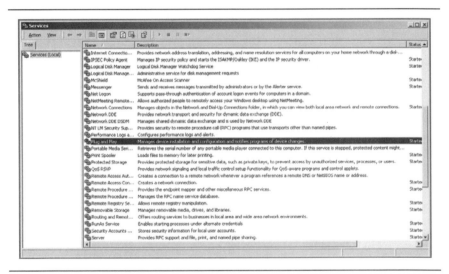

- Themes
- Uninterruptible Power Supply
- Universal Plug and Play Device Host
- Upload Manager
- Volume Shadow Copy
- WebClient
- Windows Image Acquisition (WIA) (*Leave running if computer has a scanner or digital camera connected.*)
- Windows Time (*Leave running if the computer is part of a Windows NT/2000 Domain.*)
- Wireless Zero Configuration (*Leave running if the computer uses a wireless LAN.*)
- * WMI Performance Adapter
- World Wide Web Publishing (*Leave running if using the personal edition of IIS on the computer. As mentioned earlier, this isn't a particularly good idea for a general-purpose machine.*)

Figure 4.15 (continued)   Windows XP services that should be disabled

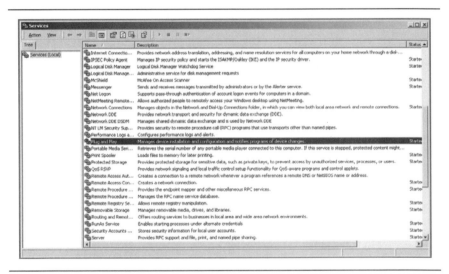

Figure 4.16   The Windows XP Services tool

provides a list of the ports on which the OS is listening, as in the fourth column from the left in Figure 4.20. But the port numbers aren't enough; you need the names of the services! To get the names, use

```
lsf -i
```

The output (for example, Figure 4.21) provides the name of the program running the service in the leftmost column.

Figure 4.17   Disabling a Windows XP service

If you are using a version of UNIX that doesn't support `chkconfig` (for example, Mac OS X), you can also disable services by editing the file `/etc/services` and commenting out any services that you don't want started at system boot.

In addition, some OSs provide GUI tools for managing services. By default, for example, Mac OS X leaves "dangerous" Internet services turned off. A user can enable specific services through a Preferences panel (see Figure 4.22).

4.5.3 Opening Ports on the Perimeter and Proxy Serving

In most cases, when you stop an operating system service, you also close the port on which the service is listening. You therefore have added protection to the specific computer. However, it does not stop a cracker from sending packets for the closed ports to your internal network. A firewall running on an edge router or a standalone firewall appliance placed between the edge router and the internal network can stop unwanted packets before they get on to your LAN.

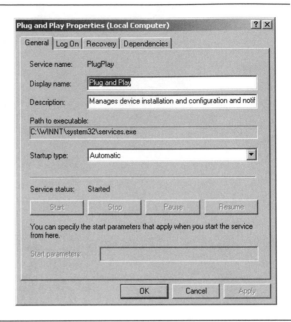

Figure 4.18   A Windows XP service that cannot be disabled

- xinetd
- inetd
- httpd
- tux
- dchpcd
- named
- portmap
- nfs
- nfslck
- sshd
- smbd (*Leave this running if you are using Samba on your internal network.*)
- nmbd
- netfs
- sendmail
- identd,
- nscd
- r* (*all of the remote access services*)
- yp*
- telnet
- ftp

Figure 4.19   UNIX services that may be disabled

```
[Desktp-G4:~] sysp% netstat -an
Active Internet connections (including servers)
Port Recv-Q Send-Q  Local Address           Foreign Address
(state)
tcp4     0      0   *.631                    *.*              LISTEN
tcp4     0      0   *.515                    *.*              LISTEN
tcp4     0      0   *.3031                   *.*              LISTEN
tcp4     0      0   *.*                      *.*              CLOSED
tcp4     0      0   *.427                    *.*              LISTEN
tcp46    0      0   *.21                     *.*              LISTEN
tcp4     0      0   *.548                    *.*              LISTEN
tcp46    0      0   *.548                    *.*              LISTEN
tcp4     0      0   *.80                     *.*              LISTEN
tcp46    0      0   *.22                     *.*              LISTEN
tcp4     0      0   *.139                    *.*              LISTEN
```

Figure 4.20   Netstat output indicating ports on which the computer is listening

```
AppleFile 524   rt    28u   IPv6 0x02566cd0   0t0    TCP *:afpvertcp (LISTEN)
AppleFile 524   rt    29u   IPv4 0x02575008   0t0    TCP *:afpvertcp (LISTEN)
xinetd    563   rt     5u   IPv4 0x01697220   0t0    UDP *:netbis-ns
xinetd    563   rt     6u   IPv4 0x02533ce4   0t0    TCP *:netbis-ssn (LISTEN)
xinetd    563   rt     9u   IPv6 0x02566e80   0t0    TCP *:ssh (LISTEN)
xinetd    563   rt    10u   IPv6 0x02566b20   0t0    TCP *:ftp (LISTEN)
xinetd    563   rt    11u   IPv4 0x02589ad8   0t0    TCP *:eppc (LISTEN)
xinetd    563   rt    12u   IPv4 0x02589008   0t0    TCP *:printer (LISTEN)
httpd     597   rt    16u   IPv4 0x025697b4   0t0    TCP *:http (LISTEN)
httpd     644   www   16u   IPv4 0x025697b4   0t0    TCP *:http (LISTEN)
slpd      693   rt     1u   IPv4 0x01ba7e50   0t0    UDP *:svrlc
slpd      693   rt     2u   IPv4 0x025747ec   0t0    TCP *:svrlc (LISTEN)
```

Figure 4.21   Lsf output showing the programs running specific services

The firewalls that run on broadband routers are usually configured to block incoming traffic on all well-known TCP ports; you must open specific ports to allow traffic through. For example, if you are hosting a Web server, you will need to open at least port 80. It also means that you will need to map the Web server's domain name to its static IP address, and that address, which is one of those on your internal network, then will be exposed to the Internet as a whole.

To shield internal static IP addresses, you hide them behind a single IP address on your edge router (the port that connects the router to the Internet). You then use a *proxy server* to redirect packets to internal IP addresses. All domain names point to the router's WAN port, which is the only IP address that is known to the Internet.

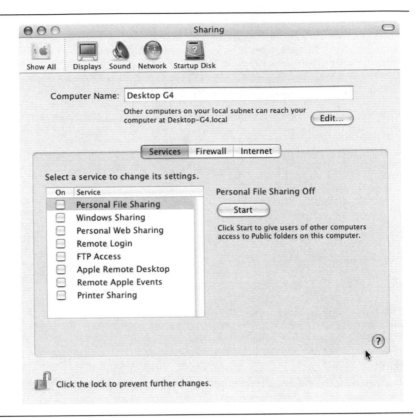

Figure 4.22   Turning on Mac OS X network services

In its simplest form, proxy server software is easy to configure. It's simply a matter of associating an incoming TCP port value with an internal IP address, as in Figure 4.23. Notice that this proxy server can not only map ports to internal IP addresses, but also can switch the external ports to different internal ports.

4.6 Summary

This chapter introduces some of the techniques that network crackers use to gather information about networks they are considering infiltrating:

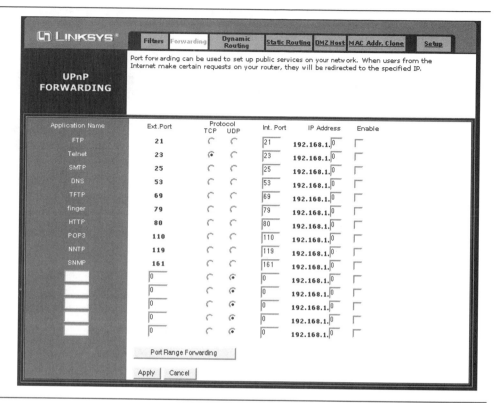

Figure 4.23 Configuring proxies (port forwarding)

◆ Social engineering: Social engineering uses a variety of in-person, telephone, and e-mail scams to convince users to divulge system access information. The best—and perhaps the only—defense against social engineering is good user education.

◆ Published information: Web pages and DNS databases can provide a wealth of information, including the names of employees, their e-mail addresses, their titles, and phone numbers. Such information can form the basis of social engineering attacks. Published information can also reveal the IP addresses of servers, which can then be targeted for further information gathering. The best defense is to limit the information revealed by public sources.

◆ Port scanning: Port scanning is a process that reveals the TCP ports on which a host is listening for Internet traffic. Open ports provide a hole through which a system cracker can launch an attack. The best defense is to close all ports that are not in use and to place servers behind firewalls that perform proxy serving, shielding the servers' actual IP addresses from the Internet.

◆ Network discovery and mapping: Network discovery and mapping provides a map of the layout of a network, showing connected devices and their IP addresses. At the very least, network mapping can indicate which hosts are up and running at any given time. The best defense is to prevent `ping` packets from entering the network so that no hosts behind the firewall respond.

In This Chapter

- ◆ Root kits
- ◆ Brute force entry attacks and intrusion detection systems
- ◆ Intrusion prevention systems
- ◆ Buffer overflow attacks

5.0 Introduction

The goal of a system cracker often is to gain access to a system, not only once, but repeatedly. If at all possible, the cracker wants to secure root (or administrator) access so that he or she can do just about anything with the system. Perhaps the cracker wants to read or copy files; perhaps the hacker wants to install software that will cause the compromised system to take part in a distributed attack on another computer. Whatever the reason, the cracker wants to establish root access, leave behind whatever is necessary to gain access again, and then exit without being detected.

The software a cracker leaves behind is known as a *root kit*, a collection of programs that allow the cracker to access the system at any desired time and gain root or administrator privileges. In this chapter we will begin by looking at root kits—what they are, where they come from, and how you can detect them—and then consider how root kits might be installed on your system in the first place and what you can do to thwart such attacks.

5.1 Root Kits

Root kits have been around since at least the early 1990s. Commonly they let a hacker

- ◆ Enter a system at any time.

- ◆ Open ports on the computer.

- ◆ Install software on the system.

- ◆ Run any software installed on the system, including software that can be used in a denial of service attack. (See Chapter 6 for in-depth coverage of denial of service attacks.)

- ◆ Become a super/administrative user, and therefore perform any actions associated with that high-level access (especially creating new accounts).

- ◆ Use the system as a platform for cracking other computers on the same local network.

♦ Capture user names and passwords.

♦ Change log files—which are discussed later in this chapter—
to erase any record of a cracker's actions.

One of the most insidious things about a root kit is that if it works as intended, you won't know that it is on your computer. A root kit hides itself, as well as the actions of the cracker who installed it. How can you
detect the presence of a root kit? It's not easy, but you can look for

♦ Unexplained decreases in available disk space.

♦ Disk activity when no one is using the system (and no background processes should be running).

♦ Changes to system files.

♦ Unusual system crashes.

Then you'll need to look for files that don't belong, not an easy task with
today's operating systems that are made up of tens of thousands of files.
In addition, on a Windows system, root kit files are invisible, although
some may appear if you boot in safe mode.

Some help is available in the form of automated file change monitoring
tools, such as Tripwire (*http://www.tripwire.com*). If the installation of a
root kit replaces system files, change monitoring software can detect the
replacement (see Figure 5.1). Software like Tripwire works by establish-
ing a baseline of clean software and can therefore make it much easier
to recover when a root kit is detected.

The only reliable way to recover from a root kit infection is to reformat
the hard drive, restore the OS from original installation media, reinstall
all applications from original installation media, and copy data files back
to the hard drive. Don't simply restore from a backup copy: You could
restore the root kit as well!

5.1.1 Root Kit Threat Level

Until 2003, UNIX systems were the primary target of root kits; there
weren't any Windows root kits. (Finally, something Windows users
didn't have to worry about!) At this time, however, there are several Windows root kits, including Slanret, null.sys, HE4Hk (a Russian effort),

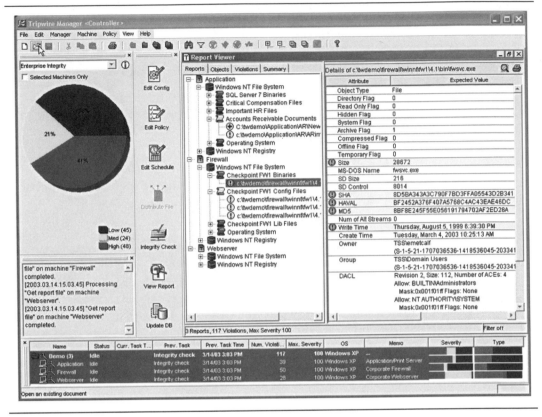

Figure 5.1 A Tripwire report screen

Hacker Defender, and FU. There are a large number of UNIX root kits, including t0rn, Knark, Are, and Rkit.

> *Note: You can learn a great deal about Windows root kits at http://www.rootkit.com. You can download root kit code and even take a course in developing a root kit.*

A root kit is made up of files left behind after a system cracker gains access to a system through some other means. The easiest way to prevent a root kit from being installed on your computers is to prevent crackers from getting in in the first place!

So, how vulnerable are your systems to a root kit? It depends on how easily your systems can be penetrated. Stop unauthorized access and you'll impede root kits as well.

5.1.2 How Root Kits Work

Most root kits hide themselves by placing themselves between calls to system routines made by program APIs and lower layers of the operating system. Whenever an application (or a portion of the OS, for that matter) makes a system call, the root kit intercepts the call and determines whether to pass the call through to the OS, handle the call itself (thus changing OS behavior), or drop the call.

The root kit handles system calls that might reveal its presence. For example, if a user were to request a listing of a directory containing root kit files, the root kit would perform the listing, but leave out any of its own files so they wouldn't be seen by the user. This also means that normal virus-detection software won't find a root kit.

UNIX root kits take advantage of the modular nature of UNIX: Most UNIX variations can be extended by *Loadable Kernel Modules* (LKMs), compiled OS modules that can be loaded into RAM while the OS is running. Current UNIX root kits—many of which load as device drivers—are LKMs that intercept system calls in the manner just described.

Reality Check: The basic technique used by root kits isn't particularly new. In the mid-1980s it was possible to set up a dumb terminal connected to a mainframe or supermini to collect user names and passwords. The system cracker wrote a script that captured input from the terminal's keyboard and wrote it to a text file. Then it passed the input on to the computer. The script passed all output directly back to the terminal screen. The user interface looked just like the normal command line; a user would have no idea that all his or her keystrokes were being logged. The cracker would start the script and walk away from the terminal. Then, some time later, the cracker would return, shut down the script, and analyze the contents of the script's log file. User names and passwords would be there, in plain text.

5.2 Brute Force Entry Attacks and Intrusion Detection

Before there were sophisticated tools for attempting to penetrate computer networks based on known system vulnerabilities, hackers would use *brute force* attacks in attempts to gain entry to systems. Such an attack involves repeatedly trying dial-up numbers, user names, and passwords in the hopes that something will work.

The hacker could write a simple BASIC program to dial a sequence of telephone numbers and record those numbers that reached a computer. Known as *war dialing*, this technique has changed with the predominance of the Internet, but not disappeared. Today, script kiddies use programs that run through a set of IP addresses, attempting to find resources such as file sharing servers (for example, Kazaa), Web servers, or Trojan horses that have been left behind by other hackers. The ranges of IP addresses used by major IPSs such as AL and Earthlink are well known. All a script kiddie needs to do is run the program, fill in the starting and ending IP addresses, and sit back and let the program run. The program reports what it finds; then the script kiddies can use other software to exploit the system he or she has found.

Crackers can use a similar technique to search for user names and passwords. Assuming that user names are not publicly available, a cracker can make educated guesses as to what administrative accounts exist on a system. Knowing employee names, the cracker can also make some reasonable guesses as to what account names might be. He or she can then try likely possibilities or, using a file containing common account names, can use software that tries every entry.

Once a cracker knows an account name, the remaining step in a brute force attack is to try to guess the password. Crackers might use clues given when users register for accounts, such as knowing that a password must be 6 to 16 characters long and must contain at least one letter and one number. Then he or she can use software that either tries random combination of letters and numbers or uses a file of possible passwords. Sometimes, the cracker gets lucky and the software stumbles upon a password that works.

You can't prevent someone from mounting a brute force attack against your network, but you can detect that such an attack is occurring and ensure that the perpetrator doesn't succeed. There are two basic tech-niques for detecting a brute force attack:

♦ Look through your network logs for patterns of repeated ac-cess attempts. Logs are usually kept by multiuser operating systems (in particular, severs) as well as firewalls. (If logging isn't turned on, turn it on!)

♦ Disable an account after a small number of unsuccessful log-in attempts. In most cases, software will lock access to an ac-count after three failed connection attempts. The user will then need to contact a help desk to get the account released.

♦ Use *intrusion detection system* (IDS) software.

An experienced security person can see patterns in system logs, but scanning the logs can take a lot of time. IDS software runs by itself and sends alerts when it detects a potential problem. However, in many sit-uations IDS software isn't as good as an experienced eye.

5.2.1 Examining System Logs

Operating systems and firewalls keep logs of the events that happen in their environments. Exactly what you see, and what you should look for, depends on the specific OS or the specific firewall.

When you set up a procedure for examining system logs, you will need to answer the following questions:

♦ If the OS or firewall allows customization of what appears in the log file, what events should be logged? At the very least, you will want to keep track of unsuccessful login attempts. A pattern of attempts to access the same account may indicate a brute force attack.

♦ How long should log files be retained? This depends on the size and activity level of your network (the larger and more ac-tive, the larger the log files), the amount of storage media available (the more storage media available, the more log files you can store), and judgements about the persistence of cracking attempts (the more persistent the crackers, the less time you need to store the log files). Keep the log files however long you feel is necessary to show patterns of unauthorized access.

♦ Where should archival log files be stored? One of the ways in which a system cracker hides his or her tracks is by altering log files. Changes for achived log files can mask a pattern of repeated access attempts. Therefore, such files should not be stored on media that are accessible to a network. The safest way to store them is on removable media, such as a CD or DVD, that can be stored away from a computer that can read the data.

♦ Which hardware should keep logs? Should each workstation keep its own logs, or is it enough that servers and firewalls keep logs? If all Internet and WAN access is through an edge router, then you may feel it is sufficient to keep logs only on those machines that are exposed to an external network along with the firewall logs. However, if you are concerned with system cracking attempts by employees, then you will also probably want to keep logs on workstations that contain sensitive information.

♦ How often will logs be examined? Is once a day enough, or should it be done several times during the day? How often you examine logs depends on the volatility of your network. The higher the traffic level, the more often you'll need to look at the logs.

You should begin monitoring system logs even before you suspect there might be a problem. Why? To see what normal activity looks like. Then, when something out of the ordinary occurs, you will be able to detect it. For example, if you see your organization's CEO logging in at 2 in the morning, you should be very suspicious (unless you know that he or she actually works at such an hour).

Windows Event Logs

Windows can keep logs of a wide variety of events. In most cases, you want to look for failed logon attempts, repetitions of which from the same source are a good indication of a brute force attack in progress. To make your life easier, Windows allows you to set up an *audit policy*, which can filter the events that are being recorded.

Note: In the long run, you may also want to look for things such as failed attempts to delete files of change security settings, but those occur after *the miscreant has already gained access to your system.*

The typical Windows system actually keeps three logs: an application log, a security log, and a system log. A Windows computer running as a domain controller also keeps a directory service log and a file replication service log. You can see a portion of a system log in Figure 5.2. Each event header contains the information in Table 5.1. (For details on access and configuring Windows system logs, see the Hands On section at the end of this chapter, beginning on page 126.)

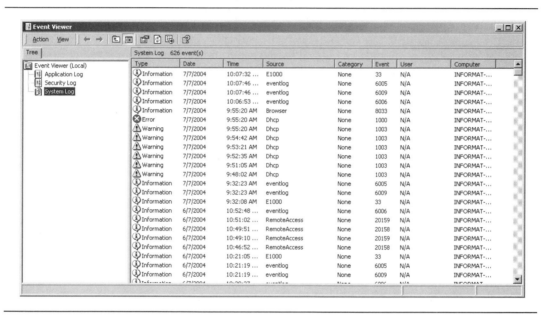

Figure 5.2 A portion of a Windows system log

UNIX System Logs

What you see in UNIX system logs will depend on the version of UNIX you are using. For example, in Figure 5.3 you can find a portion of the system log for the startup of a Macintosh OS X system, which is a variant of BSD UNIX. The system log keeps a record of just about everything the OS does. There are also logs for each user, a panic log (entries about kernel

Field	Contents
Date	The date when the event occurred.
Time	The time when the event occurred.
User	The user performing the event.
Computer	The computer on which the event occurred.
Source	The software that generated the event.
Event	An event type ID and a description of the event.
Type	The severity of the event. System and application events can be Error (a serious problem that will affect system functioning), Information (successful software action), or Warning (information about a potential problem). Security events can be Success Audit (a security event that is being logged that succeeds) or Failure Audit (a security event that is being logged that fails).
Category	A category into which the event falls, determined by the event's source.

Table 5.1 The fields in a Windows event log header

panics), crash logs (entries about software crashes), and so on. In addition, many applications, such as Web servers and database severs, keep their own log files.

Log in and log out information is usually kept in */var/log/wtmp*. A UNIX administrator will therefore probably monitor this particular log file closely. Most services write entries to */var/log/syslog* and messages about system connection attempts can be found in */var/log/messages*. These files are also important sources of data about what who is attempting to enter the system.

Because UNIX log files are text files, a user with the appropriate access rights can view them with any text editor of UNIX utility (for example, more). However, the content of the logs can be confusing to view as plain, unformatted text. Help comes in the form of a *log analyzer*, software that can extract relevant information from a log and format it for easier viewing.

```
Jul  8 07:17:40 localhost syslgd: restart
Jul  8 07:17:40 localhost syslgd: kernel bt file is /mach_kernel
Jul  8 07:17:40 localhost kernel: standard timeslicing quantum is 10000 us
Jul  8 07:17:40 localhost kernel: vm_page_btstrap: 124988 free pages
Jul  8 07:17:40 localhost kernel: mig_table_max_displ = 68
Jul  8 07:17:40 localhost kernel: IKit Component Version 7.4:
Jul  8 07:17:40 localhost kernel: Wed May 12 16:54:39 PDT 2004;
root(rcbuilder):RELEASE_PPC/ikit/RELEASE
Jul  8 07:17:40 localhost kernel: 69 prelinked modules
Jul  8 07:17:40 localhost kernel: Copyright (c) 1982, 1986, 1989, 1991, 1993
Jul  8 07:17:40 localhost kernel: The Regents of the University of California.
All rights reserved.
Jul  8 07:17:40 localhost kernel:
Jul  8 07:17:40 localhost kernel: using 1310 buffer headers and 1310 cluster I
buffer headers
Jul  8 07:17:40 localhost kernel: Local FireWire GUID = 0x3065ff:0xfee18eee
Jul  8 07:17:40 localhost kernel: Security auditing service present
Jul  8 07:17:40 localhost kernel: BSM auditing present
Jul 8 07:17:40 localhost kernel: From path: "/pci@f2000000/mac-i@17/ata-4@1f000/
@0:5,\mach_kernel", Waiting on <dict ID="0"><key>IPathMatch</key><string
ID="1">IDeviceTree:/pci@f2000000/mac-i@17/ata-4@1f000/@0:5</string></dict>
Jul  8 07:17:40 localhost kernel: Gt bt device = IService:/MacRISC2PE/
pci@f2000000/AppleMacRiscPCI/mac-i@17/AppleKeyLarg/ata-4@1f000/KeyLargATA/
ATADeviceNub@0/IATABlockStorageDriver/IATABlockStorageDevice/
IBlockStorageDriver/Maxtr 5T060H6 Media/IApplePartitionScheme/MacS@5
Jul  8 07:17:41 localhost kernel: BSD root: disk0s5, major 14, minor 5
Jul  8 07:17:41 localhost kernel: Jettisoning kernel linker.
Jul  8 07:17:41 localhost kernel: Resetting ICatalogue.
Jul  8 07:17:41 localhost kextd[88]: registering service
"com.apple.KernelExtensionServer"
Jul  8 07:17:44 localhost kernel: Matching service count = 2
Jul  8 07:17:44 localhost kernel: NVDANV10HAL loaded and registered.
Jul  8 07:17:44 localhost kernel: RM ndrv for NVDA,NVMac is to ld (0xb690c0f5)
Jul  8 07:17:44 localhost kernel: AppleRS232Serial:         0         0
AppleRS232Serial::start - returning false early, Connector of machine incorrect
Jul  8 07:17:44 localhost SystemStarter: Welcome to Macintosh.
```

Figure 5.3 A portion of a Mac OS X system log

Tip: You can find a collection of links to free and GNU licensed Linux log analyzers at http://www.linux.org/apps/all/Administration/Log_Analyzers.html.Intrusion-Prevention.

5.2.2 Intrusion Detection Software

An *Intrusion Detection System* (IDS) is software that attempts to detect a brute force or other attack that is in progress. It can then alert you to the attack or perform actions that you have specified to stop the attack.

IDSs work in one of three ways:

- Examining system logs (*host based*)
- Examining network traffic (*network based*)
- A combination of the two

Which is better? There is no simple answer because host-based and network-based IDSs have their own strengths. You can find a comparison in Table 5.2. As you can see, an IDS that uses a combination of both techniques provides the most comprehensive protection.

There are many IDSs available, some pen source and some commercial. Probably the most widely used pen source IDS for small networks is Snort (*http://www.snort.org*). Versions are available for Windows and a collection of UNIX varieties.

Snort is a network-based IDS that can run from any workstation on a network. It performs packet sniffing and logging, with its behavior controlled by a set of user-developed rules. Snort can send alerts in real time to a disk or to pop-up windows. In addition, because there are many locations using Snort, new packet filtering rules are written as soon as a new type of attack is detected over the Internet; the new rules are posted for easy downloading by Snort users.

Snort rules are written in a proprietary language. For example, the following example tells Snort to log packets going to the listed IP address destined for port 8080:

```
log tcp any any -> 10.1.1.0/24 8080
```

> *Note: For information on Linux IDSs (and IDS software in general), take a look at http://www.linuxsecurity.com/ resources/intrusion_detection-1.html.*

Host-based	Network-based
Has access to data physically stored in disk files (the log files). Conclusions of the IDS can be verified by examining the log files manually.	Works with packets as they travel over the network. Logs packets only if a problem is detected.
Is system specific. Good because the software can be tailored to a given OS, but problematic to deploy and maintain because each OS requires different software.	System independent.
Avoids problems associated with deploying an IDS across multiple collision domains in a switched network.	May present difficulties when attempting to deploy across multiple collision domains in a switched network.
Fast detection of problems, especially if the IDS is configured to check the logs as soon as they are modified.	Extremely fast detection of problems because packets are examined as they are traveling over the network; there is no need to wait for something to be written to a log.
Can't detect attacks stopped by a firewall.	Can be placed outside a firewall to detect attacks that the firewall might stop.
Can't stop a root kit from modifying a log file.	Works on packets as they travel over the network, preventing a system cracker from erasing his or her tracks.
Doesn't catch attacks that use packet headers.	Catches attacks that rely on spoofed information in packet headers, such as IP addresses.
Requires no additional hardware.	May require an additional server on the network; requires some hardware (such as a network tap[a]) to collect packets.

Table 5.2 Host-based versus network-based IDSs

a. For information on creating a passive Ethernet tap for collecting packets, see *http://www.snort.org/docs/tap/*.

Reality Check: Commercial IDSs are very expensive, costing thousands of dollars. How good are they? It depends on how well the rules for monitoring traffic are written. (Keep in mind that a rule set is always chasing a moving target: new attacks are appearing every day.) You therefore can't put all your trust in IDS software; you need to periodically monitor system logs yourself and examine packets flagged by a network-based IDS.

5.2.3 Intrusion Prevention Software

As you research network protection software, you will find *intrusion prevention systems* (IPSs) as well as IDSs. Are they really different from IDSs? In degree, yes; in intent, not really. An IPS cannot prevent a system cracker from attempting to get into your network. However, in theory IPS software works somewhat differently from IDS software.

Reality Check: Don't expect always to find a clear-cut distinction between IDS and IPS. Some software vendors use the ideas of intrusion detection and intrusion prevention interchangeably.

Intrusion detection is a passive activity in the sense that the software sits back and waits for something to occur. It is therefore reactive rather than proactive. Intrusion prevention adds learning capabilities to the software so that in some cases it can be proactive and function before an attack can penetrate your defenses. IPSs pay attention to how software on your network is supposed to act and then, using rules derived from normal behavior, identifies abnormal situations and takes action accordingly. Certainly, IPS software can't prevent an attacker from attempting to crack your network. However, it generally detects attacks in progress faster than host-based IDSs and, in many cases, is more effective than network-based IDSs.

The major drawback to an IPS is that developing the behavior rules can be difficult. You can either write them yourself or allow the software to develop them. In either case, the rules often run into trouble with unusual, but legitimate, software behavior. For example, upgrading application software on servers may trigger an IPS's anti-attack functions.

5.2.4 Honeypots

A *honeypot* is a trap set for a potential system cracker. On the surface, it looks like a real server. However, all the services are simulated. The intent is to lure a cracker to the honeypot, so he or she spends time trying to crack the honeypot, leaving the real network resources untouched. Most honeypot software raises an alert when an attack begins, giving a network administrator time to investigate the source of the attack, something you may not get with an IDS.

A honeypot can be used to detect both internal and external intrusion attempts. For internal detection, you place it behind the firewall, on the same level as any other local network server. To catch external cracking attempts, you place it outside the firewall, where it appears as a much more easily compromiseable system than anything behind the firewall.

As an example of honeypot software, consider the screen shot in Figure 5.4, the configuration screen from Specter honeypot software (*http:// www.specter.com*). Notice the variety of operating systems the software can emulate, as well the services it can simulate.

When an attack occurs on the honeypot server, the software logs what occurs and sends the preconfigured notifications. For example, in Figure 5.5 you can find the incident log records provided by Specter when a system cracker attempts to download a UNIX /etc/passwd file. (Once the cracker has the file on his/her local machine, it's easy to run password cracking software against it.)

5.3 Buffer Overflow Attacks

Buffer overflow attacks are among the most common external exploits. However, it takes a knowledgeable programmer to identify a situation where such an attack could be successful and to write a program to take advantage of one. (Once the programs are written, script kiddies can use them, but they certainly couldn't write one themselves.) Why? Because a buffer overflow attack takes advantage of a problem within the software itself.

In this context, a *buffer* is a portion of main memory set aside to hold an input value. An input buffer is surrounded on both sides by other data

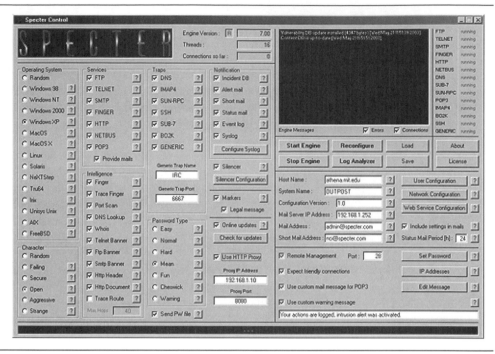

Figure 5.4 The Specter honeypot configuration screen

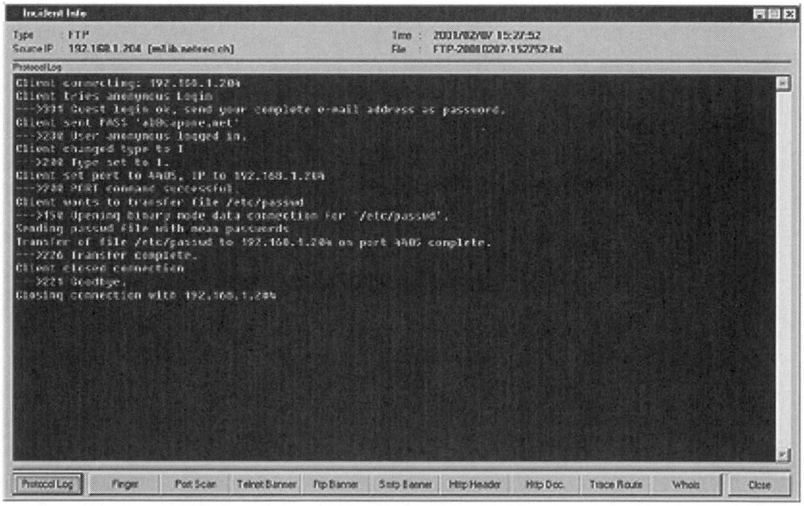

Figure 5.5 Log records from an attempt to download a UNIX `/etc/passwd` file

that a program is using. Of particular concern in a buffer overflow is what follows the input buffer.

Good programming practice requires that a program check the length (i.e., number of characters) of an input value before storing it. But it takes extra lines of code to validate the size of the value and take action if it is too long, so sometimes such validation checks aren't written into software. It is just this situation that causes a buffer overflow vulnerability.

The problem occurs when one of the pieces of data following closely in main memory to the unvalidated input is a main memory address that the program will visit to find more program instructions. (If you're a programmer, then you have probably figured out that we're talking about subroutine return addresses on the program stack. If you're not a programmer, don't worry about the technical specifics.) The writer of the software that will exploit the buffer overflow creates an input value that is long enough to overwrite the main memory address with a new address, one where the system cracker has placed his or her own software. Rather than going to another part of the current program, the computer executes the cracker's program, which could do just about anything. It could install a root kit, for example!

Reality Check: Other than malware (viruses, worms, Trojan horses, and so on), the most common security problem to reach the mass media is a buffer overflow. Problems that are caused by bad software practices seem to catch the public's attention. Media attention notwithstanding, buffer overflows are among the most common—and most troublesome—of security problems.

You can't fix a buffer overflow vulnerability yourself because the cause is a software bug. The only solution is to obtain a software patch from the software developer. For more information on patches and patch management, see "Patches and Patch Management" on page 127.

5.4 Hands On

The basic thrust of this chapter has been that you must employ a combination of human and automated tools to detect and prevent someone from gaining unauthorized root access to your computer. The automated tools are very OS-specific. Therefore, this Hands On section contains some material that applies only to a single OS, along with other resources that can help you locate software that you might choose to use.

5.4.1 Viewing and Configuring Windows Event Logs

Windows logs and the configuration of logging settings are handled through the Event Viewer application. Anyone logged into a Windows machine can view that machine's event log, but you must be logged in as an administrator to change event logging settings.

Viewing Logs

As you saw earlier in this chapter (see Figure 5.2), each Windows log that you display in the Event Viewer gives you enough data to give a knowledgeable security staff member information about repeated attempts to crack the system. Keep in mind that the logs are just that: records of what occurred. There is no intelligence (artificial or otherwise) behind them to interpret what appears; that requires the expertise of a human.

But where do you find the Event Viewer? It depends on the version of Windows you are using. For example, in Windows 2003 Family Edition, it is in the Application Tools folder; in Windows 2000, it's in the Tools folder. Best advice? Use the Search facility to find it.

Configuring Logging

You can configure the types of events that are logged and how those events are kept for each of the three system logs. To do so:

1. Open the Event Viewer.
2. Highlight the log you want to configure.
3. Choose Action->Properties.
4. Use the General panel (see Figure 5.6) to set the maximum size of the log file and what should happen when the log file is full.

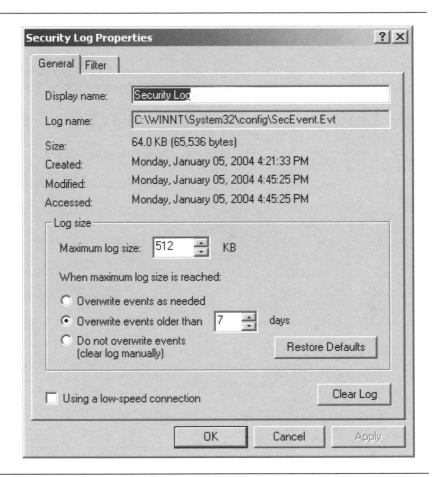

Figure 5.6 General properties for a Windows log

5. Use the Filter panel (see Figure 5.7) to configure which types of
    events will be recorded in the log. Notice that you can filter events
    by date as well as by type, source, and so on.

5.4.2 Patches and Patch Management

Because a buffer overflow attack exploits a programming flaw, there is
nothing that a security professional can do to repair the problem. You
must rely on the software developer to provide a patch that fixes the
program bug.

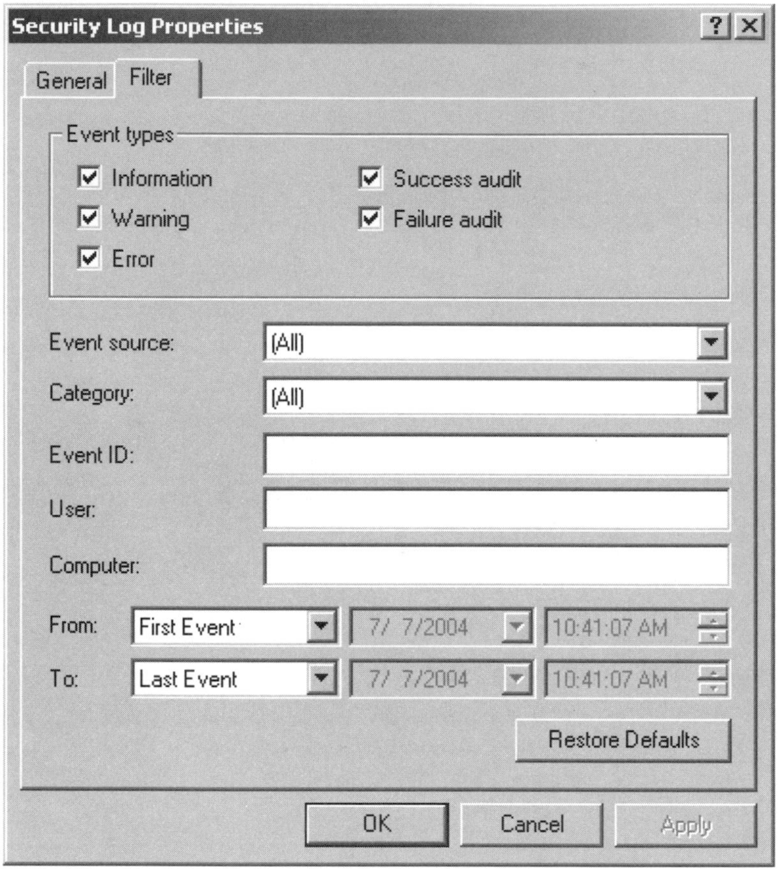

Figure 5.7 Filter properties for a Windows log

The software most vulnerable to buffer overflow attacks currently appears to be the various versions of Microsoft Windows. No other software is scrutinized so closely to reveal program bugs. Microsoft staff surely must put in long hours of overtime writing patches to fix the buffer overflow conditions identified by black and white hat hackers. And if you happen to manage the network for a large organization that relies on Windows, you may spend a great deal of your time identifying and applying patches. What makes the job even more daunting is that you need to keep track of which machines have which patches installed so that you ensure that all machines are patched to the same level of security.

Where do you find the patches? Usually on the vendor's Web site.

How do you find out that a patch is available? Usually by reading the vendor's Web site or by monitoring any of the Web sites that report security vulnerabilities (for example, *http://www.cern.org*).

And what about managing all those patches? To keep track of what's going on, you need to plan ahead:

♦ Make sure that you have a complete inventory of the hardware and software on your network so that you can identify what needs patching. This means that your inventory not only must include hardware details, but also operating system versions and patch levels.

♦ Decide how you will test new patches. Ideally, you should set aside a computer that can be detached from the network while you are installing and testing a new patch.

♦ Determine a procedure for distributing patches. Decide who will be responsible for performing the installation (e.g., the end user or IT staff). If end users install their own patches, how will you ensure that the patches actually are applied?

If you are working in a large organization, you may want to use patch management software. Among the features you can expect to find are vulnerability scanning, automated patch distribution (including scheduled deployments), and an inventory of patches applied.

Note: For a summary of the major patch management software products, see http://www.infoworld.com/infoworld/ img/25FEpatches2_ch-x.gif.

Reality Check: The college where I teach has about 5,000 nodes on a mixed OS network, although it is predominantly Windows. Because so many users attach computers not owned by the college to the network, a comprehensive patch management solution isn't feasible. The college IT department decides which Windows patches are essential. Then, when a computer that hasn't been on the network in a week or so attaches to the network, opening any browser triggers a scan of the computer. First the scan looks for viruses and, if the computer is running Windows, for the required patches. If the patches aren't present, the user is given a link for downloading the patches. The user must download and install the patches before the computer can use the network. Although the 10-minute wait to use the network after the scan is successful can be frustrating, this is probably the best the college can do, given that it can't control the types of operating systems using its network.

Reality Check: In May 2004 alone, the anti-virus developer Sophos counted 959 new viruses and worms. And that number doesn't include all the various Windows buffer overflow conditions and other exploits that seem to be multiplying at an astonishing rate. You can't hope to keep up with all of them; you'd be spending every moment of your time applying patches. You have to make judgments about which threats are the most dangerous and therefore warrant fixes.

5.5 Summary

In this chapter we have focused on the goal of serious system crackers: gaining root access without being detected and maintaining that access. One of the most primitive—yet often successful—ways of gaining root access is a brute force attack, one in which the cracker repeatedly tries to guess user name and password pairs.

Assuming that the cracker gains entry and can promote the compromised user account to root (or administrator) privileges, then the cracker will often install a root kit, software that allows the cracker to reenter the system as the root at any time.

Sophisticated crackers also can take advantage of software errors known as buffer overflows. In this case, programmers haven't added checks for the lengths of input items, and a cracker can use software that overflows the input area and redirects a subroutine to code that the cracker has installed. The result is that the cracker can execute a program that he or she has previously installed on the compromised system of any other program on the system.

The major defenses against brute force attacks include physical examination of system logs to look for unusual activity and automated tools such as intrusion detection and intrusion prevention software. In addition, it is vital to patch vendor software to prevent crackers from taking advantage of buffer overflow possibilities.

Chapter 6: Spoofing

In This Chapter

- ♦ TCP spoofing
- ♦ DNS spoofing
- ♦ IP (and e-mail) spoofing
- ♦ Web spoofing

6.0 Introduction

The term *spoofing* applies to actions that make an electronic transmission appear to originate from somewhere that it does not. Spoofing can be used to steal sensitive information, such as the social engineering attacks based on e-mail and Web spoofs (introduced in Chapter 3). By falsifying source IP addresses, a cracker can initiate a denial of service attack. In this chapter, we'll look at what can be spoofed and how you can detect when something has been faked.

Reality Check: It's impossible to stop a cracker from mounting a spoofed attack because the cracker falsifies something and then launches it at your network. You'd need contact with the cracker before the phony packet | e-mail | URL was generated to prevent such an attack. The best you can do is detect the spoofed attack and discard spoofed items.

6.1 TCP Spoofing

TCP spoofing is a technique for convincing the recipient of a TCP segment that the message is coming from a source other than the attacker. Often known as the *man in the middle* attack, it can be used to disseminate false information on which the recipient might act or to deliver payloads (attachments) that contain malware.

TCP spoofing takes advantage of the way in which the TCP processes on source and destination machines establish and maintain a connection: the *three-way handshake*. In Figure 6.1 you can see the way in which the conversation should take place.

1. The source sends a segment with a SYN request (a request to open a virtual connection between the two machines).
2. The destination replies with a SYN and an ACK, as well as a starting sequence number for the segments in the conversation.

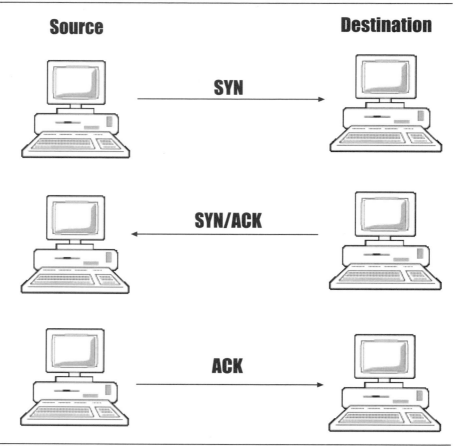

Figure 6.1 The normal TCP three-way handshake

3.   The source responds with an ACK and the connection is established.

The TCP sequence number is not a simple count of segments in a message. The first sequence number is 0 based, although the 0 may be added to a starting number. The source then counts the number of octets in the data field of the first segment. The sequence number of the second segment is the number of the first octet in that second segment. The destination host can therefore predict the sequence number of the next segment by also counting the number of octets in a received segment and adding 1. It includes the predicted next sequence number in its ACK segment. If the sequence number in an ACK segment sent by the destination isn't correct, then the source assumes that the segment did not arrive correctly and retransmits.

The goal of a cracker is to jump into the middle of the TCP exchanges, intercepting the segments and inserting his/her own segments. You can see how this can occur in Figure 6.2. The cracker detects the beginning of the three-way handshake and then intercepts segments coming from the destination, sending a spoofed SYN/ACK segment to the source. Nothing reaches the destination and eventually the destination believes that the connection has been broken. This is known as *blind TCP spoofing*.

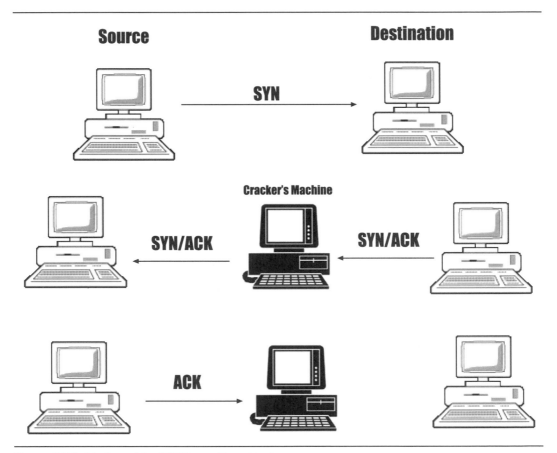

Figure 6.2 Initiating a blind TCP spoofing attack

To make TCP spoofing work, the cracker needs to know the starting sequence number of the TCP segments so that the fake segment returned to the source looks legitimate. How easy this is to do depends on the operating system of the original destination host. Some OSs use the same starting number for each TCP virtual connection. Others use random starting sequence numbers, making a connection much more difficult to spoof.

Table 6.1 contains the relative risk factors for various operating systems. As you can see, early Windows OSs are particularly vulnerable, whereas UNIX implementations (with the exception of HP/UX) tend to be less at risk for this type of attack.

Operating System	Risk
Linux	Low
FreeBSD and NetBSD	Low
OpenBSD	Low
HP/UX	Extremely high
Solaris	Low[a]
Windows 2000	Moderate
Windows NT4 SP6a	Moderate
Windows 98	Extremely high
Windows 95	Extremely high
Cisco IS 12.0 (patched)	Low
Mac OS 9	High
Mac OS X	Moderate

Table 6.1 Risks for blind TCP spoofing for various operating systems[b]

   a. Some Solaris settings can raise the risk considerably.
   b. The data from which this table was compiled can be found at *http://www.bindview.com/Support/RAZOR/Papers/2001/tcpseq.cfm*

Reality Check: Although the TCP spoofing risks for both Windows 2000 and Mac OS X are technically moderate, the Windows 2000 machine presents a much greater practical risk. Why? Because there are so many system crackers who are attempting to enter Windows systems. There aren't enough Mac OS X systems (yet ...) to make it worth their while.

TCP spoofing attacks are extremely difficult to detect. Why? Because TCP does no authentication of the parties involved in a two-way communication. Firewalls won't stop such attacks nor can IDSs/IPSs recognize them in most cases. If TCP spoofing is a concern, your best bet is to encrypt messages so that a cracker is unable to use the body of the message. (Encryption is covered in Chapter 12.)

Reality Check: How much real risk is there for TCP spoofing? Not as much as there was when the Internet was new. Why? Because an attacker needs to use a packet sniffer to grab a specific packet as it travels over the Internet and then extract the sequence number. This is very hard to do, given the volume of traffic that passes through Internet routers today. An attacker would need to examine literally tens of thousands of packets to find one of interest. For most system crackers, there are other forms of attack that are easier and less labor intensive.

6.2 DNS Spoofing

DNS spoofing is a method for redirecting users to a Web site other than the one to which a domain name is actually registered. The most common variation is *malicious cache poisoning*, which involves the modification of data in the cache of a domain name server. Any name server that specifically isn't protected against this type of attack is vulnerable.

To understand how it works, consider the following example, which is illustrated in Figure 6.3. Assume two domains, cracker.com and victim.com. The intent of cracker.com is to redirect all requests for victim.com to cracker.com's Web site:

1.   The system cracker creates a false DNS record on the cracker.com name server that maps victim.com to cracker.com's IP address.

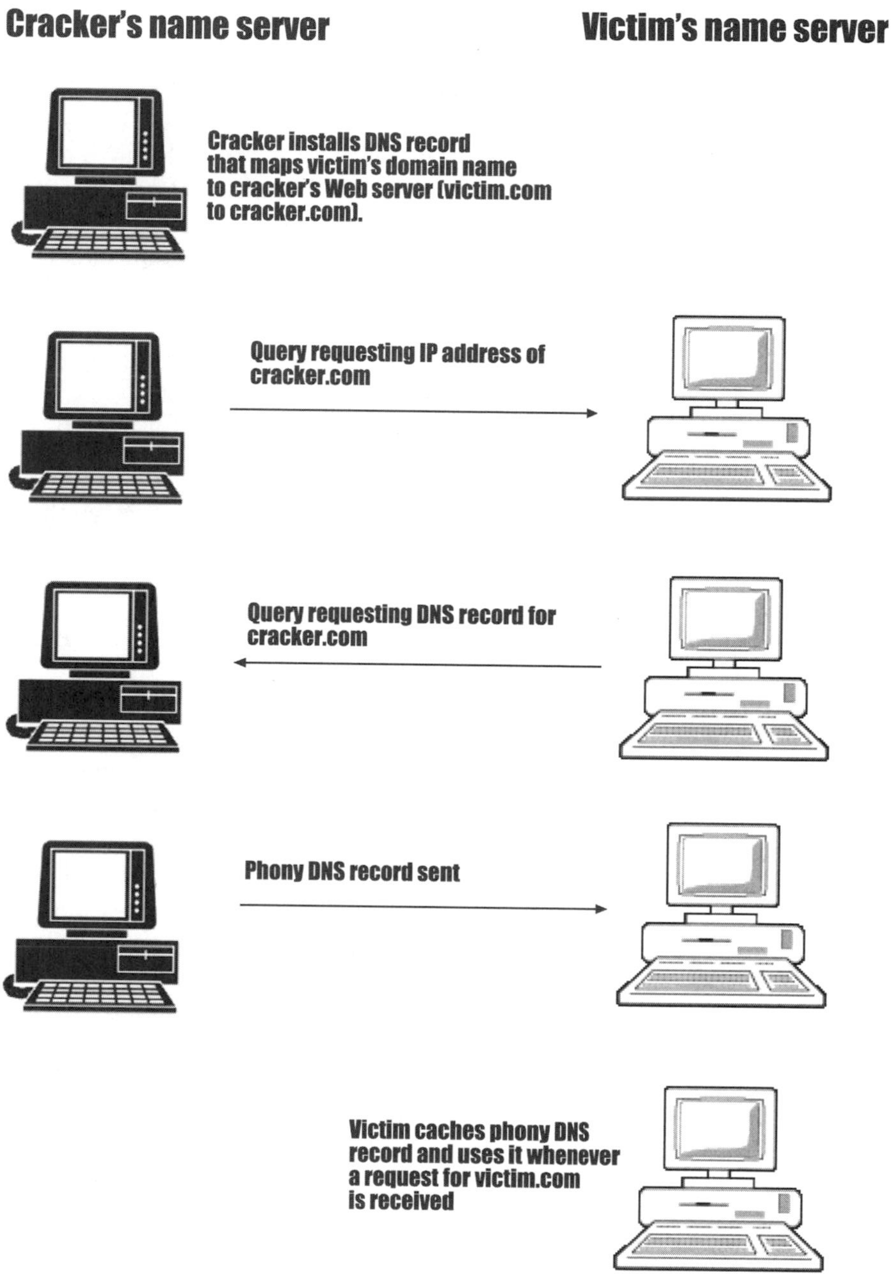

Cracker's name server   **Victim's name server**

Cracker installs DNS record
that maps victim's domain name
to cracker's Web server (victim.com
to cracker.com).

Query requesting IP address of
cracker.com

Query requesting DNS record for
cracker.com

Phony DNS record sent

Victim caches phony DNS
record and uses it whenever
a request for victim.com
is received

Figure 6.3 Setting up DNS spoofing

2. Cracker.com sends a query to victim.com, requesting DNS data for cracker.com. (Yes, you read that right. The cracker asks the victim for information about himself.)

3. The victim responds by querying cracker.com's name server for the information.

4. Cracker.com responds by sending the false DNS record.

5. The victim caches the false DNS record, which it will now use instead of whatever is in its DNS database (because it is ostensibly newer—and therefore more accurate—and faster to retrieve). All requests to victim.com for its DNS entry from other systems wil be answered with the cached, false DNS record. Any requests for victim.com's Web pages then will be redirected to cracker.com.

Alternatively, a cracker can trick a victim into thinking the cracker's machine is a DNS server. The basic method requires capturing the ID number of the UDP datagram carrying an initial DNS query. Here's how it would work if cracker.com wanted the users at victim1.com to think they were connecting to victim2.com when they were actually connecting to cracker.com (see Figure 6.4):

1. The system cracker uses a packet sniffer to intercept traffic from victim1.com.

2. When the packet sniffer detects a packet containing a DNS query about victim2.com, the cracker creates his own fake UDP datagram, using the query ID number from the intercepted packet. The fake UDP datagram contains information that maps victim2.com to cracker.com.

3. The cracker returns the fake datagram to victim1.com.

4. Victim1.com caches the information and uses it for all requests for victim2.com, which actually sends users to cracker.com.

It's virtually impossible to detect a DNS spoofing attack while it is in progress. In fact, the first hint you may have that the problem has occurred is a report from users that they aren't reaching the correct Web page. The best you can do is harden your name servers to prevent the cache poisoning from occurring.

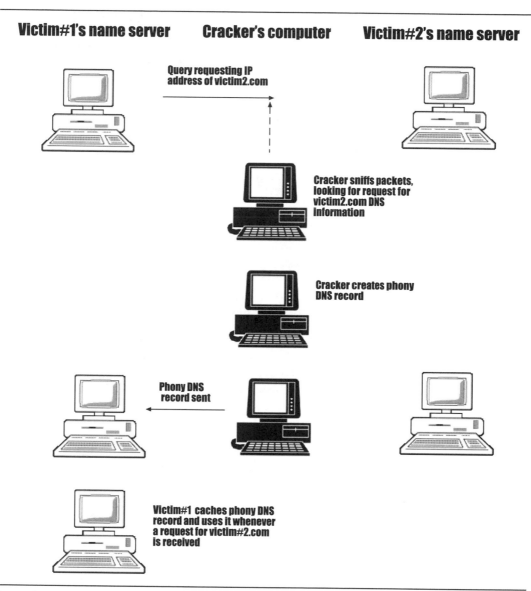

Figure 6.4 Impersonating a name server to initiate DNS spoofing

Some important techniques for safeguarding a name server include

- ◆ Use the newest version of the DNS software that you can. For the most part, each update of the software makes it more secure.

- ◆ Consider carefully how you will allow or disallow transfers of DNS information (*zone transfers*). You may want to use some form of authentication before allowing the download of full DNS records.

- ◆ Disallow recursive DNS queries (queries in which your name server queries the source of a query for information about itself).

6.3 IP (and E-Mail) Spoofing

The most common type of spoofing that you are likely to encounter is IP spoofing, used primarily to spoof the source address of e-mail. In this case, an e-mail message looks like it comes from one address, when in fact it comes from somewhere else instead. The intent is to trick the user into thinking the e-mail comes from a trusted source so that the user will open the e-mail and act on it in some way.

E-mail spoofing can be used to

- ◆ Deliver a phishing message (one that cons the user into divulging confidential information). Replying to the e-mail won't work properly, but clicking on links in the e-mail will take the user to a spoofed Web site.

- ◆ Deliver a malware payload, such as a virus, worm, or Trojan horse. The malware may come as an attachment that must be downloaded (and perhaps executed) or may be coded into the e-mail so that all the user needs to do is open the e-mail. (The malware installs itself when the e-mail is opened.)

One of the more annoying e-mail spoofing tricks is to use the contents of the e-mail address book on a compromised machine as the sources of spoofed e-mail. If you happen to receive an e-mail message such as that in Figure 6.5, then you know that your address has been harvested and used in that way.

The spoofed e-mail that generated the response in Figure 6.5 was an attempt to deliver a virus. The mailer daemon on the target machine caught the virus and blocked the delivery of the e-mail. The response e-mail was sent to the spoofed address, surprising the recipient because the owner of the spoofed address didn't send the e-mail with the attached virus.

As with other spoofing attacks, you can't stop the spoofer from sending the spoofed message. Fortunately, however, spoofed e-mail is relatively easy to detect by examining the e-mail header information and is something technologically savvy users can be taught to do. (For details, see "Detecting Spoofed E-mail" on page 149.)

If your users aren't knowledgeable enough to understand an e-mail header, then there are still some behaviors that you can insist upon to avoid much of the damage from e-mail spoofing:

♦ Train users never to download attachments from untrusted sources. Depending on the nature of your organization, you may be able to block e-mail attachments entirely.

Reality Check: Although blocking e-mail attachments sounds like a great way to stop a lot of malware from entering your system, be careful before instituting such a policy. There are very few organizations today in which workers can function without using e-mail to transfer files, be they long documents or short memos. As an alternative, it may make sense to block executables but let text and Word documents through.

♦ Insist that users avoid address book software, such as Microsoft Outlook, that is vulnerable to surfing by malware. This can go a long way to prevent the addresses in an address book from being used as spoofed addresses.

♦ Teach users to be skeptical about e-mail that promises something that is too good to be true, even if that e-mail appears to come from a trusted source. The source could be spoofed.

♦ Reiterate frequently to users that well-known sites such as PayPal and eBay never ask for confidential information in an

```
The original message was received at Tue, 20 Jul 2004 20:17:23 +0200 (MET DST)
from IDENT:root@localhost [127.0.0.1]

    ----- The following addresses had permanent fatal errors -----
<harald.haas@dfki.uni-kl.de>
    (reason: 554 5.7.1 Junkmail threshold exceeded (more than 5 hits).)

    ----- Transcript of session follows -----
... while talking to mailgate2.uni-kl.de.:
DATA
<<< 554 5.7.1 Junkmail threshold exceeded (more than 5 hits).
554 5.0.0 Service unavailable
Reporting-MTA: dns; crp-200.dfki.uni-sb.de
Received-From-MTA: DNS; localhost
Arrival-Date: Tue, 20 Jul 2004 20:17:23 +0200 (MET DST)

Final-Recipient: RFC822; harald.haas@dfki.uni-kl.de
Action: failed
Status: 5.7.1
Remote-MTA: DNS; mailgate2.uni-kl.de
Diagnostic-Code: SMTP; 554 5.7.1 Junkmail threshold exceeded (more than 5 hits).
Last-Attempt-Date: Tue, 20 Jul 2004 20:17:25 +0200 (MET DST)

From: jan.harrington@college.edu
Date: July 20, 2004 2:20:46 PM EDT
to: harald.haas@dfki.de
Subject: Mail Delivery (failure harald.haas@dfki.de)

----------------- Virus Warning Message (on crp-200)

Found virus HTML_Netsky.P in file email-body
The file email-body is moved to /tmp/virGTAH6ayWp.

If you have questions, please contact your ISG.

Found virus WRM_NETSKY.P in file message.scr
The file message.scr is moved to /tmp/virITAJ6ayWp.

If you have questions, please contact your ISG.
---------------------------------------------------------
----------------- Virus Warning Message (on crp-200)

email-body is removed from here because it contains a virus.
---------------------------------------------------------
----------------- Virus Warning Message (on crp-200)

message.scr is removed from here because it contains a virus.
```

Figure 6.5 Message sent by mailer daemon in response to spoofed e-mail

e-mail, nor do they provide links in e-mail to pages that ask for such data. If a user wants to change a password or payment option, he or she should use a browser to access the site directly.

Reality Check: The trick with all these e-mail behaviors is to get users to go against their basically trusting natures. It can be difficult to make a user suspicious of every e-mail, and most users won't be. The best you can do is refresh "safe e-mail" handling behaviors whenever possible. In the long run, most users will be relatively safe from spoofing most of the time, and some users will simply never get it. You will be removing viruses and other malware from their computers repeatedly. You can't cut off their e-mail because they need it to do their jobs. So, just try to leave some hair in your head when you get the 75th call that his or her computer keeps rebooting itself.

On the administrative end, you should update your e-mail server software frequently so that it has the most recent virus filters. (What? Your e-mail server doesn't scan incoming traffic for viruses and other nasties? Time to reevaluate that software!)

Note: It's not unusual to be thinking something like "but that's all just common sense" when reading suggestions like those in the preceding bulleted list. However, a lot of security is indeed common sense and, unfortunately, many computer users don't seem to use theirs.

6.4 Web Spoofing

You were first introduced to Web spoofing in Chapter 3 as a method of social engineering. Web spoofing involves tricking a user into thinking he or she is interacting with a trusted Web site when, in reality, the Web site is collecting personal information, usually to perpetrate an identity theft.

Spoofed Web sites look very much like the site they are imitating. The user stays within the spoofed environment until the system cracker has given the victim a chance to divulge whatever the cracker is attempting to gather.

As an example, consider the e-mail in Figure 6.6 to a PayPal member. This is a particularly good example of a phising expedition because it contains the authentic graphics of the PayPal site and the URL in the message (which was a link in the original) looks like a legitimate PayPal link. In addition, the grammar and spelling of the message are correct and professional. To make the e-mail psychologically more compelling, the phisher added a deadline and the threat of restrictions on the person's PayPal account.

As legitimate as the URL in the e-mail may appear, the URL was actually only a label for an HTML HREF tag. When the user clicked on the link, he or she was taken to the spoofed Web site. Why might the user not know that the site was spoofed? Compare Figure 6.7, the authentic PayPal login page and Figure 6.8, the spoofed PayPal login page. They are identical! This is such an easy hoax to perpetrate because the source code is available for every page on the Web. All the spoofer has to do is rewrite the code that is triggered by clicking the Log In button.

Rather than checking the PayPal user name and password, the spoofer simply collects the information in a file and displays the second page (see Figure 6.9), which is an exact copy of an information page used by PayPal.

Clicking the Continue button takes the user to the page in Figure 6.10. This page, like the preceding one, is intended to increase the user's comfort level with the spoofed site. (Notice also the threat of limited access to account balances if the user doesn't comply with the requests made by the Web page.) The real information is collected on the fourth page (see Figure 6.11). As with the eBay spoof you saw in Chapter 3, the user is asked for every piece of confidential information someone would need for an identity theft.

The spoofer wants the victim to remain in ignorance of what has occurred. Therefore, the spoofed site responds the to submitted information with a comforting Thank You page (see Figure 6.12), followed by a page that mimics PayPal's home page (see Figure 6.13). The links on the imitation home page lead to pages on the legitimate PayPal site. The user therefore leaves the spoofed site none the wiser for having been tricked.

You can't stop someone from spoofing a Web site; as long as the source code of Web pages remains freely available, spoofing a Web page or two

PayPal *The way to send and receive money online*

Dear valued **PayPal**® member:

PayPal® is committed to maintaining a safe environment for its community of buyers and sellers. To protect the security of your account, PayPal employs some of the most advanced security systems in the world and our anti-fraud teams regularly screen the PayPal system for unusual activity.

Recently, our Account Review Team identified some unusual activity in your account. In accordance with **PayPal**'s User Agreement and to ensure that your account has not been compromised, access to your account was limited. Your account access will remain limited until this issue has been resolved. This is a fraud prevention measure meant to ensure that your account is not compromised.

In order to secure your account and quickly restore full access, we may require some specific information from you for the following reason:

We would like to ensure that your account was not accessed by an unauthorized third party. Because protecting the security of your account is our primary concern, we have limited access to sensitive **PayPal** account features. We understand that this may be an inconvenience but please understand that this temporary limitation is for your protection.

Case ID Number: PP-040-187-541

We encourage you to log in and restore full access as soon as possible. Should access to your account remain limited for an extended period of time, it may result in further limitations on the use of your account.

However, failure to restore your records will result in account suspension. Please update your records on or before July 30, 2004.

Once you have updated your account records, your **PayPal** session will not be interrupted and will continue as normal.

To update your **Paypal** records click on the following link:
https://www.paypal.com/cgi-bin/webscr?cmd=_login-run

Thank you for your prompt attention to this matter. Please understand that this is a security measure meant to help protect you and your account. We apologize for any inconvenience.

Sincerely,
PayPal® Account Review Department
PayPal Email ID PP522

Figure 6.6   Phishing e-mail that provides entry to the spoofed Web site

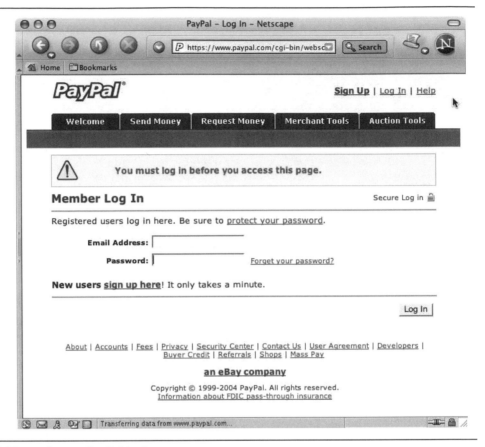

Figure 6.7 The authentic PayPal login page

or three or four…,will continue to be easy to do. The best you can do is to educate your users so they can recognize Web spoofing when they encounter it. (For details, see "Detecting Spoofed Web Sites" on page 153.)

6.5 Hands On

If you are blessed with a technologically savvy user base, you can teach the users to recognize spoofed e-mails and Web sites by examining e-mail headers and URLs, respectively. This hands-on section looks at doing both in detail.

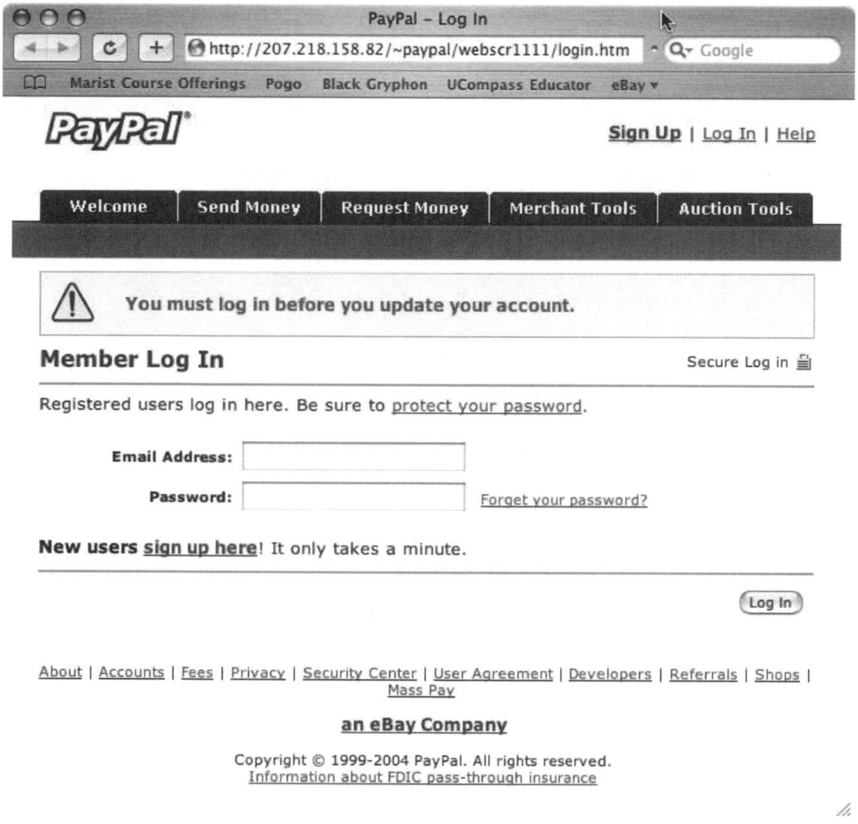

Figure 6.8 The spoofed PayPal login page

6.5.1 Detecting Spoofed E-mail

Each e-mail sent over the Internet is accompanied by a lengthy header that indicates where it came from and the path it took to reach its destination. In Figure 6.14 on page 155 you can see the header for an e-mail that was not spoofed. The most important lines to look at are From and Return Path. As you can see, they match, and they should.

In contrast, consider the e-mail header in Figure 6.15 on page 156. It's from *victorj@ntcity.com (Janulaitis, Victor),* but the return path is *bounced@fcsmail.com.* Not only do they not match, but the return path is just a wee bit suspicious....

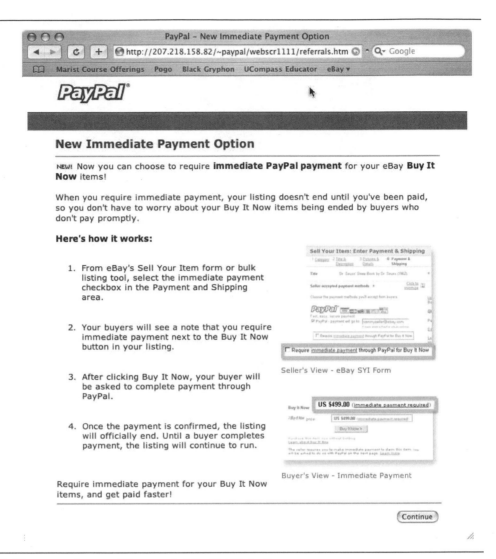

Figure 6.9 The second page of the spoofed PayPal Web site

There are some exceptions to this rule, in particular when the e-mail has come from a mailing list, such as the header in Figure 6.16 on page 157. Because the sender of the message is really the mailing list computer rather than the original poster of the message, From and Return Path don't match. In this case, users need to keep track of the mailing lists from which they receive e-mail so they can recognize authentic mailing list messages.

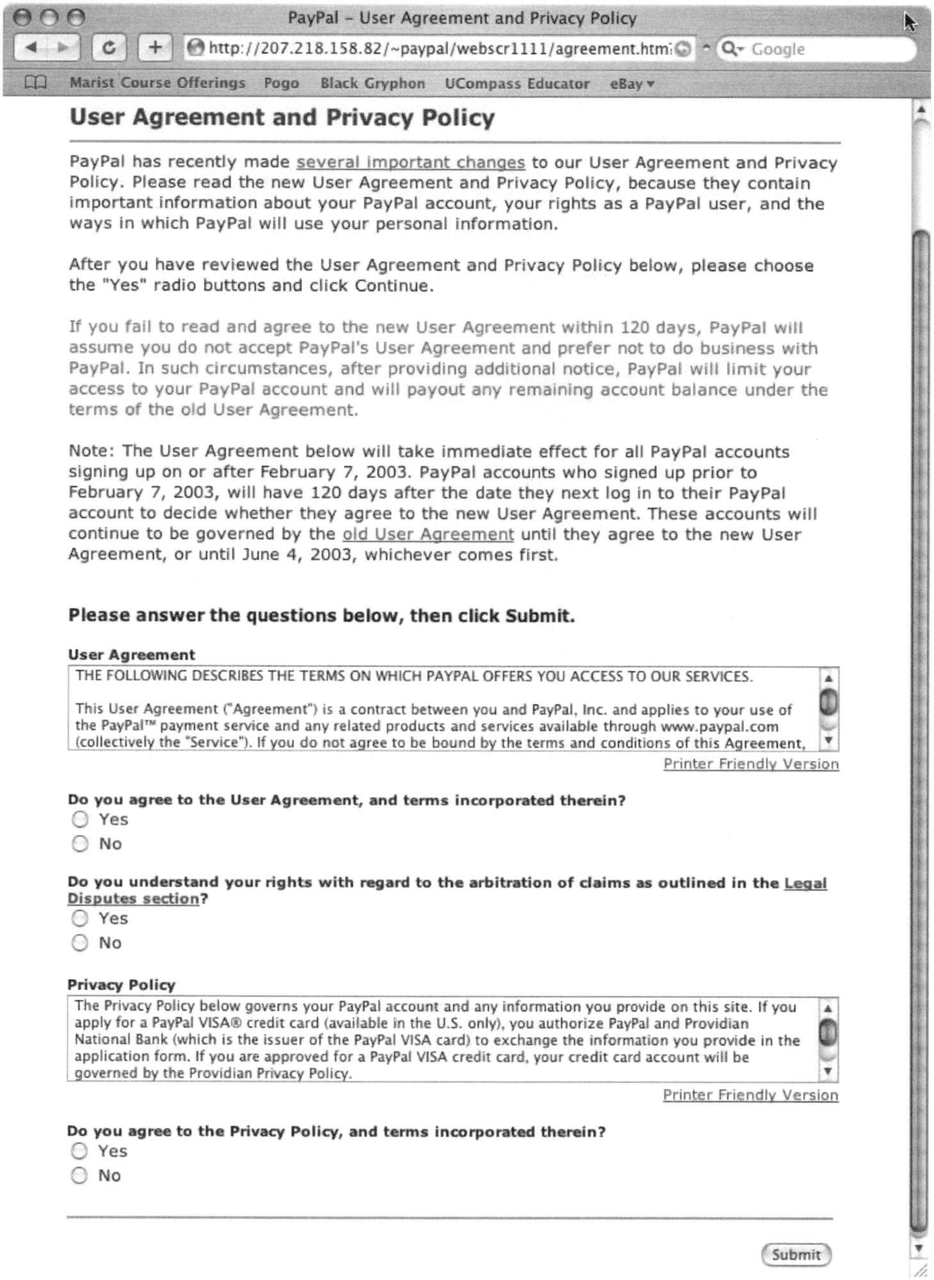

Figure 6.10 The third page of the spoofed PayPal Web site

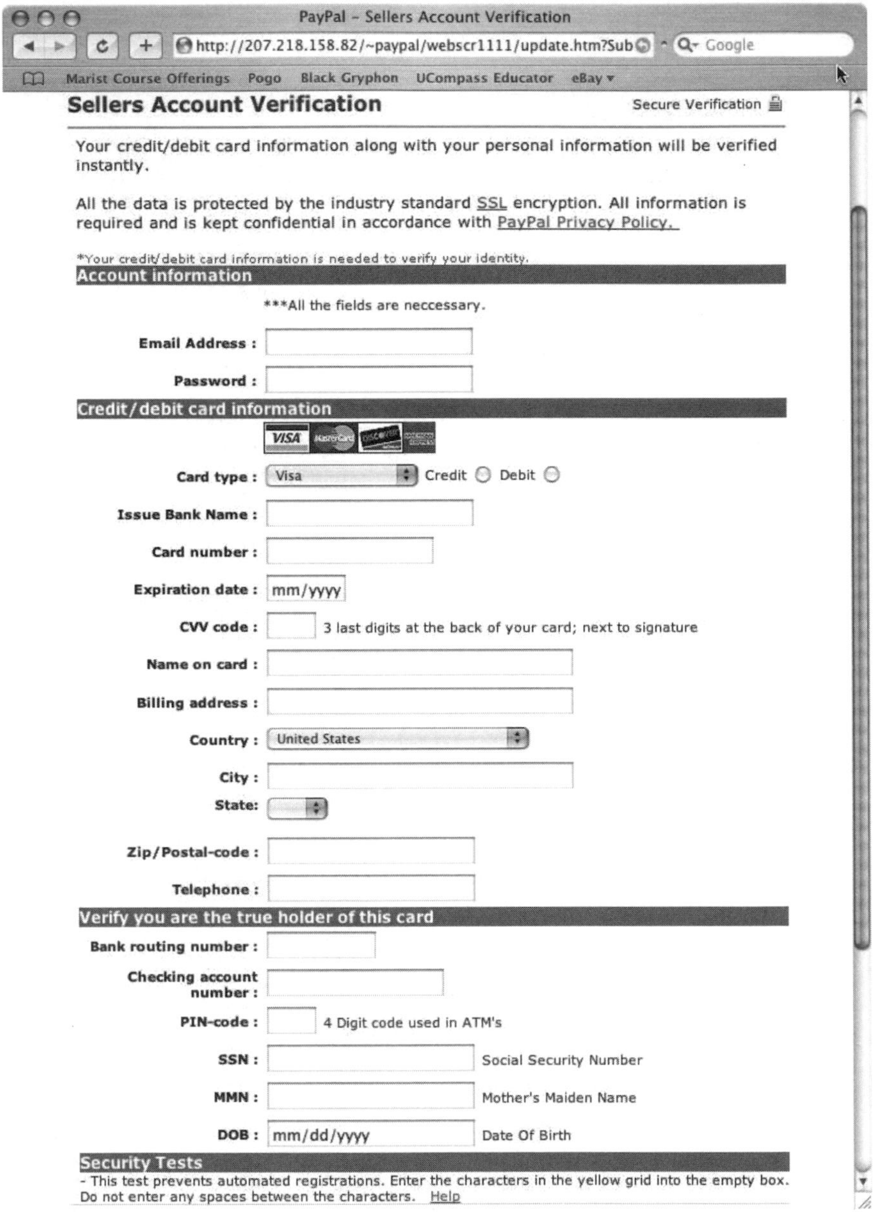

Figure 6.11 The fourth page of the spoofed PayPal Web site

Figure 6.12 The fifth page of the spoofed PayPal Web site

6.5.2 Detecting Spoofed Web Sites

Detecting a spoofed Web site is actually quite easy, but, if not done carefully, may result in the accidental downloading of malware. All a user needs to do is compare the URL of the site to which he or she is being directed to the URL of the authentic site.

As an example, consider the spoofed PayPal Web site that you saw as an example earlier in this chapter. The true PayPal login page has the URL *https://www.paypal.com/cgi-bin/webscr?cmd=_login-done*. In fact, if you look back at the e-mail in Figure 6.6 on page 147, you'll notice that this URL appears as the link in the body of the e-mail. However, if you click on the link you'll be taken to *http://207.218.158.82/~paypal/webscr1111/login.htm*.

Figure 6.13 The final page of the spoofed PayPal Web site

The spoofer is attempting to hide the location of the site by using a numeric IP address rather than a domain name, the latter of which would be a dead giveaway that the user wasn't at a real PayPal site. Users should be trained that any site with a URL that includes an IP address rather than a domain name is highly suspicious.

The easiest way to find the spoofed URL is to click on the link in the e-mail. However, doing so can be risky because some links trigger the downloading of malware. Therefore, it is safer to right-click (or CTRL-

```
        From:                              or.Adams@Elsevier.com
        Subject:                           FW: status report no ms
        Date:                              July 20, 2004 3:03:25 PM EDT
        to:                                blackgryphon@verizon.net
        Return-Path:                       <or.Adams@elsevier.com>
        Received:                          from mail-relay2.elsevier.c.uk
([192.168.1.3]) by mta011.verizon.net (InterMail vM.5.01.06.06 201-253-122-130-
106-20030910) with ESMTP id <20040720191320.JCVJ5111.mta011.verizon.net@mail-
relay2.elsevier.c.uk> for <blackgryphon@verizon.net>; Tue, 20 Jul 2004 14:13:20
-0500
        Received:                          from mail-relay2.elsevier.c.uk
(193.131.223.6) by sc018pub.verizon.net (MailPass SMTP server v1.1.1 -
121803235448JY) with  ESMTP id <1-8083-10-8083-2559-1-1090350798> for
mta011.verizon.net; Tue, 20 Jul 2004 14:13:20 -0500
        Received:                          from elsxfs30373.elsevier.c.uk (unverified)
by mail-relay2.elsevier.c.uk (Content Technologies SMTPRS 4.3.14) with ESMTP id
<T6aea90cceac183df06514@mail-relay2.elsevier.c.uk> for
<blackgryphon@verizon.net>; Tue, 20 Jul 2004 20:04:51 +0100
        Received:                          by elsxfs30373.elsevier.c.uk with Internet
Mail Service (5.5.2657.72) id <P19MANOZ>; Tue, 20 Jul 2004 20:02:58 +0100
        Message-Id:
<6CF59C1AC9DB56458DF1DD7561B4CF3107765632@elssdgs02685>
        Importance:                        high
        X-Priority:                        1
        Mime-Version:                      1.0
        X-Mailer:                          Internet Mail Service (5.5.2657.72)
        Content-Type:                      text/plain; charset="is-8859-1"
```

Figure 6.14 An authentic e-mail header

click with a one-button mouse) to show the link's pop-up menu. Copy the target address of the link to the clipboard and paste it into a text editor document so you can see the link. Then you can examine it to see if it really points where you think it should.

If looking at the URL doesn't give you enough information to determine whether the site is authentic, try querying the top-level domain using a program like whois. In Figure 6.17, for example, you can see the result of a search for the spoofed PayPal site that used the IP address from the URL of the spoofed pages. The most important information here is that the IP address is owned by Global Crossing and not by PayPal. In fact, Global Crossing would probably be grateful if you used their "abuse" address to report the spoofed site that was residing on one of its servers.

```
Return-Path: <bounced@fcsmail.com>
Received: from rly-xm02.mx.al.com (rly-xm02.mail.al.com [172.20.83.103]) by air-
xm04.mail.al.com (v100.23) with ESMTP id MAILINXM43-5f640fd3a2da5; Tue, 20 Jul
2004 11:29:33 -0400
Received: from  mail.fcsmail.com (mail.fcsmail.com [66.100.152.200]) by rly-
xm02.mx.al.com (v100.23) with ESMTP id MAILRELAYINXM26-5f640fd3a2da5; Tue, 20 Jul
2004 11:28:46 -0400
Received: from mail.fcsmail.com (localhost.localdomain [127.0.0.1])
     by mail.fcsmail.com (8.11.6/8.11.6) with ESMTP id i6KFSgZ22728
     for <blgryph@aol.com>; Tue, 20 Jul 2004 11:28:42 -0400
Message-Id: <200407201528.i6KFSgZ22728@mail.fcsmail.com>
Content-Transfer-Encoding: binary
Content-Type: multipart/alternative; boundary="_----------=_109033562274460"
MIME-Version: 1.0
From: victorj@ntcity.com (Janulaitis, Victor)
to: blgryph@aol.com
Subject: CI Productivity & IT Alignment Kit
Date: Tue, 20 Jul 2004 11:00:22 -0400
Reply-to: victorj@ntcity.com (Janulaitis, Victor)
Organizatin: FCSMail
Comments: mail.fcsmail.com:ID10902561503smY:ID1090264925JbNE:ID1090265116ZsXz
X-Mailer: FCS Mailer 1.6
X-AL-IP: 66.100.152.200
X-AL-SCLL-SCRE: 1:XXX:XX
X-AL-SCLL-URL_COUNT: 19
```

Figure 6.15 An e-mail header containing a spoofed return address

6.6 Summary

Spoofing is a technique for tricking an end user into believing that an e-mail or Web site comes from somewhere other than its actual source. In most cases, the intent is to make the user think that the origin is a trusted source (either a known individual or a well-respected organization).

There are several kinds of spoofing, each with a slightly different intent:

♦ TCP spoofing: TCP spoofing involves intercepting a TCP segment being returned from a legitimate destination to a legitimate source. The spoofer masquerades as the destination host and communicates directly with the source. The purpose is often to steal trade secrets or financial information.

♦ DNS spoofing: DNS spoofing replaces the information in a name server that maps a domain name to an IP address with

```
From:    John.Smith@marist.edu
   Subject:              [MARFAC] Employee ID Cards
   Date:                 March 30, 2004 10:24:40 AM EST
   to:                   MARFAC@VM.MARIST.EDU
   Reply-to:             John.Smith@marist.edu
   Return-Path:          <owner-marfac@VM.MARIST.EDU>
   Received:             from mailer390.marist.edu ([192.168.1.6]) by
mta011.verizon.net (InterMail vM.5.01.06.06 201-253-122-130-106-20030910) with
ESMTP id <20040330153729.LFSP1450.mta011.verizon.net@mailer390.marist.edu>; Tue,
30 Mar 2004 09:37:29 -0600
   Received:             from mailer390.marist.edu (148.100.80.47) by
sc007pub.verizon.net (MailPass SMTP server v1.1.1 - 121803235448JY) with  ESMTP
id <2-1540-105-1540-160727-1-1080661048> for mta011.verizon.net; Tue, 30 Mar 2004
09:37:29 -0600
   Received:             from VM.MARIST.EDU (vm.marist.edu [148.100.80.40]) by
mailer390.marist.edu (Postfix) with ESMTP id 920AD12FBA; Tue, 30 Mar 2004 10:37:07
-0500 (EST)
   Received:             by VM.MARIST.EDU (IBM VM SMTP Level 430) via spool with SMTP
id 8936 ; Tue, 30 Mar 2004 10:37:28 EST
   Received:             from VM.MARIST.EDU (NJE origin LISTSERV@MARIST) by
VM.MARIST.EDU (LMail V1.2b/1.8b) with BSMTP id 4259; Tue, 30 Mar 2004 10:37:29 -
0500
   Received:             from VM.MARIST.EDU by VM.MARIST.EDU (LISTSERV release 1.8e)
with NJE id 3501 for MARFAC@VM.MARIST.EDU; Tue, 30 Mar 2004 10:37:28 -0500
   Received:             from MARIST (NJE origin SMTP@MARIST) by VM.MARIST.EDU (LMail
V1.2b/1.8b) with BSMTP id 4254; Tue, 30 Mar 2004 10:37:27 -0500
   Received:             from ntes.marist.edu [148.100.49.11] by VM.MARIST.EDU (IBM
VM SMTP Level 430) via TCP with SMTP ; Tue, 30 Mar 2004 10:37:26 EST
   X-Mailer:             Lotus Notes Release 5.0.10  March 22, 2002
   X-Mimetrack:          Serialize by Router no Shakespeare/Marist(Release 5.0.11
|July 24, 2002) at 03/30/2004 10:37:01 AM
   Mime-Version:         1.0
   Content-Type:         text/plain; charset=us-ascii
   Approved-By:          John Smith <John.Smith@MARIST.EDU>
   Message-Id:           <F9CBA2C24.6F73F4C9-N85256E67.004B3DE3-
85256E67.0054A32C@marist.edu>
   Sender:               Marist Faculty <MARFAC@VM.MARIST.EDU>
   Comments:             to: marfac@marist.edu, marstaff@marist.edu
   Precedence:           list
```

Figure 6.16 An authentic e-mail header from a mailing list

a phony mapping stored in the name server's cache. The result is the redirection of the domain name to the site of the spoofer's choice. The purpose is often to divert customers from a legitimate Web site (perhaps to steal information for identify theft). DNS spoofing may also be used to humiliate the operators of the legitimate Web site.

```
OrgName:    Global Crossing
OrgID:      GBLX
Address:    14605 South 50th Street
City:       Phoenix
StateProv:  AZ
PostalCode: 85044-6471
Country:    US

ReferralServer: rwhis://rwhis.gblx.net:4321

NetRange:   207.218.0.0 - 207.218.191.255
CIDR:       207.218.0.0/17, 207.218.128.0/18
NetName:    GBLX-20
NetHandle:  NET-207-218-0-0-1
Parent:     NET-207-0-0-0-0
NetType:    Direct Allocation
NameServer: NAME.PHX.GBLX.NET
NameServer: NAME.RC.GBLX.NET
NameServer: NAME.JFK1.GBLX.NET
NameServer: NAME.SNV.GBLX.NET
Comment:    ADDRESSES WITHIN THIS BLOCK ARE NON-PORTABLE
RegDate:    1996-10-14
Updated:    2002-12-06

OrgAbuseHandle: GBLXA-ARIN
OrgAbuseName:   GBLX-Abuse
OrgAbusePhone:  +1-800-404-7714
OrgAbuseEmail:  abuse@gblx.net

OrgNCHandle: GBLXN-ARIN
OrgNCName:   GBLX-NC
OrgNCPhne:   +1-800-404-7714
OrgNCEmail:  gc-nc@gblx.net

OrgTechHandle: IA12-RG-ARIN
OrgTechName:   GBLX-IPADMIN
OrgTechPhone:  +1-800-404-7714
OrgTechEmail:  ipadmin@gblx.net
```

Figure 6.17 whois search for spoofed site

♦ IP (e-mail) spoofing: IP spoofing makes it appear that an e-mail comes from a source different that its actual origination. The purpose of such a spoof is to trick the user into opening the e-mail and trusting the contents. It might be used to deliver a malware payload or to redirect the user to a spoofed Web site.

♦ Web spoofing: Web spoofing is the counterfeiting of an entire Web site, usually to steal confidential information from the user. The information is used as the basis for identity theft or simply to steal money from the victim.

Chapter 7: Denial of Service Attacks

In This Chapter

- SYN flood attacks
- Other single-source DoS attacks
- Distributed DoS
- Stopping DoS attacks

7.0 Introduction

A *denial of service* (DoS) attack attempts to prevent legitimate users from accessing a computing resource. DoS attacks can take several forms:

♦ Overwhelm a network: The attack can flood a network with so many packets that legitimate traffic slows to a crawl.

♦ Overwhelm a server: The attack can flood a single server with so much traffic that legitimate users can't access the server.

♦ Bring down a server: The attack can cause a server to crash.

You can't prevent an attacker from launching a DoS attack, but you can detect one in progress and take steps to mitigate its impact. In addition, you can prevent hosts on your network from being unwitting parties to a *distributed DoS*, a DoS attack in which the source is multiple computers.

7.1 Single Source DoS Attacks

The earliest DoS attacks were launched from a single source computer. They are attractive types of attacks to system crackers because they don't require any account access. The attacker launches packets from his or her machine that compromise the victim by taking advantage of the victim's natural behavior to communication requests.

7.1.1 SYN Flood Attacks

A simple type of DoS attack comes from a single source computer. one of the earliest to appear was the *SYN flood attack* (see Figure 7.1), which takes advantage of the TCP three-way handshake that we reviewed in Chapter 5. The general technique of the attack is to send a flood of SYN segments to the victim with spoofed—and usually invalid—source IP addresses. The victim responds with SYN/ACK segments that go nowhere, tying up the victim with a multitude of unfinished virtual connections. As a result, the victim slows down and can't handle legitimate traffic in an acceptable time frame.

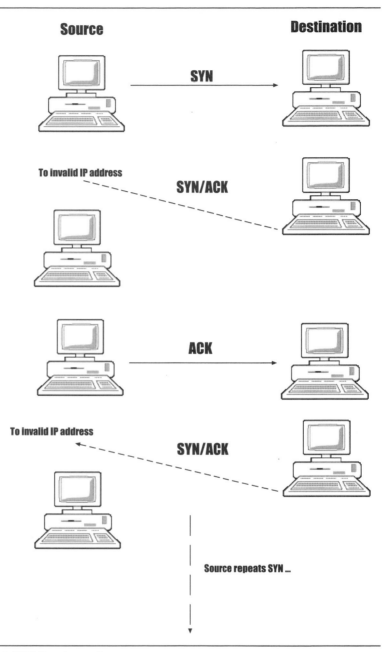

Figure 7.1 A SYN flood attack

7.1.2 Ping of Death

A simple way to mount a DoS attack is to flood the victim system with multiple, oversized ping requests. (This *ping of death* attack first appeared in 1996.) The attacker sends a ping in a packet that has too much data in its data field, creating a packet that is too long (more than 65,536 octets). The victim receives these oversized packets and is likely to crash, hang, or even reboot.

What makes the ping of death so insidious is that all the attacker needs to know is the victim's IP address. Today, however, most operating systems have been patched so that they react more appropriately to oversized packets, mitigating the effects of the attack. However, if your network has older operating systems (for example, Windows 95, MacOS 7.x and earlier, or Novell Netware 3.x and earlier), then you are vulnerable.

In addition, the ping of death can be launched against hosts that aren't computers. Anything with an IP address is vulnerable, such as routers and printers.

7.1.3 Smurf

Smurf is a DoS attack that takes advantage of ICMP (Internet Control Message Protocol) and IP broadcast addresses. (ICMP forms the basis for ping, for example.) Smurf works in the following way:

1. An attacker creates an ICMP echo request packet with a spoofed return address (the IP address of the attack's victim) and a broadcast destination address.
2. The attacker then sends the packet to another target, usually a router that doesn't block ICMP echo requests to broadcast addresses.
3. The router sends the packet to all systems on its network.
4. Each system that received the echo request packet responds to the victim, flooding the victim with packets that tie up its network bandwidth.

7.1.4 UDP Flood Attacks

A UDP flood attack (sometimes called *pingpong*) takes advantage of the chargen service, which is used legitimately to test hosts and networks. An attacker mounts it in the following manner:

1. The attacker spoofs the return IP address of a UDP datagram that makes a request of the chargen service. Typically, the spoofed return address will point to a host on the victim network.
2. The attacker sends the datagram to the victim.
3. The victim's chargen service responds with a random string of characters, which goes to the spoofed IP address on its own network.
4. The two systems continue to send characters to each other, slowing both their own processing and network traffic.

An attacker can also mount a similar type of attack using echo requests.

7.2 Distributed DoS Attacks

A distributed DoS attack uses multiple source computers to disrupt its victims. This does not mean that the attack is coming from multiple attackers, however. The most typical architecture, in fact, is a single attacker or small group of attackers who trigger the attack by activating malware previously installed on computers throughout the world.

> *Note: It's not unusual for an attack to combine multiple techniques. For example, Web spoofing relies on social engineering to draw victims to the spoofed site. In the case of distributed DoS attacks, client malware needs to be installed on an intermediate system before the DoS attack can be launched. This often means that the attacker must gain root or administrative access to the machine to install the client, change system configuration files (if necessary), hide the modifications, and erase traces of his or her activity.*

There are some well-known DoS attacks, as well as new ones seemingly appearing daily. In this section you will become familiar with the well-known varieties to help you understand the strategies behind such attacks.

7.2.1 Tribe Flood Network

Tribe flood network (TFN) uses client software on compromised hosts to launch attacks on a victim or victims. Once the client software has been installed, an attacker can direct the compromised host to begin a single source DoS attack, such as a SYN flood, ping of death, or smurf attack. The problem presented by the attack is that a single victim may receive attack packets from multiple sources, making the actual source of the attack extremely difficult to trace.

The TFN client communicates with TFN *daemons*, the programs on the compromised hosts that actually launch the attack (see Figure 7.2). The daemons use a list of IP addresses as targets for their attacks. Therefore, the TFN attack can be directed at specific systems or use IP addresses selected randomly. Later, more sophisticated versions of TFN use encrypted IP address lists. Therefore, even if you determine that the client and daemon software are installed on a computer, you may not be able to identify the systems targeted for the attack

TFN client and daemon software runs primarily on UNIX systems. (Of course, the attack can be directed to any machine running TCP/IP, regardless of operating system.)

Reality Check: It takes a great deal of expertise to write the software to mount a DoS attack. However, most of the source code is available on the Internet. A script kiddie with a modest amount of skill can compile the code and run it. Assuming that the script kiddie has a way to deliver the client and daemon software to a host, he or she can launch a DoS attack. Alternatively, the script kiddie can scan the Internet looking for hosts that have been previously compromised with the client and daemon software and use the existing compromised host for an attack.

7.2.2 Trinoo

The architecture of a trinoo DoS attack is similar to that of TFN (the attacker communicating with daemons on a compromised host). However, it is used to launch UDP flood attacks from multiple sources.

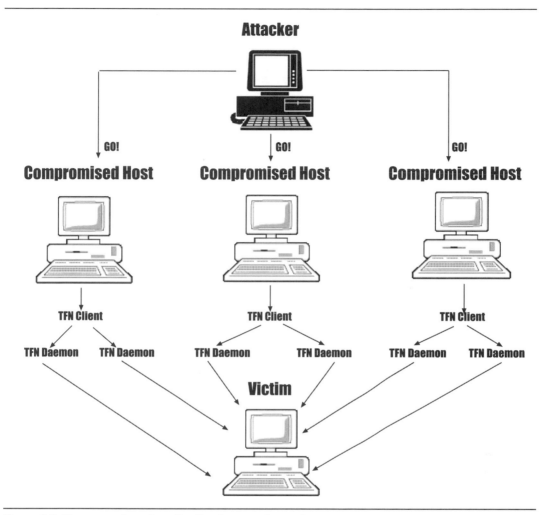

Figure 7.2 The operation of a tribe flood network attack

A trinoo daemon knows the IP address of the computer that installed it. Whenever the daemon launches, it lets its *master* know that it is available. It is therefore to the attacker's advantage to configure the compromised host system to launch the trinoo daemons at system startup.

In addition, a trinoo master also stores the IP addresses of all the daemons known to it. The master can send a broadcast to those daemons to verify their availability.

7.2.3 Stacheldraht

In late February 2000, several large Web sites (for example, eBay and Yahoo) were brought down by a variation of TFN and trinoo called *stacheldraht*. Its architecture is identical to TFN, although its parts are called the *client* (the software run by the attacker), the *handler* (the software running on the compromised host in the middle of the attack), and the *agent* (the daemon that launches the attack packets from the compromised host).

The client, which runs on UNIX systems, communicates with handlers using encrypted communication from a command line similar to `telnet`. Each handler can control up to 1024 agents, each of which can launch multiple packets toward a victim.

Handlers are password protected. The attacker running the client must supply the correct password to control the client. This prevents attackers other than the one who compromised the middle host from launching an attack. (It certainly goes a long way toward preventing script kiddies from taking advantage of a serious system cracker's work.)

Stacheldraht uses both TCP and ICMP to mount attacks. In other words, it combines the attack methods of both TRN and trinoo. Additionally, stacheldraht allows the attacker to automatically update agent software on compromised hosts.

> *Note: Some types of malware also create DoS attacks, without any effort by the attacker once the malware is released on the network. You can find more information in Chapter 8.*

7.3 Hands On

In most cases, DoS attacks don't damage what is stored on a network's hosts, but they can cause major losses of business revenue because they prevent an organization from functioning normally. It is therefore important to harden your network against them as much as possible and to monitor computers on your network for software related to distributed DoS attacks.

7.3.1 Using an IDS to Detect a DoS Attack

For the most part, IDSs work by looking for patterns of network and/or host activity. One part of the IDS logs network events (or looks at existing system logs). The analyzer then examines the event log to determine if suspicious activity is occurring. The rules that the analyzer uses are based on knowledge of previous attacks and known system vulnerabilities.

> *Note: As you might guess, the "heart" of an IDS is its event analyzer. The better it is at detecting unusual activity— without generating false positives—the more effective it is.*

Reality Check: Like most network and host protection software, an IDS that uses pattern matching needs to be updated frequently so that it has analysis rules that can handle current software vulnerabilities. (IDSs that use heuristic detection do not require updating.) If you're going to rely on a pattern matching IDS, then your organization needs to make a commitment to provide the funds for upgrades as they become available. And when it comes to patching, your IDS should be at the top of the list!

In some cases, IDSs look for specific types of activity. For example, an IDS can detect TFN and trinoo activity by looking for communication between the client and the daemons. This is one instance where a host-based (as opposed to network-based) IDS can be invaluable.

IDSs are generally quite effective at detecting DoS attacks that consume network resources such as bandwidth. Along with a firewall, they are your best line of defense against DoS attacks. However, if an attacker knows that an IDS is in place, he or she can launch DoS attacks that attempt to disable the IDS. Any of the following techniques have been known to work:

♦ An attack can tie up CPU cycles on the hardware running the IDS by sending packets that cause the IDS to check large numbers of packets. For example, the attacker might send fragments of many messages that the IDS would attempt to assemble into complete messages.

♦ An attack can consume the RAM on the hardware running the IDS. Each message fragment that the IDS encounters, for example, requires a RAM-based message queue to save the parts of the message until the entire message is assembled. Therefore, the attack mentioned in the previous bullet can be used to tie up RAM as well as CPU cycles.

♦ An attack can send events to the IDS that need to be stored on disk. A flood of such events can consume all available disk space.

♦ An attack can overwhelm network bandwidth by flooding the network with meaningless packets. (This kind of attack is certainly a double-whammy because it affects not only the IDS but all hosts on the network as well.)

♦ If an IDS is capable of reacting automatically to DoS attacks, it can be susceptible to "false positives," attacks that repeatedly cause it to react to a nonexistent attack. An IDS may take many types of action, but usually it will shut down the TCP communication with the source of packets used in a DoS attack; each time it does this, it must send traffic over the local network. The IDS itself therefore becomes the middle man in a DoS on its own network. Because many IDSs are vulnerable to this type of problem, you may want to configure an IDS to trigger alarms only, rather than to take attack countermeasures on its own.

The bottom line is that an IDS is as vulnerable to a DoS attack as any other piece of software on your network. A good practice is to use an IDS to trigger alarms to which a network security professional will respond. In many cases, only a human can determine the best reaction in a specific situation, whether it be shutting down TCP connections or shutting down the entire network.

7.3.2 Using System Logs to Detect a DoS Attack

If you notice significant network congestion, receive reports of your Web site becoming inaccessible, or systems begin crashing without explanation—and you're not running an IDS or your IDS hasn't triggered an alert—then you need to resort to manual methods to look for evidence of a DoS attack.

The best way to detect such an attack is to check your firewall's log. If you see a lot of packets coming repeatedly from the same sources, then you've probably identified a DoS attack. As an example, consider the small log extract in Figure 7.3. The system under attack was a single host using a dial-up connection! Notice that the attack packets, using port 4313, are coming rapidly from just a few source systems. (What was the attacker's aim? Given that the attack was against a single system, the attacker was probably a script kiddie out to make mayhem. However, the number of packets was so small that it was only a chance look at the system log that detected the attack; processing never slowed down because the bandwidth usage wasn't high enough.) The log shows that the attacking packets were dropped at the firewall's external interface and that the attack had no effect on the intended victim system.

If you are running an IDS, the IDS should be configured to alert you when the software detects evidence of a DoS attack. You will then need to examine the IDS logs to determine exactly what is occurring so that you can stop the attack or at least minimize its effects.

As an example, consider the part of an IDS log in Figure 7.4 (generated by GFI LANGuard). The specific events that are logged are determined by filters created by the software administrators. The software also keeps additional detail about each recorded event that you can display as needed (for example, Figure 7.5).

7.3.3 Handling a DoS Attack in Progress

What can you do if you or your software determines that your network (or a host on your network) is the victim of a DoS attack? The easiest solution is to shut down the affected host or network. (It may not be enough to isolate the network from the Internet if malware is propagating packets around the network.) That may sound extreme, but it is just about the only way to ensure that the attack doesn't continue. Shutting down will give you time to examine your computers to see if any DoS client software has been installed.

```
6/25/03  2:11:09 PM  Denied   Unknown   4313   TCP   24.191.100.133    1-18bf6485.dyn.ptnline.net
6/25/03  2:11:10 PM  Denied   Unknown   4313   TCP   24.191.100.133    1-18bf6485.dyn.ptnline.net
6/25/03  2:11:10 PM  Denied   Unknown   4313   TCP   208.63.162.145    adsl-63-162-145.mb.bellsouth.net
6/25/03  2:11:11 PM  Denied   Unknown   4313   TCP   24.191.100.133    1-18bf6485.dyn.ptnline.net
6/25/03  2:11:19 PM  Denied   Unknown   4313   TCP   204.131.27.6      crwcd-ntserver.crwcd.gv
6/25/03  2:11:20 PM  Denied   Unknown   4313   TCP   24.191.26.231     1-18bf1ae7.dyn.ptnline.net
6/25/03  2:11:22 PM  Denied   Unknown   4313   TCP   204.131.27.6      crwcd-ntserver.crwcd.gv
6/25/03  2:11:23 PM  Denied   Unknown   4313   TCP   24.191.26.231     1-18bf1ae7.dyn.ptnline.net
6/25/03  2:11:24 PM  Denied   Unknown   4313   TCP   172.136.60.3      ac883c03.ipt.al.cm
6/25/03  2:11:27 PM  Denied   Unknown   4313   TCP   68.81.136.107     pcp01328601pcs.chrstn01.pa.cmcast.net
6/25/03  2:11:27 PM  Denied   Unknown   4313   TCP   172.136.60.3      ac883c03.ipt.al.cm
6/25/03  2:11:27 PM  Denied   Unknown   4313   TCP   69.0.120.136      69.0.120.136.adsl.snet.net
6/25/03  2:11:28 PM  Denied   Unknown   4313   TCP   204.131.27.6      crwcd-ntserver.crwcd.gv
6/25/03  2:11:29 PM  Denied   Unknown   4313   TCP   24.191.26.231     1-18bf1ae7.dyn.ptnline.net
6/25/03  2:11:29 PM  Denied   Unknown   4313   TCP   68.81.136.107     Unknown
6/25/03  2:11:30 PM  Denied   Unknown   4313   TCP   69.0.120.136      Unknown
6/25/03  2:11:33 PM  Denied   Unknown   4313   TCP   172.136.60.3      Unknown
6/25/03  2:11:34 PM  Denied   Unknown   4313   TCP   68.81.136.107     Unknown
6/25/03  2:11:36 PM  Denied   Unknown   4313   TCP   69.0.120.136      Unknown
6/25/03  2:11:41 PM  Denied   Unknown   4313   TCP   67.86.181.180     Unknown
6/25/03  2:11:45 PM  Denied   Unknown   4313   TCP   172.136.60.3      Unknown
6/25/03  2:11:45 PM  Denied   Unknown   4313   TCP   67.86.181.180     Unknown
6/25/03  2:11:48 PM  Denied   Unknown   4313   TCP   137.21.88.157     Unknown
6/25/03  2:11:49 PM  Denied   Unknown   4313   TCP   24.166.75.20      Unknown
6/25/03  2:11:51 PM  Denied   Unknown   4313   TCP   24.166.75.20      Unknown
6/25/03  2:11:51 PM  Denied   Unknown   4313   TCP   67.86.181.180     Unknown
6/25/03  2:11:53 PM  Denied   Unknown   4313   TCP   68.185.149.239    Unknown
6/25/03  2:11:55 PM  Denied   Unknown   4313   TCP   65.33.46.46       Unknown
6/25/03  2:11:56 PM  Denied   Unknown   4313   TCP   68.185.149.239    Unknown
6/25/03  2:11:57 PM  Denied   Unknown   4313   TCP   24.166.75.20      Unknown
6/25/03  2:11:58 PM  Denied   Unknown   4313   TCP   65.33.46.46       Unknown
6/25/03  2:12:00 PM  Denied   Unknown   4313   TCP   68.57.124.77      Unknown
6/25/03  2:12:01 PM  Denied   Unknown   4313   TCP   68.185.149.239    Unknown
6/25/03  2:12:03 PM  Denied   Unknown   4313   TCP   68.57.124.77      Unknown
6/25/03  2:12:04 PM  Denied   Unknown   4313   TCP   65.33.46.46       Unknown
6/25/03  2:12:09 PM  Denied   Unknown   4313   TCP   68.57.124.77      Unknown
6/25/03  2:12:09 PM  Denied   Unknown   4313   TCP   67.100.17.120     Unknown
6/25/03  2:12:13 PM  Denied   Unknown   4313   TCP   68.99.19.118      Unknown
6/25/03  2:12:13 PM  Denied   Unknown   4313   TCP   67.100.17.120     Unknown
6/25/03  2:12:16 PM  Denied   Unknown   4313   TCP   68.99.19.118      Unknown
6/25/03  2:12:16 PM  Denied   Unknown   4313   TCP   165.24.250.47     Unknown
6/25/03  2:12:17 PM  Denied   Unknown   4313   TCP   67.100.17.120     Unknown
6/25/03  2:12:18 PM  Denied   Unknown   4313   TCP   68.49.152.132     Unknown
6/25/03  2:12:19 PM  Denied   Unknown   4313   TCP   165.24.250.47     Unknown
6/25/03  2:12:19 PM  Denied   Unknown   4313   TCP   12.207.17.128     Unknown
6/25/03  2:12:21 PM  Denied   Unknown   4313   TCP   68.49.152.132     Unknown
6/25/03  2:12:22 PM  Denied   Unknown   4313   TCP   12.207.17.128     Unknown
6/25/03  2:12:22 PM  Denied   Unknown   4313   TCP   68.99.19.118      Unknown
6/25/03  2:12:25 PM  Denied   Unknown   4313   TCP   165.24.250.47     Unknown
6/25/03  2:12:26 PM  Denied   Unknown   4313   TCP   12.207.17.128     Unknown
6/25/03  2:12:28 PM  Denied   Unknown   4313   TCP   68.49.152.132     Unknown
6/25/03  2:12:43 PM  Denied   Unknown   4313   TCP   68.210.107.135    Unknown
6/25/03  2:12:47 PM  Denied   Unknown   4313   TCP   12.250.130.200    Unknown
6/25/03  2:12:47 PM  Denied   Unknown   4313   TCP   68.210.107.135    Unknown
6/25/03  2:12:48 PM  Denied   Unknown   4313   TCP   137.21.88.157     Unknown
6/25/03  2:12:50 PM  Denied   Unknown   4313   TCP   12.250.130.200    Unknown
6/25/03  2:12:52 PM  Denied   Unknown   4313   TCP   68.210.107.135    Unknown
6/25/03  2:12:54 PM  Denied   Unknown   4313   TCP   66.26.68.208      Unknown
6/25/03  2:12:54 PM  Denied   Unknown   4313   TCP   68.185.149.239    Unknown
6/25/03  2:12:55 PM  Denied   Unknown   4313   TCP   63.229.25.180     Unknown
6/25/03  2:12:56 PM  Denied   Unknown   4313   TCP   12.250.130.200    Unknown
6/25/03  2:12:57 PM  Denied   Unknown   4313   TCP   68.185.149.239    Unknown
6/25/03  2:12:57 PM  Denied   Unknown   4313   TCP   66.26.68.208      Unknown
6/25/03  2:12:58 PM  Denied   Unknown   4313   TCP   63.229.25.180     Unknown
6/25/03  2:13:03 PM  Denied   Unknown   4313   TCP   68.185.149.239    Unknown
6/25/03  2:13:03 PM  Denied   Unknown   4313   TCP   66.26.68.208      Unknown
6/25/03  2:13:04 PM  Denied   Unknown   4313   TCP   63.229.25.180     Unknown
6/25/03  2:13:24 PM  Denied   Unknown   4313   TCP   155.201.35.53     Unknown
6/25/03  2:13:29 PM  Denied   Unknown   4313   TCP   155.201.35.53     Unknown
```

Figure 7.3 An excerpt from a firewall log showing a distributed DoS in progress

6/25/03 2:13:29 PM	Denied	Unknown	4313	TCP	24.49.99.191	Unknown
6/25/03 2:13:33 PM	Denied	Unknown	4313	TCP	155.201.35.53	Unknown
6/25/03 2:13:38 PM	Denied	Unknown	4313	TCP	24.49.99.191	Unknown
6/25/03 2:13:50 PM	Denied	Unknown	4313	TCP	67.84.72.191	Unknown
6/25/03 2:13:58 PM	Denied	Unknown	4313	TCP	64.252.7.27	Unknown
6/25/03 2:13:58 PM	Denied	Unknown	4313	TCP	67.84.72.191	Unknown
6/25/03 2:13:59 PM	Denied	Unknown	4313	TCP	67.84.72.191	Unknown
6/25/03 2:13:59 PM	Denied	Unknown	4313	TCP	65.105.166.186	Unknown
6/25/03 2:14:01 PM	Denied	Unknown	4313	TCP	64.252.7.27	Unknown
6/25/03 2:14:02 PM	Denied	Unknown	4313	TCP	65.105.166.186	Unknown
6/25/03 2:14:02 PM	Denied	Unknown	4313	TCP	68.34.220.31	Unknown
6/25/03 2:14:05 PM	Denied	Unknown	4313	TCP	68.34.220.31	Unknown
6/25/03 2:14:07 PM	Denied	Unknown	4313	TCP	64.252.7.27	Unknown
6/25/03 2:14:08 PM	Denied	Unknown	4313	TCP	65.105.166.186	Unknown
6/25/03 2:14:11 PM	Denied	Unknown	4313	TCP	68.34.220.31	Unknown
6/25/03 2:14:14 PM	Denied	Unknown	4313	TCP	68.193.145.171	Unknown
6/25/03 2:14:14 PM	Denied	Unknown	4313	TCP	68.74.69.12	Unknown
6/25/03 2:14:15 PM	Denied	Unknown	4313	TCP	68.198.53.157	Unknown
6/25/03 2:14:17 PM	Denied	Unknown	4313	TCP	68.193.145.171	Unknown
6/25/03 2:14:17 PM	Denied	Unknown	4313	TCP	68.74.69.12	Unknown
6/25/03 2:14:18 PM	Denied	Unknown	4313	TCP	68.198.53.157	Unknown
6/25/03 2:14:20 PM	Denied	Unknown	4313	TCP	192.104.254.78	Unknown
6/25/03 2:14:23 PM	Denied	Unknown	4313	TCP	68.193.145.171	Unknown
6/25/03 2:14:23 PM	Denied	Unknown	4313	TCP	68.74.69.12	Unknown
6/25/03 2:14:23 PM	Denied	Unknown	4313	TCP	192.104.254.78	Unknown
6/25/03 2:14:24 PM	Denied	Unknown	4313	TCP	68.198.53.157	Unknown
6/25/03 2:14:27 PM	Denied	Unknown	4313	TCP	192.104.254.78	Unknown
6/25/03 2:14:50 PM	Denied	Unknown	4313	TCP	80.134.177.56	Unknown
6/25/03 2:14:54 PM	Denied	Unknown	4313	TCP	216.158.45.214	Unknown
6/25/03 2:14:54 PM	Denied	Unknown	4313	TCP	80.134.177.56	Unknown
6/25/03 2:14:57 PM	Denied	Unknown	4313	TCP	216.158.45.214	Unknown
6/25/03 2:14:57 PM	Denied	Unknown	4313	TCP	141.157.64.226	Unknown
6/25/03 2:14:59 PM	Denied	Unknown	4313	TCP	141.157.64.226	Unknown
6/25/03 2:14:59 PM	Denied	Unknown	4313	TCP	68.164.7.217	Unknown
6/25/03 2:14:59 PM	Denied	Unknown	4313	TCP	80.134.177.56	Unknown
6/25/03 2:15:02 PM	Denied	Unknown	4313	TCP	68.164.7.217	Unknown
6/25/03 2:15:03 PM	Denied	Unknown	4313	TCP	216.158.45.214	Unknown
6/25/03 2:15:05 PM	Denied	Unknown	4313	TCP	68.164.7.217	Unknown
6/25/03 2:15:05 PM	Denied	Unknown	4313	TCP	141.157.64.226	Unknown
6/25/03 2:15:07 PM	Denied	Unknown	4313	TCP	65.41.187.130	Unknown
6/25/03 2:15:11 PM	Denied	Unknown	4313	TCP	80.134.177.56	Unknown
6/25/03 2:15:11 PM	Denied	Unknown	4313	TCP	68.164.7.217	Unknown
6/25/03 2:15:11 PM	Denied	Unknown	4313	TCP	65.41.187.130	Unknown
6/25/03 2:15:14 PM	Denied	Unknown	4313	TCP	68.164.7.217	Unknown
6/25/03 2:15:15 PM	Denied	Unknown	4313	TCP	24.118.45.103	Unknown
6/25/03 2:15:16 PM	Denied	Unknown	4313	TCP	65.41.187.130	Unknown
6/25/03 2:15:17 PM	Denied	Unknown	4313	TCP	24.118.45.103	Unknown
6/25/03 2:15:32 PM	Denied	Unknown	4313	TCP	24.118.45.103	Unknown
6/25/03 2:15:32 PM	Denied	Unknown	4313	TCP	68.164.7.217	Unknown
6/25/03 2:16:08 PM	Denied	Unknown	4313	TCP	24.44.145.104	Unknown
6/25/03 2:16:08 PM	Denied	Unknown	4313	TCP	68.164.7.217	Unknown
6/25/03 2:16:18 PM	Denied	Unknown	4313	TCP	24.44.145.104	Unknown
6/25/03 2:16:18 PM	Denied	Unknown	4313	TCP	38.72.192.220	Unknown
6/25/03 2:16:20 PM	Denied	Unknown	4313	TCP	68.8.4.173	Unknown
6/25/03 2:16:20 PM	Denied	Unknown	4313	TCP	38.72.192.220	Unknown
6/25/03 2:16:23 PM	Denied	Unknown	4313	TCP	68.8.4.173	Unknown
6/25/03 2:16:26 PM	Denied	Unknown	4313	TCP	38.72.192.220	Unknown
6/25/03 2:16:29 PM	Denied	Unknown	4313	TCP	68.8.4.173	Unknown
6/25/03 2:16:42 PM	Denied	Unknown	4313	TCP	219.57.16.49	Unknown
6/25/03 2:16:44 PM	Denied	Unknown	4313	TCP	198.107.58.66	Unknown
6/25/03 2:16:45 PM	Denied	Unknown	4313	TCP	219.57.16.49	Unknown
6/25/03 2:16:47 PM	Denied	Unknown	4313	TCP	198.107.58.66	Unknown
6/25/03 2:16:49 PM	Denied	Unknown	4313	TCP	64.203.194.247	Unknown
6/25/03 2:16:51 PM	Denied	Unknown	4313	TCP	68.82.71.109	Unknown
6/25/03 2:16:51 PM	Denied	Unknown	4313	TCP	219.57.16.49	Unknown
6/25/03 2:16:52 PM	Denied	Unknown	4313	TCP	64.203.194.247	Unknown
6/25/03 2:16:53 PM	Denied	Unknown	4313	TCP	198.107.58.66	Unknown
6/25/03 2:16:54 PM	Denied	Unknown	4313	TCP	68.82.71.109	Unknown

Figure 7.3 (continued) An excerpt from a firewall log showing a distributed DoS in progress

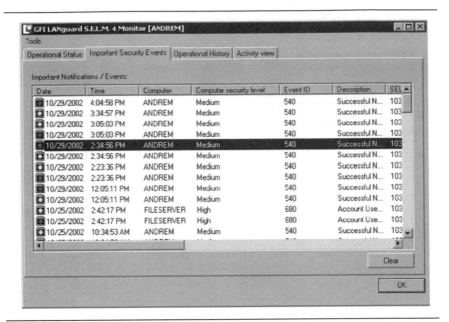

Figure 7.4   An IDS event log (taken from GFI LANGuard)

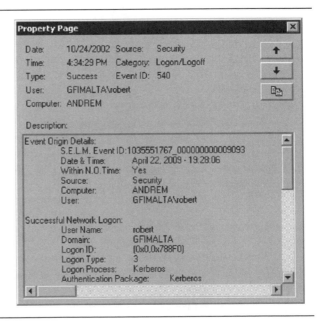

Figure 7.5   IDS event detail

Reality Check: The thought of shutting down a corporate network can cause heart palpitations in a lot of people. In many cases today, when the network is down, the organization simply can't function. You therefore need to have some type of backup solution in the event that you have to shut down. This is an instance where a hot site can come in very, very handy.

There are less extreme alternatives, of course. As you read earlier, one alternative is to close down the TCP connections to the source(s) of the packets involved in the DoS attack. This is certainly practical for a single-source attack, but may require too much bandwidth for a distributed DoS. In addition, you need to regain control of your network, and the only sure way is to cut it off from the source of the attack. In other words, shut down Internet access! (If the attack is coming from an internal source, you will need to shut down the local network as well.)

The next step is to make a backup of any computers that have been involved in the attack. This will give you something to analyze even after you have restored the network. It will also give you evidence for any legal investigations that might occur once the attack is over.

At this point, you can begin examining involved network hosts for software used in the attack. Look for DoS attack clients and agents/daemons, network sniffers (software that grabs network packets and deciphers them), and backdoor software that gives an attacker access to a host. To detect these files, you'll need to look for unauthorized modification to system files and for user files that neither the system administrator or the user can identify.

Once you've identified which hosts on your network have been compromised, you can recover. You'll need to

- Install a clean copy of the operating system.
- Install all vendor patches.
- Disable unused services.
- Use all new passwords.

Be very careful if you choose to restore data files from a backup: The backups may be compromised, depending on how long an attacker's software has been on a host.

Reality Check: As you can see, the cost of a DoS doesn't come from physical damage. Instead, it comes from the intensive labor involved in recovering as well as business lost while the network is unavailable.

7.3.4 DoS Defense Strategies

Although you can never stop all DoS attacks, there are a number of techniques that can stop some of the well-known attacks:

◆ Most of today's operating systems and network devices have been modified to respond gracefully to oversized IP packets. However, as mentioned earlier, if you have older OSs on your network, then you need to be aware of the potential for ping problems. The best solution is to upgrade OS software on all devices.

◆ To stop smurf attacks, disable IP broadcast packets addressed to your edge router. You can also configure hosts so they don't respond to ICMP echo request packets that have broadcast destination addresses.

◆ To stop UDP flood attacks, turn off chargen. For a UNIX system, edit */etc/inetd.conf* to comment out the two chargen lines. For Windows, turn off Simple TCP Services.

◆ You can stop many DoS attacks by disabling ICMP. However, many applications use ICMP and you may find that turning it off will cripple your network.

◆ The best way to prevent the hosts on your network from being used in a single source or distributed DoS attack is to make sure that the client malware can't be installed by an attacker. At the very least, make certain that virus scanning software is up to date and that it runs each time a host boots.

7.3.5 Finding Files

In addition to the techniques described in the preceding section, it pays to assume that despite all your efforts, distributed DoS attack middle-ware may still creep onto one or more of your network's computers. Your best defense is therefore to check machines regularly for such files.

The general technique is to scan the content of files for strings of text that are known to exist in the code. For example, a stacheldraht client contains the strings in Figure 7.6; the agent contains those in Figure 7.7.

```
connection closed.
usage: ./sclient <ip/host>
    [*] stacheldraht [*]
 (c) in 1999 by ...
trying to connect...
unable to resolv %so
unable to connect.
connection established.
-------------------------------------
enter the passphrase :
authentication
failed
authentication failed.
entering interactive session.
./0123456789abcdefghijklmnopqrstuvwxyzABCDEFGHIJKLMNOPQRSTUVWXYZ
huhu
```

Figure 7.6 Strings in the stacheldraht client program

Note: For further information on detecting stacheldraft files, see http://staff.washington.edu/dittrich/misc/ stacheldraht.analysis. The same information about trinoo can be found at http://staff.washington.edu/ dittrich/misc/trinoo.analysis. For TFN, see http:// staff.washington.edu/dittrich/misc/tfn.analysis.

Another way to protect files is to install software that checks for changes made to stored files. For example, Tripwire—open source soft-ware for Linux is available at *http://www.tripwire.org;* other versions are commercial—detects changes to the binary signature of a file, its size, and so on. Such software can alert you to the presence of artifacts left by DoS attacks.

```
%d.%d.%d.%d
ICMP
Error sending syn packet.
tc: Unknown host
3.3.3.3
mservers
randomsucks
skillz
ttymn
rm -rf %so
rcp %so@%so:linux.bin %so
nhup ./%so
1.1.1.1
127.0.0.1
lpsched
on masterserver config found.
using default nes.
available servers: %i - working servers : 0
[*] stacheldraht [*] installation failed.
found a working [*] stacheldraht [*] masterserver.
masterserver is gone, looking for a new one
sicken
in.telne
./0123456789abcdefghijklmnopqrstuvwxyzABCDEFGHIJKLMNOPQRSTUVWXYZ
```

Figure 7.7 Strings in the stacheldraht agent file

7.4 Summary

A denial of service attack is an attack against a network that prevents legitimate users from accessing resources over a network. An attack may flood a network with packets to tie up network bandwidth, or it may use up resources such as memory, disk space, or CPU cycles on one or more network hosts.

Single source DoS attacks are launched by a single attack computer. Distributed DoS attacks use compromised systems to launch an attack; the compromised systems may be controlled by a single master system.

DoS attacks can be detected by IDSs or by examining system logs for repeated patterns of attempted network access. In either case, once an attack has been detected, the best solution is to shut down the network while you recover.

Although it is impossible to prevent a DoS from being directed at a network, you can prevent systems from being used in a distributed DoS attack by hardening the systems against system intrusions, especially the delivery of unauthorized software.

Chapter 8: Malware

In This Chapter

- ◆ Types of malware
- ◆ Infection mechanisms
- ◆ Protecting yourself against malware
- ◆ Malware detection software
- ◆ Lockdown schemes

8.0 Introduction

If there is any computer security threat with which the average person is familiar, it is a virus, one type of malicious software known generally as *malware*. Malware does nothing useful and, more often than not, is nasty and destructive.

There are several types of malware, each of which propagates differently and has a different goal:

♦ Virus: A virus is a self-propagating piece of software that runs as an executable program on a target machine. It is not, however, a stand-alone piece of software. It must piggyback itself on something else, such as a piece of e-mail or other application program, and is "installed" on a victim machine when the user accesses the host software. A virus's effect can be relatively benign—such as displaying a dialog box—or it can be seriously destructive, deleting files from a hard disk, causing a computer to reboot repeatedly, and so on. Some viruses are known to be *polymorphic*, meaning that they can change themselves as they propagate so that each copy looks a bit different from all others.

♦ Worm: A worm is a self-propagating piece of stand-alone software that has effects similar to a virus. It can be the cause of a denial of service attack or can damage items stored on a computer.

♦ Trojan horse: A Trojan horse is a piece of software that appears to be one thing, but is, in fact, another. Some Trojan horses are installed by crackers for their use as back doors into a system they have cracked. Others might record a user's keystrokes to a file that can later be retrieved by a system cracker.

♦ Spyware: Spyware originally was intended as a tool for shareware authors to include advertising in their software as a way to raise revenue. The spyware (originally called *adware*) was to be installed with the shareware, show pop-up advertising, and—most importantly—send information about the computer on which it was running back to the advertiser. The idea was that the advertiser would collect only demographic information for use in targeted advertising campaigns. However, today spyware collects private information without the knowledge or consent of the person whose information is being collected and uses the victim's own Internet bandwidth to transmit the information.

Malware is easily disseminated. Not only can it be delivered through e-mail, but it travels quite nicely on removable media, such as floppy disks, CDs, DVDs, and CD-ROM flash drives.

This chapter looks at the ways in which malware travels, how you can detect it, and ways in which you can prevent its spread.

8.1 A Bit of Malware History

Malware has been around since the dawn of personal computers. To help you put today's efforts in perspective, take a look at Table 8.1. As you can see, the continuing trend is not only to generate malware that propagates further and faster, but to target individual applications. Both Microsoft and applications that run on Web pages are favorites.

> *Note: For in-depth coverage of virus history, see http://www.cknow.com/vtutor/vthistory.htm. The page at the URL contains an overview article, with links at the bottom leading to more detailed coverage.*

8.2 Types of Malware Based on Propagation Methods

In the introduction to this chapter you read about the four general classes of malware that are found floating around the Internet today. There is, however, another way of classifying malware: the way in which they operate and propagate. This section looks at malware from that point of view.

Year	Malware Name	Comments
1981	Elk Cloner	Supposedly originated at Texas A&M University; propagated on Apple II floppy disks and displayed a benign poem on the screen.
1983		Experimental virus created on a VAX 11/750 (running UNIX) and demonstrated by Fred Cohen at a security seminar. Term *virus* was coined by Len Adleman.
1986	Brain	First MS-DOS virus; infected boot sector of a floppy disk; programmers were probably Basit and Amjad.
	PC-Write Trojan	First application malware, a Trojan horse that infected PC-Write, an early word processor.
1987	Lehigh	First virus to infect COMMAND.COM.
	Suriv-02	First virus to infect .EXE files.
	IBM Christmas worm	Worm spread rapidly to IBM mainframes; reportedly replicated as many as 500,000 times per hour.
1988	MacMag	First Hypercard stack virus.
	Scores	First Macintosh virus.
	Internet worm	The first Internet worm, written and released by Robert Morris, stalled a significant amount of Internet traffic.
1989	AIDS Trojan	Propagated by disguising itself as a file of information about AIDS; encrypted hard drives and then requested extortion money for the decryption key.
1991	Tequila	First polymorphic virus.
1992	Michelangelo	First virus reported widely on the popular media; impact of virus was much less than predicted.
1995	Concept	First Word macro virus.
1996	Boza	First Windows 95-specific virus.
	Laroux	First Excel macro virus.

Table 8.1   Malware history

Year	Malware Name	Comments
	Staog	First Linux virus.
1998	Strange Brew	First Java virus.
	Back Orifice	First Trojan horse that allowed remote administration of a Windows machine over the Internet.
		First Access macro viruses.
1999	Melissa	First virus to use entries in Outlook address books as destinations for virus propagation; virus was written in Visual Basic for Applications as part of a Word document and was triggered when the document was opened.
	Corner	First virus to target MS Project files.
	Tristate	First virus that affected Word, Access, and Project.
	Bubbleboy	First virus that was triggered by simply opening the e-mail to which it was attached; user no longer needed to download and execute a file.
2000	Love Letter/ ILOVEYOU	Fast spreading worm that shut down e-mail all over the world; transmitted as an e-mail attachment that executed when users double-clicked on the attachment to open it.
2001	Gnuman/ Mandragore	First worm to attack a file-sharing service (Gnutella); appeared as a downloadable MP3.
	PeachyPDF-A worm	First malware to affect Adobe PDF files.
	Nimda	Wide-spread virus with many ways to infect Windows files; installed as a resource in .EXE files; infects Web pages hosted by Microsoft IIS; use any host on a network to scan for other vulnerable hosts.
	Code Red	Microsoft IIS worm that slowed Internet traffic at *www.whitehouse.gov* by launching a DDoS attack at the White House site from infected machines.

Table 8.1 (continued) Malware history

Year	Malware Name	Comments
2002	LFM-926	First worm targeted at Shockwave Flash files.
	Donut	First worm targeted at .NET files.
	Sharp-A	First worm written in C#.
	SQLSpider	First worm to target SQL Server installations; written in JavaScript.
	Benjamin	First malware to use KaZaa's file sharing capabilities to propagate itself.
	Perrun	First virus to infect JPEG files; required stripped programming running on the infected victim computer to detach virus from the JPEG.
	Scalper	First worm to attack FreeBSD and Apache Web servers.
2003	Sobig	First virus that distributed its own replacement version of SMTP; propagated through Windows file sharing; left behind a Trojan horse component that system crackers could later use to send spam e-mail.
	Slammer	First malware to target SQL 2000 servers.
	Sobig.F, Blaster, Welchia, Min-mall	Worms that exploited a buffer overflow opportunity in Windows Distributed Component Object Model (DCOM) Remote Procedure Call (RPC) programming interface; all hit during August.
2004	Xombe	Trojan horse that instructed users to install an attached service pack for Windows XP; appeared to come from Microsoft Windows Update.
	Witty	First worm to target security software such as RealSecure, Proventia, and BlackICE.
	Sasser	First worm to take advantage of a Windows buffer overflow that allowed the worm to use FTP rather than e-mail to propagate itself.
And so on …		

Table 8.1 (continued) Malware history

Downloadable Executable Malware

The earliest viruses were hidden within legitimate programs that a user might download from a bulletin board system (BBS). When the user executed the program, the virus extracted itself from its host and ran its own code.

> *Note: If you're a young person, then you may not be familiar with BBSs. They were the precursor to Web sites and existed before the Web. In most cases, you reached a BBS through a direct dial-up connection; although the Internet existed, it wasn't used extensively to reach places where files were shared. A BBS typically provided files for downloading (both legal and illegal software) as well as supported message boards like those found on Web sites today. Anyone with an extra PC, an available phone line, and some BBS software could set up his or her own bulletin board.*

The virus would perform two types of actions. First, it would propagate itself by writing its code into one or more files. When those files were transferred—either over data communications lines or on a disk—the virus infected the destination computer.

A virus's second task was to perform some sort of nasty action on the victim machine. The effect of the virus could be as benign as displaying a dialog box containing a funny poem or as destructive as erasing files on the victim computer's hard disk.

The major limitation of an executable virus is that it can run only when the program it uses as a host is launched by the user. If it happens to be infecting a program that isn't commonly used, its ability to do damage and propagate itself is curtailed.

Reality Check: Executable viruses are rarely found anymore. They are nowhere near as much of a risk today as e-mail malware and malware transmitted by Web page code. Why? Because so many computers are attached to the Internet, and it is easier and faster to propagate a virus through e-mail or the Web than it is to rely on the installation of an application program. In addition, today's secure OSs make it much harder for virus software to obtain the access rights it needs to infect an application program. (The virus would need to supply an administrator or superuser password to modify the application program code.)

Boot Sector Viruses

Boot sector viruses were created to overcome the major limitation of executable viruses: By loading the virus into the boot sector—the portion of a disk that contains the code needed to boot a computer—the virus writer could be certain that the virus would run every time the computer was booted.

Boot sector viruses propagated themselves by installing themselves in the boot sector of every disk inserted into the machine. (This became an enormous problem when floppy disks were the primary means of transferring files from one computer to another!)

Like executable viruses, boot sector viruses not only propagated themselves, but performed some type of malicious action on the infected computer. Erasing files on hard disks was a favorite trick, for example.

Reality Check: The combination of read-only installation media and stronger operating systems have made boot sector viruses mostly an unpleasant memory. However, if you have users who still may be booting from removable media (floppy disks, USB flash drives, or CDs from untrusted sources), be careful.

Macro Viruses

A *macro virus* is a virus that is embedded in macros written primarily for Microsoft Office applications, most commonly Word. Spread whenever an infected file is transferred, most macro viruses are relatively benign.

They might display a message on the screen or insert some text into a document.

Probably the most famous macro virus is the Melissa virus, which struck in March 1999. It created such a severe problem with illegitimate e-mail traffic that Microsoft was forced to shut down its e-mail system until the virus was eradicated.

Distributed as a Microsoft Word file attached to an e-mail message, Melissa worked in the following manner:

1. The user downloaded and opened the infected file.
2. The macro code (written in Visual Basic for Applications) was loaded into main memory and executed automatically.
3. The macro copied the virus into Word's normal.dot template. (This template is used to set the format for documents that don't use a custom template.)
4. The macro wrote an entry in Windows registry:

```
HKEY_CURRENT_USERSoftwareMicrosoftOffice"Melissa?"="...by Kwyjibo"
```

5. The macro created a Microsoft Outlook object.
6. The macro loaded the object with the first 50 entries in the victim's Outlook address book.
7. The macro sent the infected document to the addresses culled from the address book.

Melissa-infected e-mails typically had the same subject line—

```
Subject: Important Message From <name>
```

—where <name> was the name of the user who theoretically sent the message.

Like most macro viruses, Melissa didn't destroy anything, but did create an denial of service situation because of the high volume of e-mail traffic it generated.

The best way to avoid macro viruses is through user education. However, because macro viruses are often undetectable until they have been run or because their hosts (for example, e-mail messages) appear to come from trusted sources, you may want to resort to stronger avoidance methods. Most macro viruses attack Microsoft Office software. You can therefore mitigate most of their effects by avoiding that software. At the very least, users should turn off macros, preventing any macro viruses from executing.

> *Note: Although macro viruses can be transmitted to computers that don't run the Windows OS, they have no effect.*

E-Mail Malware

Today, much malware is propagated through e-mail. The first e-mail malware was sent as an attachment to e-mail. The user would download the attachment, double-click on the file to open it, and launch the malware. The malware would then search the victim computer for e-mail addresses to which it could send itself. (As noted in the preceding section, Microsoft Outlook address books are favorite targets of such searches.)

The malware could then do whatever tasks it had been programmed to do. In some cases, the malware would send out so many copies of itself that it created a DoS attack on the victim computer. In other cases, the malware simply installed itself and lay sleeping until a system attacker came looking for it—the proverbial Trojan horse.

E-mail attachment malware is not confined to .EXE files. In fact, one of the most famous e-mail attachment viruses—Melissa, which you read about in the preceding section of this chapter—was actually encoded into a Word document.

Notice that e-mail attachment viruses require the "cooperation" of the recipient of the e-mail to do their nasty work. If the user doesn't download the attachment and open it, nothing happens. This means that the best preventative measure against such malware is user education.

Reality Check: Because e-mail attachment malware is executable code, each must be written for one specific operating system running on one type of CPU. Although there are certainly those that will work on UNIX systems, most malware of this type has been written to attack Windows computers. If you are running UNIX, then your risk is less (although certainly not nonexistent) than if your computers are running some version of a Microsoft product. Microsoft products are in such wide use that they make the most appealing targets for malware writers.

As users have become more sophisticated in their handling of e-mail attachments, malware authors have also become more sophisticated. Using JavaScript, they can embed code in the body of an e-mail that will execute when the user opens the message; nothing needs to be downloaded. The limitation of this technique is that the e-mail recipient needs to be running a mail reader that can accept HTML encoded messages. If the e-mail reader is configured for text-only, the malware code won't be able to run.

It's tough to defend against e-mail that contains embedded malware at the user end. Most of us commonly receive e-mail from people we don't know in the normal course of a working day; blocking such e-mail would make it almost impossible to do our jobs. The best solution is to invest in an e-mail server that can scan incoming messages for malware. (For more detail on malware detection software, see "Hands On" on page 192.)

Reality Check: Just to make life more difficult, malware writers have created attacks that work through Microsoft Outlook's preview mode. The user doesn't even have to open the message; all that is necessary is that a part of it show up in the preview pane. (Moral to the story: If you must use Outlook—and that may not be a safe decision— don't use preview mode.)

Web Site Malware

Users get smarter, and so the malware authors get trickier. It's a never-ending spiral. The effectiveness of e-mail attachment malware has gone down because users are more careful. Therefore, malware authors have resorted to embedding malware in Web pages. When a user visits a Web page—downloading the HTML and associated files that make up that page—he or she downloads malware as well. The malware downloads automatically, just as any other file that is part of a Web page downloads to a browser for display.

Most Web site malware is written in JavaScript, so one way to avoid it is to disable Java in a browser. Unfortunately, more and more Web content relies on JavaScript, so disabling Java severely limits what is available to a user.

8.3 Hands On

Handling malware is both the easiest and hardest thing security personnel have to do. It's easy in the sense that there is a great deal of software designed to detect and remove malware. It's hard because the malware authors are usually one-step ahead of the software developers. In this Hands On section we'll consider the software that's available and how you can use it to the best advantage, despite the never-ending cycle caused by malware authors and the software developers who attempt to keep up with them. We'll finish by looking at system lockdown schemes that can prevent malware from entering a system by restricting what users can do.

8.3.1 "Virus" Scanners

Because viruses were the first malware, the software that detects and removes malware is still known as "virus" software, although such programs have been upgraded over time to handle all types of malware. At one time, there were many virus detection software packages available. As with most software arenas, however, time has shaken out the marketplace, leaving several leading products that have shown to have staying power.

> *Note: I've tried to avoid talking about specific commercial products wherever possible throughout this book (other than to use them as examples). Virus checking software, however, has become so well established and is so important that, in this case, I'm going to violate that policy. The vendors chosen for this discussion provide multiplatform products.*

You can perform malware detection at two places: on each host or on your servers. In particular, it is well worth the investment to purchase an e-mail server that includes malware detection. Because malware can enter a computer through a vehicle other than e-mail, you should also have virus checkers installed—and preferably run automatically—on all computers as well.

Reality Check: Some of your users may be savvy enough to disable the running of a virus checker that has been configured to run when a computer is booted. If you want to prevent this, consider running the checker whenever the computer connects to your network. The college where I teach has a rather Draconian—but effective— means of enforcing virus scanning. Any machine that attempts to connect to the network and hasn't been connected in the past week is scanned for viruses by a network server. The machine isn't allowed to use the network unless it passes the virus check. This way, if a user chooses to disable local virus detection and doesn't pass the network-based virus check, the onus is on the user to clean up his or her own machine. At least other machines on the network won't be infected.

Host-Based Virus Detection Software

The simplest type of virus detection software is host-based. Its job is to scan a single computer, looking for any malware that is stored on the host's hard disk, either as separate files or embedded in other files. Such software is usually reasonably priced and, in most cases, should be configured to run automatically whenever the computer is booted.

Reality Check: Because new and improved malware is constantly appearing, virus checking software goes out of date rapidly. If a virus checker doesn't provide constant and free updates to its malware-recognition database, then the product isn't worth your money. The major vendors provide automatic update options: When configured properly with a live Internet connection, the software checks the vendor's Web site at predetermined intervals and downloads any new virus detection information that is available.

Symantec. Symantec is one of the oldest developers of virus detection software. Having acquired Norton Software, they now market the Norton AntiVirus line for individual desktop machines. When installed on an end system, the software detects worms, viruses, and Trojan horses; it will remove them automatically. It also detects viruses in e-mail attachments, spyware, and keystroke logging programs. In addition, it can scan file archives (for example, ZIP archives) for malware before files have been extracted.

Like all good virus checking software, Norton AntiVirus provides a simple user interface that even those who aren't technologically savvy can use (see Figure 8.1). All the user needs to do to start a scan is to click the Scan Now button. At the end of the scan, the software presents its results (see Figure 8.2).

Like any worthwhile virus checking software, Norton AntiVirus can update itself automatically from the vendor's Web site (see Figure 8.3). When choosing antivirus software, be sure to look into whether the updates are free or require a subscription. Also find out how often updates are made available (for example, as needed to handle new virus threats or on a predetermined schedule).

Reality Check: On the day this section of this chapter was being written, Symantec's Web site reported a new Trojan horse, Backdoor.Nemog, that affected Windows OSs from Windows 95 on. The site explained the operation of the malware—it allows a compromised host to be used by a system cracker as an e-mail relay (creating a DoS situation) or an HTTP proxy—and presented a threat assessment (medium) as well as techniques for removing the malware. You can find a wealth of current malware information at sites such as www.symantec.com. Don't discount the commercial sites. Yes, they are in business to sell you software, but, given the nature of their software, it behooves them to provide you with as much information about threats (especially given that their software can remove them) as they can.

McAfee.   McAfee VirusScan is the major competitor to Norton Anti-Virus. As you can see in Figure 8.4, the software can detect spyware as well as the more traditional viruses and Trojan horses. As with any good virus checker, it alerts the user to the presence of any suspicious files and—unless configured for automatic removal—takes no action until the end user directs it to do so (see Figure 8.5). VirusScan also detects malware in incoming and outgoing POP3 e-mail attachments.

Note: Automatic updates require a yearly subscription fee.

Note: VirusScan is a Windows application; the McAfee product for the Macintosh is the venerable Virex.

Sophos.   Although not as well known to end users as Symantec and McAfee, Sophos provides a heavy-duty suite of products for protecting

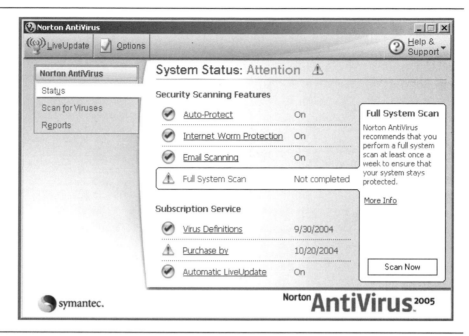

Figure 8.1 The Norton AntiVirus user interface

Figure 8.2 The results of a Norton AntiVirus scan

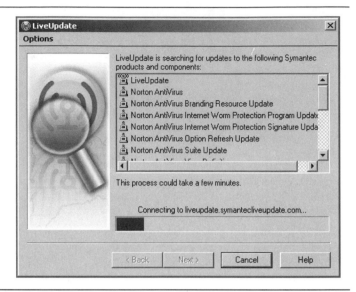

Figure 8.3 Getting virus definition updates for Norton AntiVirus

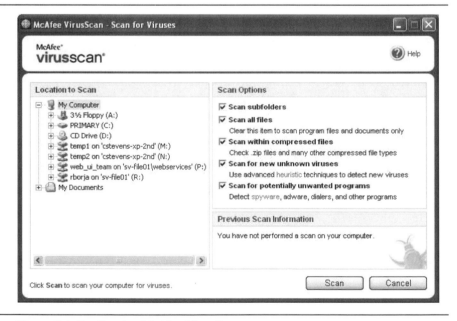

Figure 8.4 Configuring McAfee VirusScan

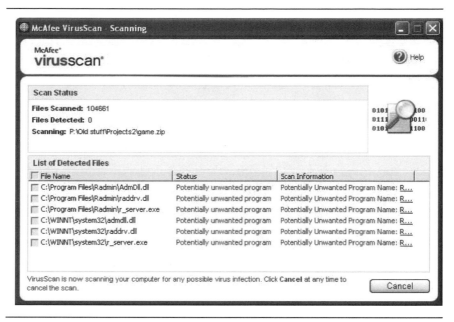

Figure 8.5 The results of a malware scan performed by McAfee VirusScan

end user systems. Its simple user interface (see Figure 8.6) makes it suitable for users who aren't terribly technologically savvy.

Network- and Server-Based Virus Detection Software

All the vendors discussed in the preceding section provide network and server-based malware control software. Network-based virus detection software centralizes malware detection. The beauty of server-based control is that it prevents malware from ever getting onto individual machines. It means that you don't have to rely on users either running their own virus checking software or avoiding risky behavior (for example, downloading and opening questionable e-mail).

Symantec.   Symantec's Symantec AntiVirus is intended to protect an entire network. It provides centralized management of software that scans servers as well as end user systems. Like Norton AntiVirus, it handles worms, viruses, Trojan horses, and spyware as well as scanning incoming and outgoing e-mail attachments. The major difference between the "Symantec" label and the "Norton" label is the ability to control all copies of the software from a single computer. This ensures that all

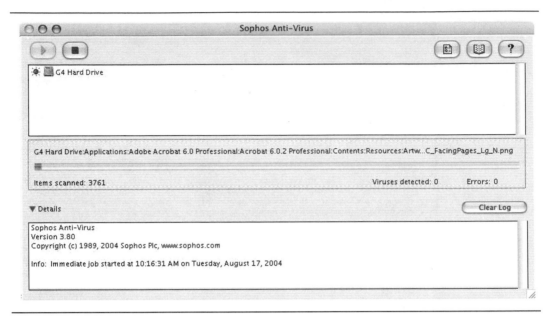

Figure 8.6 The Sophos Anti-Virus user interface

copies are configured in the same way and makes it easier to propagate updates. It also makes it easier to determine if an end user is attempting to avoid using malware detection software.

Large networks, however, may want software that works directly on specific server software. For example, Symantec Mail Security for SMTP works directly with a variety of SMTP-based mail servers, providing malware detection and spam control. Symantec also provides application-specific products that add malware security to Web servers.

McAfee.   Like Symantec, McAfee provides a product (McAfee Active VirusScan SMB Edition) that centralizes both end user and server malware detection and control. It detects and stops viruses, worms, Trojan horses, and spyware. It can also scan file archives without decompressing them and handles both MAPI and POP-3 e-mail attachments. In addition, the product scans Web transfers for malware.

McAfee's enterprise-level product (McAfee VirusScan Enterprise) isn't directed so much at specific servers, but instead adds more overall network security features to malware detection. In particular, it protects against known buffer overflow problems in specific software products and also looks for unknown software that might creep onto a network. (Such unknown software could be part of a root kit, for example.) Finally, VirusScan Enterprise provides features to combat a virus, worm, or DoS attack in progress.

> *Note: McAfee also provides a specific product for handling malware on Linux systems—LinuxShield—and another for Novell Netware (NetShield for Netware).*

Sophos.   Sophos Anti-Virus for networks, like the offerings of the preceding vendors, is a network-based solution for end user systems and servers. It provides the same centralized control as its competitors and works with a wide range of platforms (all versions of Windows, NetWare, OS/2, various flavors of UNIX, Mac OS, and OpenVMS).

Sophos's PureMessage Small Business Edition is designed to protect Exchange and SMTP e-mail servers, controlling both malware and spam. Its control panel (see Figure 8.7) provides an overview of e-mail traffic to give you quick information about the state of your e-mail.

Reality Check: Most enterprise-level virus detection products scan e-mail attachments, but they are limited in the languages they "understand." For example, Sophos PureMessage Small Business Editions works with English and Japanese only (and the anti-spam feature is effective for English only). This can be a major roadblock for organizations with heavy international e-mail traffic.

8.3.2 Dealing with Removable Media

If you listen to the popular media, you'd think that the only way malware is spread is through e-mail or the Web, but as you read earlier in this chapter, removable media can become a transport vector as well. Floppy disks were the original culprits: Employees carried viruses from home to office and from office machine to office machine; students carried viruses from bulletin boards to school labs. The demise of the floppy has helped curb "sneaker net" malware transmission, although viruses can still creep onto recordable CDs and DVDs—and let's not forget the increasing use of USB flash drives! Those little keychain solid state conveniences have in large measure replaced the floppy disk, and are as susceptible to malware as any other disk.

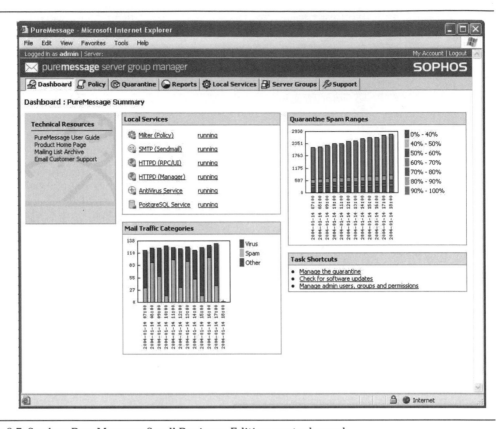

Figure 8.7 Sophos PureMessage Small Business Edition control panel

In most organizations today, people carry files from work to home and back again. Regardless of whether they're burning CDs or using key-chain drives (or even still using floppies), the risk remains. The major problem is that it is very hard to control removable media. The files don't travel over your network, nor do they necessarily originate on a machine under your control.

There are two strategies that can help you control the effects of removable media:

♦ Forbid the use of removable media altogether. (This may work in an organization with a high level of security, such as a government organization, but isn't terribly practical in most environments.)

♦ Configure virus detection software to run automatically whenever a disk is mounted. This is probably the most practical solution because it ensures that all files are scanned before being used. (If your virus detection software can't be configured to do this, then you may want to look at a different product.)

8.3.3 Lockdown Schemes

If you have public access computers—whether they be in a school lab, Internet cafe, or library—you will have very little control over what users do. They aren't your employees; they're your customers. The best solution in such a situation is to lock down the computer so that users can't engage in unwanted activities.

What does it mean to lock down a computer? With appropriate software, you can prevent

♦ System restart, shutdown, or logout

♦ Installation of new software

♦ Access to the command line

♦ Access to the system control panel or preferences panels

♦ Access to task management

♦ Cutting, copying, or pasting

♦ Use of removable media drives

♦ Access to operating system components

Note: As an example of lockdown software, check out SpyLock, at http://www.topsecretsoftware.com/pc-lockdown.html.

In some cases, such as a school lab, you can't really lock down the computers too tightly because users need access to a wide range of activities, including searching the Web and downloading files to their own removable media. Such situations almost guarantee that malware is going to creep onto the computers.

The solution isn't to lock down the software, but to *reimage* the hard disks at regular intervals. What this means is that you keep a clean copy of the hard drive on a computer, complete with operating system and application software, on a network server. Then, at predetermined times, you erase the current contents of the public workstation's hard drive and reload it from the clean copy on the server. Users have free access to the computer, including restarts and software installation, but whatever they place on a computer will be erased the next time the disk is reimaged.

The drawback to reimaging is that there needs to be a master image for each system configuration. The larger your organization, the larger the number of images you will likely need to maintain.

> *Note: Reimaging can also be handy when a corporation needs to distribute software to large numbers of users.*

There are many ways to make disk images, depending on the operating system and the way in which you plan to restore the target hard disks. However, the first step is to configure a clean hard disk from which you create the image file. Many types of backup software, such as Retrospect (*www.dantz.com*), will take care of that for you. Once you have the image, you can restore it to hard disks as needed.

8.4 Summary

Malware—viruses, worms, Trojan horses, and spyware—enters computer systems through e-mail, downloads from Web sites and bulletin boards, and removable media. Viruses can be destructive, destroying files on a hard drive. Worms typically aren't destructive, but tie up system resources, often causing DoS conditions.

Trojan horses remain quietly on a host computer until activated by a system cracker. For example, they may be used in a DoS attack on another computer or to regain root access on the infected host.

Spyware collects information about what is stored on a computer and sends it to the spyware's owners, usually without the knowledge of the person whose information is being collected.

Although good practices such as being wary of e-mail attachments and unknown removable media can help prevent the spread of viruses, the best solution is good virus detection software. The software should be run each time the computer boots; updates to the virus recognition database should be provided automatically by the software vendor.

Large networks can be protected by virus detection software that can be controlled centrally. Such software protects servers as well as end user systems. Other virus detection software is directed specifically at e-mail servers, attempting to stop malware before it gets onto the network.

Computers that are accessible to the public (an uncontrolled user population) may need to be locked down to prevent unwanted activities. Alternatively, hard drives can be reimaged from a master copy at regular intervals to destroy unwanted software.

Chapter 9: User and Password Security

In This Chapter

♦ Deciding who has access to what
♦ Social aspects of password policy
♦ Creating strong passwords
♦ Securing password files
♦ Password audits
♦ Automating password management

9.0 Introduction

Passwords are both the bane and the foundation of network security. Until recently, a matching user name and password pair were the only form of user identification available to most network installations. Nonetheless, despite the increasing affordability and accessibility of biometric identification devices, passwords still remain the most widely used way to provide secure access to computing facilities.

In this chapter, we'll discuss the issues surrounding passwords and password management, including password audits. The chapter-ending Hands On section covers password management software, both from a network and an individual point of view.

9.1 Password Policy

In Chapter 1, you saw an example of a password policy. Do you really need a written password policy with the kind of detail you saw there? In any organization that has more than a handful of employees, probably you do. Given that passwords are a network's first line of defense, it pays to be overly cautious.

General password wisdom says that users should create strong passwords—more on strong passwords shortly—and that passwords should be changed every 60 days or so. New passwords should not use any portion of the preceding password. For example, users shouldn't take a word and simply add a different number at the end each time they recreate their password, nor should they be able to reuse passwords that have been used in the recent past. In addition, users should use different passwords for each account.

Certainly you want strong passwords, but should passwords be changed so frequently? The theory behind changing passwords frequently is that a moving target is much harder to decipher. At the same time, however, a password that is changed frequently is much harder to remember, and when users can't remember their passwords, they write them down. You might find a password on a sticky note stuck to a monitor or on a little slip of paper in the middle drawer of a desk. The problem, of course, is exacerbated when users are dealing with passwords for multiple accounts.

You can handle the problem in several ways:

- ◆ Don't insist that passwords be changed frequently. If users pick strong passwords, this may be acceptable.

- ◆ Insist that passwords be changed frequently and stress good password behavior. If you believe that your users will not write passwords down, then this is a good alternative.

- ◆ Provide users with host-based password management software (see "Hands On: Password Management Software" on page 218) and insist that the master password is changed frequently and never written down. This strategy has the advantage of requiring users to remember only a single password, while changing passwords as recommended, and can therefore be a good solution to the problem of multiple Internet account passwords.

- ◆ Use software that provides *single sign-on* at the network level. This allows users to authenticate themselves once and then gain access to all resources they have on a network, providing a solution to the problem of multiple local network logins. Its major drawback is that because a single password unlocks all network resources for a user, the overall security level for a user drops to the level of the least secure system to which the user has access. (For more about single sign-on, password synchronization, and network-based password management solutions, see "Centralized Password Management" on page 218.)

Note: The last two solutions in the preceding list are certainly not mutually exclusive.

9.2 Strong Passwords

Most password policies include some mention of *strong passwords*, passwords that are not easily guessed or decrypted by password cracking software. Strong passwords have the following characteristics:

- Have eight or more characters. Longer is better than shorter.

- Use a combination of letters, numbers, and punctuation marks. They should not consist of a single word or number.

- Not contain more than two paired letters or numbers. For example, XXYY2 would be acceptable, but XXXYYY2 would not.

- Contain words that have no special meaning to the person creating the password. Names of family, friends, or pets, birthdates, telephone numbers, and so on should be avoided at all costs.

- If passwords are case sensitive, contain a mix of upper- and lowercase characters.

There are several simple ways to construct strong passwords:

- Join two simple and easily remembered, but unrelated, words with a punctuation mark. For example, "green*knee" is easy to remember but very difficult for either a human or password cracking software to guess.

- Take a short phrase and substitute numbers for some of the letters. For example, "greenway" could be changed to "gr33nway" by substituting "3" for "e." You could also change "domino" to "d0m!n0." Both of these samples preserve the properties of being easy to remember yet hard to guess. The second is more secure, however, given that password cracking software has become sophisticated enough to identify single numbers replacing single letters.

- Select a phrase, take the first letters of each word in the phrase, and then exchange some of the letters for numbers. For example, choose "My very elderly mother just swept up nine pins" and extract the letters "Mvemjsunp." Then substitute 3 for "e," producing "Mv3mjsunp." The seemingly random string of letters with a number in the middle will be very hard to guess.

- Use a very long (and hopefully, nonsense) phrase.

- Combine any of the preceding.

If you are using a recent version of Windows, you can configure the OS to set strong passwords. Head for Control Panel->Administrator Tools->Security Settings. As you can see in Figure 9.1, you can determine whether the OS keeps a list of previously used passwords (to prevent users from reusing passwords too frequently), the length of time a user can retain the same password, the minimum length of a password, and so on. Also setting lockout options (see Figure 9.2) can make it significantly more difficult for a brute force password cracking attack to succeed.

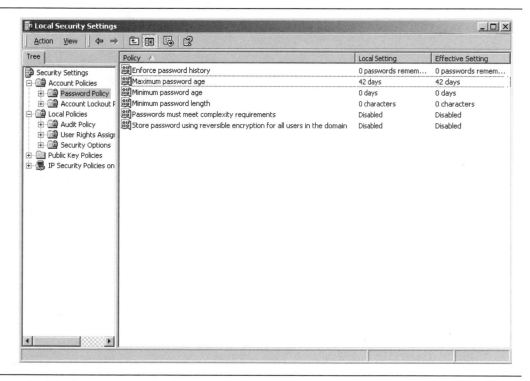

Figure 9.1 Windows password policy settings

9.3 Password File Security

Passwords are stored somewhere on the servers into which users log. Because password files are sitting passively on a disk, they are frequent targets for system crackers. If a cracker can get a copy of a password file, he or she can download that file and then use a variety of resources in

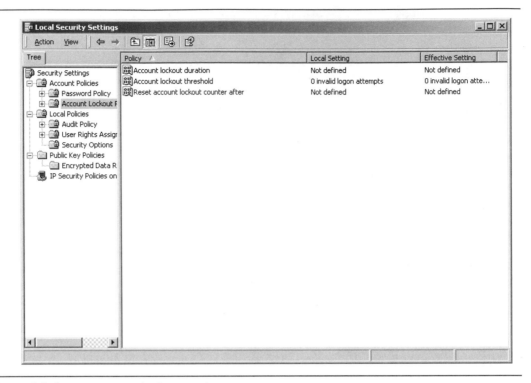

Figure 9.2 Setting account lockout options

an attempt to crack the contents of the file. In this section, we'll look at where Windows and UNIX store passwords and how such files can be protected.

9.3.1 Windows

The way in which passwords are handled depends on the version of Windows you are using. As you will see, password management has improved significantly since Windows 9x!

Windows 9x

Windows 95 and 98 store passwords in *password list* (.pwl) files. They can be found in a variety of places throughout a hard disk, although by default they are stored in the Windows directory. Any cracker with access to the computer can use a simple find command to locate the password list files.

> *Note: Because .pwl files are a Microsoft creation, they are used primarily by Microsoft software. You may therefore be unable to store many application passwords using Windows's native capabilities.*

A .pwl file is a text data file with three fields:

- ◆ The resource type; for example, dial-up networking is 6 and Web resources used by Internet Explorer are 19.

- ◆ The resource name.

- ◆ The resource password.

The entire contents of the file are encrypted and stored with the user name and a checksum.

There is at least one .pwl file for each user, with a maximum of 256 entries per file. Each .pwl file is recorded in the System Registry, in the [Password Lists] section of the *system.ini* file, with an entry in the format

```
USERNAME=path_to_pwl_file
```

These versions of Windows do not store a login password in a .pwl file. Instead, when a user logs in, Windows uses the password supplied to decrypt the associated .pwl file. It then recomputes the file's checksum. If the computed checksum matches the stored checksum, then the user is authenticated and has access to all resources associated with that .pwl file.

> *Note: .pwl file names are a maximum of eight characters. If a user name is more than eight characters, Windows truncates the name. For example, the user FirstUser will have an initial .pwl file named FirstUse.pwl. When that file fills, Windows will create a secondary file named First000.pwl. The next file will be First001.pwl, and so on.*

Tip: If you have upgraded users from Windows 98 or Windows Me to Windows XP, you may discover that some saved passwords have disappeared. This is because Windows XP uses stronger encryption for passwords than earlier versions of the OS and won't allow the less secure passwords. Even uninstalling Windows XP won't restore the lost passwords. If there is a chance that you may lose some passwords with an upgrade, back up the .pwl files to removable media before upgrading. Then you can reinstall them if you downgrade the machine. However, there is nothing you can do to get XP to use those stored passwords; they will need to be reentered as the user accesses the resources they protect.

Windows NT and Beyond

More recent versions of Windows store encrypted passwords in the Windows Registry. In other words, there are no specific password files as there are in earlier versions of the OS.

The passwords in the Registry are encrypted and are never decrypted. When a user logs in, the OS encrypts the password the user enters and compares the encrypted version (the *password hash*) with what is stored in the Registry. If the two hashes match, the user is authenticated and allowed onto the computer.

Tip (and a Warning): The RDISK utility creates a compressed copy of the password hashes and stores them in %SystemRoot%\repair\sam_. A valid use of this file would be to restore the passwords to a new copy of the OS. However, a system cracker with access to the backup file can use it to crack passwords. Here is another good reason to secure your backup media!

Warning: Watch out for sophisticated Windows users who may attempt to edit their system registry to enable automatic login. There will be a DefaultUserName and DefaultPassword entry in the Registry file, and the password will appear in plain text.

9.3.2 UNIX

UNIX stores passwords in *⁄etc⁄passwd,* which can be read (but not modified) by any user with an account on the system. The file is plain text, but the passwords are encrypted. UNIX never decrypts passwords. When a user logs in, the OS encrypts the password the user enters and compares the result to the contents of *⁄etc⁄passwd*. If the two ciphers match, then the user is authenticated. The appearance of powerful password cracking software, however, made it unwise to allow users access to the main password file. Therefore, many UNIX implementations today use *shadow passwords*, where the password ciphers are stored in a secondary file.

When shadow passwords are in effect, the shadow file is usually *⁄etc⁄ password*. This file can be read only by the root account, making it much less likely that a casual user can run password cracking software against it. (A system cracker would need to have root access to obtain a copy of the file.)

As you can see in Figure 9.3, the leftmost column of a shadowed UNIX *⁄etc⁄passwd* file contains the name of the account, followed by an asterisk (*) in the field where the password would ordinarily appear. (Some UNIX implementations use ! or x in place of the password.)

```
nobody:*:-2:-2:Unprivileged User:/:/usr/bin/false
root:*:0:0:System Administrator:/var/root:/bin/sh
daemon:*:1:1:System Services:/var/root:/usr/bin/false
smmsp:*:25:25:Sendmail User:/private/etc/mail:/usr/bin/false
lp:*:26:26:Printing Services:/var/spool/cups:/usr/bin/false
postfix:*:27:27:Postfix User:/var/spool/postfix:/usr/bin/false
www:*:70:70:World Wide Web Server:/Library/WebServer:/usr/bin/false
eppc:*:71:71:Apple Events User:/var/empty:/usr/bin/false
mysql:*:74:74:MySQL Server:/var/empty:/usr/bin/false
sshd:*:75:75:sshd Privilege separation:/var/empty:/usr/bin/false
qtss:*:76:76:QuickTime Streaming Server:/var/empty:/usr/bin/false
cyrus:*:77:6:Cyrus User:/var/imap:/usr/bin/false
mailman:*:78:78:Mailman user:/var/empty:/usr/bin/false
appserver:*:79:79:Application Server:/var/empty:/usr/bin/false
unknown:*:99:99:Unknown User:/var/empty:/usr/bin/false
```

Figure 9.3 The contents of a UNIX *⁄etc⁄passwd* file

Reality Check: Allowing any user to read UNIX systems files is not necessarily a safe thing to do. A side effect of the way UNIX file permissions work may give users more access than you intended, with potentially disastrous consequences. See Chapter 12 for more details.

9.4 Password Audits

How can you ensure that your users have created strong passwords? You perform a password audit, in which you essentially take the role of a system cracker and attempt to break existing passwords. The easiest way to perform the audit is to use password cracking software, some of which is readily available over the Internet.

How often should you audit? That depends on your password policies. If you require that passwords be changed every 60 days, for example, that would be the minimum interval between audits. If you also have controls in place to keep users from changing their passwords too often (to keep them from cycling back to a favorite password), then a shorter interval probably isn't warranted. However, if your user management software isn't (or can't be) configured in that way, then you may want to audit more frequently than the required password-change interval.

When you perform a password audit, what should you look for? You look for passwords that can be cracked in a reasonable amount of time using high-end hardware. The assumption is that system crackers will have all the time in the world to run password cracking software and that they will have the money to purchase fast computers. If, for example, a password can be cracked in 24 hours, then it probably isn't good enough for your network. (Some system crackers are *very* patient, but if a password doesn't crack in 24–48 hours, then it's probably a good one.)

9.4.1 UNIX: John the Ripper

John the Ripper is an open source UNIX password cracking program. You can download the software or purchase a distribution on CD, much like you would a Linux distribution!

John the Ripper uses a dictionary-style attack in which it encrypts words and phrases and compares them to the contents of a UNIX password file. It can crack most three- to four-character passwords in less than a second, but can be stumped by passwords made up of nonsense characters. In other words, if John the Ripper can extract a password, then the user needs to change it to a stronger password; if John the Ripper can't identify it in a reasonable amount of time, then the password is acceptable.

Reality Check: A sample run of John the Ripper against a UNIX password file cracked three-letter passwords almost instantaneously. Five and six character passwords took several hours; strong passwords of eight or more characters were still uncracked after 12 hours. Longer is definitely better when it comes to passwords.

9.4.2 Windows: L0phtCrack

L0phtCrack is a now-commercial password cracking tool that works with Windows 95 and beyond. According to vendors, it can break approximately 90 percent of Windows passwords in about 48 hours. Like John the Ripper, it uses a dictionary-style attack and allows the user to use customized dictionaries along with those supplied by the software. In addition, it supports brute force password cracking (trying every possible combination of characters in a character set) and a combination of dictionary-style and brute force. The output of the software includes the user, the password, the time it took to crack the password, and how the password was cracked (see Figure 9.4).

Note: L0phtCrack version 3 handles Windows 95, 98, and NT. You need at least version 4 to include XP, NT, or 2000. At the time this book was written, the software had been upgraded to version 5 (see http://www.atstake.com/products/lc/). This version also supports auditing UNIX passwords. Mac OS X users can find information about a port of l0phtCrack 1.5 at http://l0phtcrack.darwinports.com/ for port information.

Note: Some older, open source versions of L0phtCrack are still floating around the Internet.

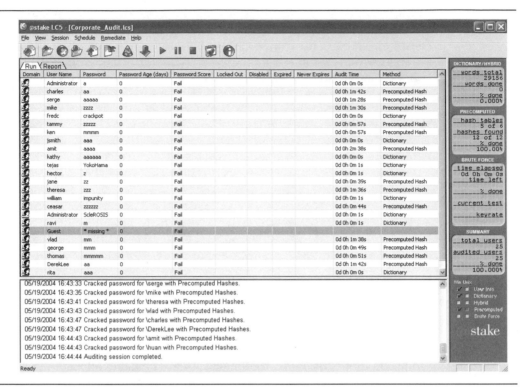

Figure 9.4 L0phtCrack output

As far as a system cracker is concerned, L0phtCrack is an excellent tool, in particular because it supports distributed password cracking. In other words, the password cracking task can be split between multiple machines.

Reality Check: John the Ripper is a part of many UNIX distributions. Why? Ostensibly to help a system administrator recover lost passwords. But let's be real here: Any tool that can be used to audit passwords can also be used by system crackers in attempts to gain unauthorized access. When you are doing inventories of the software on client machines on your network, be sure to search for password cracking software. There is no reason end users should have such software (assuming that network administrators are performing regular password audits).

9.5 Enhancing Password Security with Tokens

As discussed in Chapter 3, it is possible to equip your users with devices that they must have in their possession to be authenticated for network access. One of the most widely used—SecurID from RSA Security—provides a typical adjunct to password security.

Although there are many devices that work with RSA SecurID software, RSA sells the device in Figure 9.5, which generates a new, one-time use password every 60 seconds. The device is small enough to fit on a user's keychain and is supplied with a lifetime battery.

Figure 9.5   The RSA SecurID device that generates a one-time use password

There are three major advantages to a system of this type:

♦ Users are authenticated by two factors: something they have (a one-time password from the SecurID device) and something they know (a PIN).

♦ The one-time use password eliminates some problems with password management because users don't need to remember or change their own password, although users do need to manage their PINs, just as they would any other password.

♦ Authentication using the hardware token requires no software on the desktop, although it does require authentication server software. The server software, as you might expect, is the most complex component of the system.

On the down side, unless the network provides single sign-on capabilities, a user will need a separate SecurID device for each account to which he or she has access.

If a company chooses, it can use software SecurID tokens instead of hardware devices. The SecurID client software (for example, Figure 9.6) works like the hardware, generating a one-time use password that the user enters when signing on to network resources. The software is available for Windows computers, Palm handhelds, Blackberry handhelds, and many mobile phones.

Figure 9.6   SecurID software

Note: For more information on RSA's SecurID system, see http://www.rsasecurity.com/node.asp?id=1156.

9.6 Hands On: Password Management Software

Password management software can be used at the network level to provide the same services to all network users or can be deployed on individual hosts so end users can manage their own passwords. Depending on your particular environment, you may find that you need both types of software.

9.6.1 Centralized Password Management

The first solution to the problem of managing passwords is to provide network-based password management. Many packages provide password synchronization—updating all passwords when one is changed—as well as single sign-on—supporting a single password for access to all local network resources—that was introduced earlier in this chapter.

Most centralized password management programs are designed for UNIX and Windows computers, with a few products able to handle mainframe OSs as well. When shopping for a product, you should expect to find the following features:

♦ Enforcement of strong passwords.

♦ Enforcement of password change intervals.

♦ Automation of password reset requests. Research by the Gartner group suggests that as much as 30 percent of calls to corporate help desks involve help with passwords. You may therefore be able to significantly reduce help desk costs and improve help desk performance by removing the need to handle password reset requests manually. Users authenticate themselves by answering a series of personal questions, the answers to which have been stored previously. Once the questions have been answered, a user's password is reset.

♦ Password synchronization (also known as *single sign-on*).

Reality Check: Although I keep saying that I want to avoid mentioning specific products in this books, it's really hard to stick to that pronouncement. So, here are some Web sites for vendors of enterprise-level password management products: *http:www.symark.com*, *http://ca.com* (yes, that's the correct URL ...), and *www.netegrity.com*. There are many, many choices available.

9.6.2 Individual Password Management

As mentioned earlier in this chapter, one of the biggest drawbacks to requiring different passwords for all accounts (including Web site accounts) and frequent password changes is that users can't remember their passwords and tend to write them down. You can help ensure that users adhere to your password rules and yet don't write down their passwords by providing them with individual password management software.

Password management software provides a place for users to store account names and passwords, typically securing the entire collection with a single master password. If all the user needs to remember is the master password, then he or she is much more likely to keep that single password memorized rather than writing it down. To show you how such software works, this section looks at two examples, one for Windows and one for Mac OS X.

Norton Password Manager

Norton Password Manager (sold by Symantec and known as NPM) is a stand-alone application for Windows Me, 98, 2000 Professional, and XP Home/Professional. It stores Internet and application account and password information as well as other confidential information (for example, credit card numbers) that a user might need. Because the user can add addresses and telephone numbers, it can also double as an online address book. (For an example of the user interface, see Figure 9.7.)

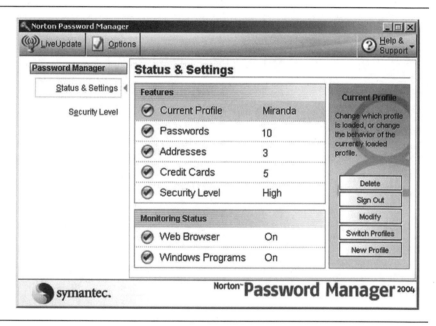

Figure 9.7 The Norton Password Manager user interface

Note: The Windows XP Stored User Names and Passwords tool automatically records user names and passwords for shared network resources, but can't handle Web sites, credit cards, and so on.

As you navigate using a supported Web browser (IE 5.01 SP2 and higher, and AOL 8.0 and higher), NPM records your logins and passwords. The next time you visit those sites, NPM handles the logins automatically.

Each copy of NPM supports multiple "profiles," collections of secure information protected by a password. Users can therefore organize groups of related information into profiles or a single computer can maintain separate profiles for multiple users. NPM includes password auditing software to help users choose strong passwords.

> *Note: Windows XP includes a keyring that is a tool for managing passwords ("credentials," in XP terminology) for XP resources. It handles only stored user names and passwords and is not intended as a general password/secure information management utility. However, for users who have multiple Windows XP accounts, it can be useful. To access the keyring, go to Control Panel->User Accounts, where you will see a list of all credentials stored in the keyring. You can then add, change, or delete credentials.*

Mac OS X Keychain

The Mac OS X Keychain is a password management facility supplied with and integrated into the OS itself. As you can see in Figure 9.8, a keychain is a collection of Internet and application passwords. The password access application—Keychain Access—supports multiple keychains, each locked and unlocked with its own master password.

Once a keychain is unlocked, the user can view all information about each entry in the keychain *except* the password or secure note. Clicking the Show Password button requires the user to reenter the keychain password (see Figure 9.9). This second layer of security protects the items in a keychain that has been left unlocked for a period of time.

Like NPM, the OS X Keychain application supports multiple sets of secure information, each of which can have its own password. However, users can enter accounts and passwords manually, rather than relying solely on the keychain application to record them automatically.

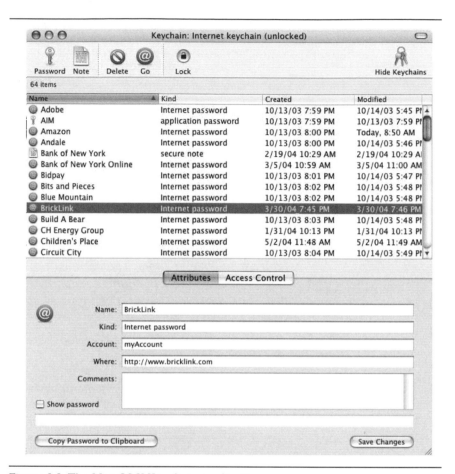

Figure 9.8 The Mac OS X Keychain application

Figure 9.9 Viewing a keychain item's password

The OS X keychain supplies account names and passwords only for applications that are "keychain aware." At the time this book was written, that included primarily Apple's Safari Web browser.

> *Note: Some Web browsers—in particular, Netscape—have their own password manager. Netscape can remember account names and passwords and enter them automatically for you. The drawback to using this feature is that there is no security layer protecting the passwords. Anyone using the copy of Netscape storing passwords has access to the accounts protected by those passwords.*

> *Note: Why isn't there a section here about a host-based password manager for UNIX? Because in all my research, I haven't been able to find one! There is network-level password management, however, that preselects passwords and lets users choose from a list of acceptable passwords. Used primarily in government applications where strong passwords are required, such software does not provide a single sign-on function.*

9.7 Summary

Password and user name pairs continue to provide the front line of security for most computer systems. This means that security administrators must ensure that users choose strong passwords and that they adhere to password maintenance policies set by the organization.

Strong passwords are easy to remember and hard to guess. Longer passwords work better than short ones, and combinations of letters, numbers, and special characters are also effective. Passwords need to be easy enough to remember that users don't write them down.

Password policies can be enforced automatically through the use of centralized password management software that monitors password change intervals and the composition of passwords.

To determine whether users are choosing strong passwords, an organization should conduct frequent password audits, during which security personnel attempt to crack passwords. Any password that can be cracked by generally available password cracking software in a reasonable amount of time is not a strong password and needs to be changed.

Strong passwords should be changed frequently. However, the need to remember which password is in use, along with the many other passwords that users may have, make it difficult to avoid writing down the passwords. One solution is to provide users with password management tools that store user accounts and passwords for them. The password management software is secured with a single master password that can be changed as frequently as an organization requires. The user then needs to remember only one password.

Chapter 10: Remote Access

In This Chapter

- ◆ Security vulnerabilities introduced by remote access
- ◆ VPNs
- ◆ OS VPN support

10.0 Introduction

Are all your users physically located close to your network hardware (in the same building or on the same campus) all the time? Chances are, they're not. Many people work from home all or part of the week; many networks are designed for remote access by a variety of clients. Your salespeople in the field, personnel away from the office (for business or pleasure), users who pay you for network access—all need to connect to your network and use it as if they were physically local to its resources.

Remote access of any kind—whether it be through a dial-up connection or the Internet—adds significant security problems. In this chapter we'll first look at how the various types of remote access present security problems. Then we'll discuss ways in which you can secure that access.

10.1 Remote Access Vulnerabilities

Whenever network traffic leaves your premises, it becomes much more vulnerable than it is on the local network because it presents opportunities for system crackers to intercept that traffic. The presence of remote access to your network also provides additional entry points for crackers to try.

Users establish remote access connections physically in one of two ways: They dial into the network using a modem or they connect over the Internet. Once connected, they can interact with the local network using remote control software, a browser interface, or remote control commands.

10.1.1 Dial-In Access

Dial-in access to a network is inherently insecure, given that anyone who has access to a modem's telephone number can attempt to dial in and log on. It provides a nice open spot for a system cracker to creep in, although in most cases it isn't particularly stealthy: Most networks log dial-in access attempts and can lock accounts after a specified number of failed attempts (usually three). However, if a system cracker gains access to account names and passwords, he or she may have free access to your network through a dial-in connection.

There are at least two things you can do to secure a dial-in connection. First, you can keep the telephone number of the dial-in modem private. Don't publish the number anywhere; give it only to users who have a real need to use it. Unfortunately, the more people who know something secret, the greater the chance of it being revealed. Keeping the number secret is effective only if the number is used by a small number of people.

> *Note: Even the most secret dial-in number is still vulnerable to "war dialers," software that dials a range of telephone numbers automatically, reporting back to the software user any numbers that are answered by a computer or fax machine.*

Second, you can use a *callback* system, where the user sets up a telephone connection, logs in, and then hangs up. The network modem then calls the user back at a number that has been stored for the user on a network server. The user's modem answers the call and the user logs in again. Then the user is ready to use network resources.

The drawback to a callback system is that it requires that the user always be located at the same telephone number. This is fine for someone who is dialing in from home, but won't help traveling users.

> *Note: Callback servers are not difficult to set up. For instructions on configuring a Linux system for callbacks, see http://www.linuxgazette.com/issue77/sunil.html.*

Reality Check: To make your network as secure as possible, you want to limit the number of ways a system cracker could gain access. Your Internet connection is probably your major security focus, and securing access over that major pipe may overshadow other access methods. If you can—and admittedly this is not possible in some environments—avoid providing dial-in access so that there is only one pipe into your network from the outside world.

10.1.2 Remote Control Software

One way Internet users can gain access to local network resources is to use remote control software. As well as supporting file transfers, remote control software allows users to either view what is happening on another computer or to control another computer. The advantage of such software is that it provides GUI access to network resources; the major disadvantage is that it doesn't provide protection for the data being transferred over the remote connection.

As an example, consider the two screen shots in Figure 10.1 and Figure 10.2, taken using Timbuktu Pro, one of several programs that provide such functionality. Figure 10.1 shows a full Macintosh screen appearing in a window on a Windows 2000 computer. When Timbuktu Pro is the foreground application and the mouse pointer is over the Timbuktu Pro window, the pointer changes to appear as a Macintosh pointer and mouse movements affect the remote Macintosh, rather than the host Windows machine. The exact opposite is occurring in Figure 10.2, where movement of the mouse pointer over the Timbuktu Pro window controls a Windows 2000 machine.

> *Note: Timbuktu Pro is well suited for a mixed OS environment. If you have a Windows-only network, then you can also use pcAnywhere. These are the two most widely used remote control software packages, although there are certainly others available.*

Remote control software does not connect the remote user as if he or she were working locally. Instead, it gives the remote user the ability to observe or control a computer on the network, as well as transfer files. It is therefore very useful for users who need to access their office computers while located elsewhere. All he or she needs to do is have the remote control software installed on his or her office machine and laptop, and to remember to leave the office machine turned on. However, it doesn't gives users the access to all system resources, and won't allow them to use client/server applications.

Most of today's remote control software supports connections using TCP/IP. You must be able to supply either a domain name or IP address of the target system. Some packages support dial-in connections as well, although a remote connection over the Internet is usually most convenient for users working from long distances away from the local network.

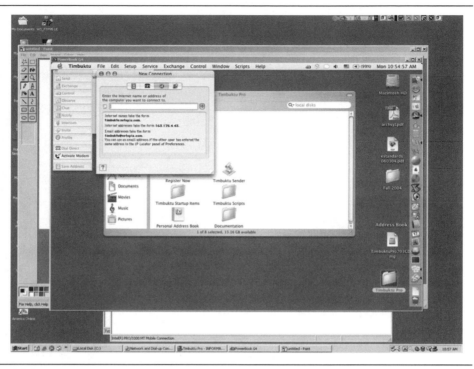

Figure 10.1   A Macintosh being controlled by a Windows 2000 machine

Note: Remote control software can also be used locally, and is particularly useful for technical support because it allows tech support personnel to see what is happening on an end user's computer without physically going to the user's location.

How secure is this type of remote access? More secure than you might think. First, the software must be installed on both the remote and local computers. A hacker would somehow need to get the software onto the target machine. The cracker would also need to configure the software to allow the remote control (or even observation) to occur. This configuration can be done only by sitting at the target computer. By default, remote control software installations allow no remote access; each type of access must be enabled individually.

Even if a system cracker has physical access to a target computer, there is an icon (in the menu bar or task bar, depending on the OS) that indicates

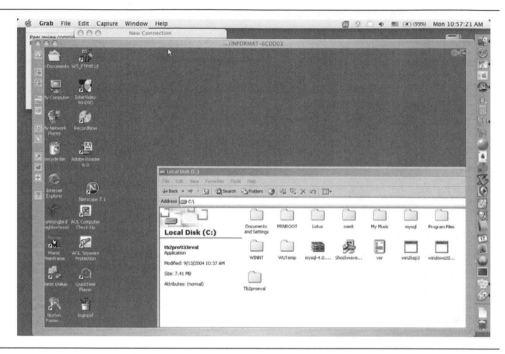

Figure 10.2 A Windows 2000 computer being controlled by a Macintosh machine

the presence of the remote connection. However, other than that, it is difficult for an observed or controlled host to detect the presence of the remote user. However, if the end user of the machine is observant enough to notice something odd and to report it to someone, then a stealthy attempt to control a machine in this way would likely fail.

The biggest threat placed by remote control software is that it could be installed by a system cracker using a social engineering attack that convinced the computer's end user that the remote control was authorized by the end user's organization. User education to prevent social engineering of this kind is the best defense.

10.1.3 Remote Access Commands

The most traditional way to gain remote access to local network resources is to use remote access commands such as telnet. Originally a UNIX utility, telnet is now available for Windows as well.

A telnet program provides the user with a command-line interface to a remote computer. Assuming that you have a full-time Internet connection or have established a dial-in connection to a network, then you can use the Windows Run dialog box or the UNIX command line to establish a `telnet` session. The computer to which you are attempting to connect must be configured to accept an incoming `telnet` connection. Because `telnet` provides only a command-line interface, it is most commonly used to connect to UNIX systems.

Windows Telnet Connections

To establish a `telnet` connection from a Windows machine, a user would

1. Type `telnet` in the Run dialog box (see Figure 10.3).

Figure 10.3 Starting a Windows telnet connection

2. Click OK to display a command line window running the `telnet` client program (see Figure 10.4).
3. Type the `telnet` command to connect to the destination machine.
4. Once the connection is established, the destination computer displays a `login` prompt.
5. Type the account name. The destination computer displays a `password` prompt.
6. Type the account's password.

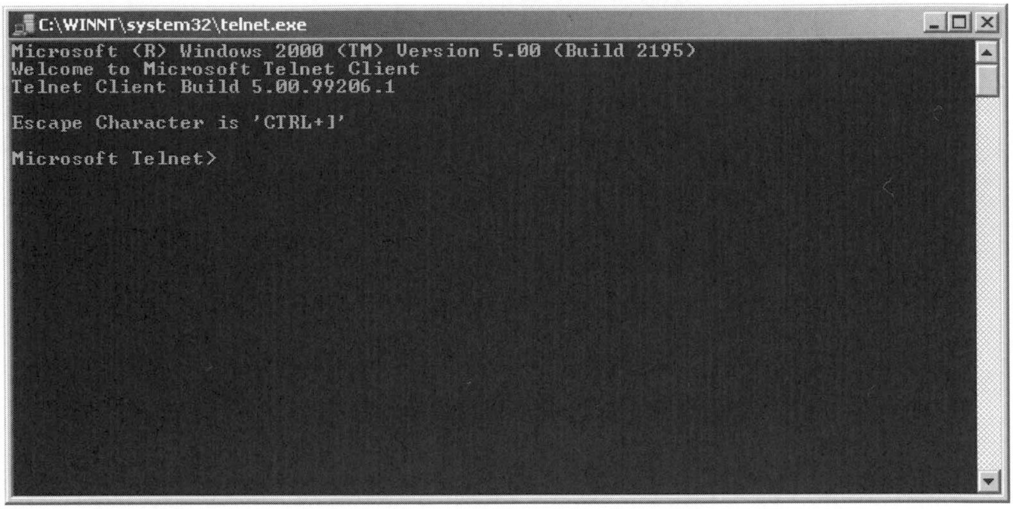

```
C:\WINNT\system32\telnet.exe                                        _ □ ×
Microsoft (R) Windows 2000 (TM) Version 5.00 (Build 2195)
Welcome to Microsoft Telnet Client
Telnet Client Build 5.00.99206.1

Escape Character is 'CTRL+]'

Microsoft Telnet>
```

Figure 10.4 The telnet command line window

Once the password and account name pair are validated, the user is logged in and has command-line access to everything the account name is allowed to access. To end the telnet session, the user types exit.

UNIX Telnet Connections

To start a telnet session from a UNIX system, a user would

1. Go to the command line (if working with a GUI).
2. Type

    telnet *host_name_or_IP_address*

3. The destination computer displays a login prompt. Type the account name.
4. The destination computer displays a password prompt. Type the password.

At this point, the user has access to the account on the destination computer. To end the telnet session, the user types exit.

Telnet's Vulnerability

Today, you will find that very few servers support `telnet`. Why? Because it has a known security hole: `Telnet` does not encrypt any portion of a remote conversation. A system cracker can collect data by placing a sniffer program on the network and then looking for specific packets, including `telnet` password packets. Intercepted packets can be read or modified in a classic man-in-the-middle attack. In addition, because `telnet` does not authenticate users, IP and DNS spoofing attacks are relatively easy to perform.

> *Note: FTP also sends user names and passwords in the clear.*

Other UNIX Remote Access Commands

There is a group of UNIX commands that can be used for remote system access, including `rsh` (open a remote shell), `rcp` (remote copy), and `rlogin` (remote login). Like `telnet`, they are inherently insecure. None require passwords; they allow connections from trusted hosts based on the host having a trusted IP address.

ssh: The Secure Alternative

The best alternative to `telnet` (and the other remote shell commands) is `ssh`, the secure shell. Not only does `ssh` encrypt passwords and the rest of the conversation, but it also supports X Window display information, providing some GUI support for remote access.

Connecting in using `ssh` is very similar to using `telnet`:

```
ssh -l account_name domain_name_or_IP_address
```

Using `ssh` for remote access protects against a number of types of system cracking:

♦ Man-in-the-middle attacks in which the system cracker intercepts packets in the middle of a transmission and either hijacks the session or modifies packets before they are sent on to their destination.

♦ IP spoofing, that lets the cracker make the packet appear to come from a trusted host and may convince the recipient to download malware.

♦ DNS spoofing, through which the cracker modifies the cache on a DNS server so that a domain name points to the wrong IP address. The effect is to redirect users to a spoofed Web site where the cracker will in all likelihood collect information to be used for identity theft.

♦ IP source routing, where a system cracker routes packets from a computer rather than allowing a router to make routing decisions. Like IP spoofing, this can convince the target machine that the packet is coming from a trusted host.

To secure remote access through shell access, you should shut down or disable `telnet` and the other remote access commands. Allow connections through `ssh` only. This will ensure that packets are encrypted, thus protecting the communications session.

Note: You'll find more about the type of encryption used by ssh in Chapter 12.

An Aside: `ssh` does not support the logging of attempts to connect to a system. To add that capability, look into TCP wrapper (implemented by the program `tcpd`). TCP wrapper provides some access control using the source and destination addresses of the connection request. It also logs both successful and unsuccessful connection attempts. For information on using and installing TCP wrapper, see *http://www.cert.org/security-improvement/implementations/i041.07.html.*

10.2 VPNs

The major secure alternative for remote access that has emerged in the past few years is *virtual private networks*, or VPNs. The intent behind a VPN is to allow geographically removed users to send data over an existing WAN—most commonly the Internet—in a secure fashion. The basic technique provides a secure transmission path known as a *tunnel* between two systems. The tunnel can connect two systems or two networks.

Currently there are at least four competing VPN technologies, each of which has drawbacks and benefits when used for remote access.

IPSec VPNs

As originally defined, the TCP/IP protocol stack is very weak in terms of security. IPSec is a group of protocols that were added to IP to provide encryption for data traveling over the Internet. Because IPSec works at the network layer of the protocol stack, it is independent of any specific application program. One of its biggest advantages, therefore, is that applicatons don't need to be written specifically to take advantage of it.

> *Note: According to some sources, the original protocol name was written IPsec. However, current common usage tends to write it IPSec, which is what I'm using in this book.*

When used for a VPN, IPSec establishes a *tunnel* between a client machine running IPSec client software and an IPSec server located at the destination end of the connection (*tunnel mode*, as illustrated in Figure 10.5).

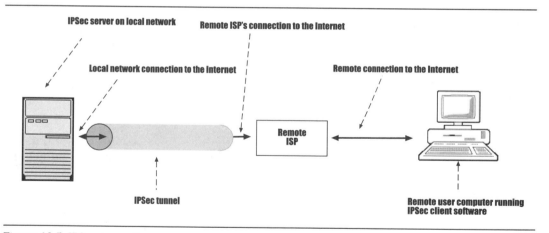

Figure 10.5 IPSec tunneling

In tunnel mode, IPSec's encryption is in place only as data travel over the Internet. It does not encrypt data on the local network or between a remote host and its connection to the Internet. Therefore, if you have a remote office that needs to access the home office LAN on a regular basis,

IPSec is a good VPN solution. You can place an IPSec server at either end of the connection, alleviating the need for each client machine at the remote office to run IPSec client software. You can then use an Internet connection to share the VPN tunnel among the remote office users.

> *Note: IPSec servers generally are sold as hardware appliances rather than as software you can add to an existing network machine. For example, Cisco (www.cisco.com) provides a plug-in module for its Catalyst 6500 Series Switch and 7600 Series Internet Router to provide VPN services. Other vendors, such as SSi (www.ssimall.com) add IPSec VPN support to their security appliances, providing firewall and proxy serving along with the VPN.*

An Aside: IPSec can provide end-to-end (host to host) encryption—when it is running in *transport mode*. However, to use transport mode you must have control over the entire length of the transmission, something that isn't supported with a VPN that requires users to connect to the Internet using an ISP provided by some other organization.

If you need to connect mobile or widely scattered remote users securely, an IPSec VPN may not be the best solution:

♦ IPSec allows users to access the destination LAN as if they were connected directly to that LAN. This may not be desirable for some remote users (for example, customers or other business partners who aren't employees).

♦ Most intermittent remote users must connect to an ISP before they connect to the Internet, and data are not subject to IPSec protection as they move from remote user to ISP.

♦ IPSec tunneling is not compatible with most firewalls and can't make its way through a router using *network address translation* (NAT). To ensure compatibility with firewalls and NAT, you'll need to purchase hardware (such as the SSi appliance described in the previous *Note*) that specifically provides such capabilities.

♦ IPSec requires that client software from the same vendor that supplied the IPSec server (or software from a compatible vendor) be installed on each remote host. This is fine if all your remote users are working with computers owned by your organization, such as laptops for users who are traveling. However, remote users may need to use hardware that you don't own, such as the Internet access provided in a hotel room or Internet cafe. An IPSec VPN isn't accessible in such environments.

More on IPSec: IPSec has two protocols. The first, *Authentication Header* (AH), takes care of verifying the identity of a message sender (*authentication*) and ensures that the message isn't modified during transmission (*message integrity*). The second protocol, *Encapsulating Security Payload* (ESP), provides encryption for the data field of the IP packet, as well as authentication. Both protocols can operate in one of two modes: *tunnel mode*, as described previously, provides the secure IP tunnel used by VPNs; *transport mode* provides host-to-host security. Because transport mode works between two hosts only, it isn't practical for a VPN, which needs to support sharing of the tunnel among multiple users.

IPSec authenticates both users and computers. For user authentication, it can require as little as a user name and password. It also supports two-level authentication, where a user needs to supply an additional piece of information, such as a one-time password or a token. Some VPNs finish the authentication process at this point. However, IPSec can also authenticate hardware by setting up a *security association* (SA), in which a third-party agency issues a *certificate* indicating that the computer is a trusted host. (You will read more about certificates of authority and how they work in Chapter 12.) Once the user and computer are authenticated, IPSec is said to have established the security association.

Reality Check: In theory, hardware authentication sounds like a great idea for preventing a system cracker from inserting a rogue machine into a network. Unfortunately, hardware authentication using third-party certifying authorities isn't widely implemented. Not only does it add cost to a VPN implementation, but there doesn't appear to be wide-spread agreement on which certificate issuing organizations are to be trusted. In addition, you can't authenticate hardware from users whose hardware you don't control.

PPTP VPNs

One alternative to an IPSec VPN for remote access is to use a protocol based on a dial-up protocol, such as *point-to-point tunneling protocol* (PPTP). This VPN solution avoids some of the problems with using IPSec for remote access, including the issue of firewall and NAT incompatibility. (NAT compatibility requires an editor for PPTP packets, however.) And because PPTP VPN support is part of operating systems by Microsoft and Apple, you don't need to purchase extra client software. Network operating systems from both vendors also provide PPTP server software.

PPTP has been designed as a wrapper for *point-to-point protocol* (PPP), the protocol used by most dial-up connections between the client computer's modem and an ISP's modem. It takes the PPP frame, encapsulates the frame using *Generic Routing Encapsulation* (GRE), and then encapsulates it once more into an IP packet.

PPTP encrypts the data in the PPP frame. However, the encryption doesn't begin until after the PPP connection is established. This means that the exchange of authentication information—in particular, the user name and password—is sent in the clear.

PPTP also can't authenticate hardware, although as mentioned in the preceding sidebar, hardware authentication isn't being widely practiced. On the other hand, PPTP doesn't require certificates of authority (CAs) at all, simplifying its implementation.

L2TP/IPSec

IPSec and PPTP work only with TCP/IP networks. If the WAN over which remote traffic will be traveling uses another protocol (for example, X.25, Frame Relay, or ATM), then neither IPSec nor PPTP is a viable solution. *Layer 2 Tunneling Protocol* (L2TP), which is suppported by both Microsoft and Apple, functions over the alternative WAN protocols, as well as IP. When used with IP, it provides tunneling over the Internet.

In contrast to PPTP, which uses TCP, L2TP uses UDP datagrams to control its tunneling. Each PPP frame is encapsulated by L2TP, then by UDP, and finally by IP.

L2TP can work with IPSec to provide end-to-end security. The combination—known as L2TP/IPSec, uses IPSec encryption to encode the PPP data field. Because IPSec establishes an SA before beginning transfer of any message packets, the encryption is in place prior to the beginning of PPP user authentication. This ensures that the user name and password are encrypted, rather than being sent in the clear as they are with PPTP. However, the IPSec authentication does require that mechanisms for CAs be in place.

L2TP has problems getting through routers with NAT. However, if both the client and VPN server are running *IPSec NAT traversal* (NAT-T) then NAT will function.

SSL VPNs

The final major VPN alternative is *secure socket layer* (SSL), which made its debut as a protocol for securing Web browser traffic. For applications with a Web browser interface, SSL supports VPN access using any browser on a client machine. It also avoids any problems with NAT by incorporating proxies that direct a VPN connection to a specific application.

More on SSL: SSL is a protocol developed by Netscape for encrypting data sent from Web browsers. Its first uses included encrypting credit card numbers, for example. SSL is an unusual protocol in that it doesn't fit neatly within any of the existing layers of the TCP/IP protocol stack. Instead, it sits between the network and application layer, providing services both to applications and to TCP. SSL provides server and client authentication, message integrity, and encryption.

SSL authenticates both clients and servers using digital certificates. (Have you ever seen a browser message that a site's certificate has expired?) You will read about digital certificates in Chapter 12.

Many vendors advertise their SSL VPN solutions as "clientless." However, SSL VPNs avoid client software only when the application to be used through the VPN has a Web browser interface. To access non-browser-enabled applications, the SSL VPN server must be able to handle proxies to pass browser traffic through to the needed applications. In addition, most SSL VPN vendors also supply client software that provides access similar to that provided by an IPSec VPN, where the client computer has full access to the local network.

10.3 Remote User Authentication

A task that we haven't looked at in much detail is the authentication of remote users. How does a network determine that a remote user is entitled to use the resources that he or she is trying to access? In most cases, we rely on the user name–password combination. But what makes the task so difficult is that system crackers are attempting to glean that information while it is being exchanged between the remote user and the remote access server.

10.3.1 RADIUS

One of the biggest problems with remote access has been handling authentication when there are a great many remote users (for example, users of a single ISP). The solution is to dedicate a server to remote user authentication, typically using the *Remote Authentication Dial-In User Service* (RADIUS) protocol.

> *Note: Although the name of the RADIUS protocol suggests that it is just for dial-in access, it has been updated to include support for VPNs, wireless access points, DSL modems, Ethernet switches, and so on.*

The RADIUS server stores user authentication information. Therefore, when a RADIUS client—some type of remote access server, such as a VPN server or modem pool server—receives an access request, it sends the user's information (user name and password, for example) to the RADIUS server, which then attempts to authenticate the user. The RADIUS server then responds to the access server, indicating whether authentication succeeded.

RADIUS messages travel between the RADIUS server and access server as UDP datagrams. Security is provided by a *shared secret*, a passphrase theoretically known only to the two servers.

RADIUS servers and the communications between them and access servers do have some security vulnerabilities:

♦ There is no protection against spoofing of the IP address of the access client. When the RADIUS server receives a datagram, it verifies that the source IP address represents what it knows to be a legitimate access server. However, there is nothing to keep a system cracker from spoofing that source IP address. The solution is to configure the access server to attach a *message digest* to the datagram using the shared secret as an encryption key. (You will find information about message digests in Chapter 12.)

♦ A shared secret, like any password or passphrase, needs to adhere to the rules for strong passwords. Otherwise, it is vulnerable to brute force and dictionary cracking attacks. The RFCs that describe the standard suggest shared secrets of no less than 22 characters (or 32 hexadecimal digits). In addition, use a different shared secret for each access client/RADIUS server combination.

♦ The entire RADIUS datagram should be encrypted. The standards suggest the use of IPSec with ESP and a strong encryption algorithm.

10.3.2 Kerberos

Kerberos is an authentication protocol designed for client/server applications. Developed by MIT, it is available as an open source product as well in commercial software.

> *Note: The protocol is named after the three-headed dog from Greek mythology, whose job it was to guard the entrance to Hades.*

Kerberos facilitates user authentication and provides strong encryption for a network. To facilitate authentication, it maintains a database of users and their secret encryption keys. For end users, the key is an encrypted password; other network services negotiate secret keys with a Kerberos server when they register with the server. The Kerberos server then acts as the middle man between the application server (for example, a database server) and the client attempting to gain access. It accepts authentication information from the client, checks the information against its own database, and responds to an application server's query that the user has been verified.

Kerberos may also distribute a secret encryption key generated by an authentication server for use during one communications session that it distributes to the two clients in a conversation. Kerberos uses its own *ticket* to distribute the key to the two clients.

One of Kerberos's major weaknesses is that it isn't particularly effective against brute force password guessing attempts. If a user hasn't chosen a strong password, a system cracker can guess the password and be authenticated. Kerberos also works only with software that has been modified to use its services.

10.3.3 CHAP and MS-CHAP

Challenge Handshake Authentication Protocol (CHAP) and the Microsoft extension to it (MS-CHAP) are authentication protocols designed for dial-in access. CHAP was designed originally to handle users logging in to an ISP, for example.

The authenticator (e.g., the ISP) has a database of user names and passwords. Assuming that the communications link has been established, CHAP works in the following way:

1. The authenticator issues a "challenge" message to the client.
2. The client machine encrypts its user name and password and sends it to the authenticator.
3. The authenticator compares what it receives to the encrypted version of the client's stored password. If the two match, the client is authenticated and permitted onto the network.

CHAP reissues the challenge message at random intervals during the communications session. This helps ensure that the session hasn't been hijacked by a system cracker.

Microsoft's extensions add more information to the challenge message and the challenge response. The challenge message includes an arbitrary "challenge string." The client responds with its user name, password, an encrypted version of the challenge string, and another challenge string that it generates. The authenticator uses all the information in the challenge response to validate the client.

10.4 Hands On: OS VPN Support

Many of today's mainstream operating systems provide built-in support for VPNs. In this section we'll look at how you can connect to a VPN using Windows and Macintosh OS X, without adding any additional software to the computer. In addition, you'll find some remarks about the support that Windows and Macintosh server software provides for VPNs.

> *Note: Setting up a Linux machine for use as a VPN client or server, especially if it's behind a firewall and a router using NAT, isn't trivial. Nonetheless, you can find a good tutorial at http://www.tldp.org/HOWTO/ VPN-Masquerade-HOWTO.html.*

> *Note: This section discusses operating system support for VPNs. However, it is important to recognize that many VPNs, especially those using IPSec, rely on specific vendor appliances and users, therefore, will be running client software from the hardware vendor. For example, one of the major IPSec VPN appliance suppliers is Cisco, and users of those VPN appliances run the Cisco client software.*

10.4.1 Windows VPN Support

Windows desktop operating systems include support for PPTP and L2TP clients; Windows Server 2003 can act as a VPN server without additional software.

The Windows 2003 Server Interface

If your organization needs only a few—say, 128 or less—simultaneous VPN connections, then you may find that a desktop computer running Windows Server 2003 can act as a VPN server. The operating system includes support for that role and provides tools to make the setup and management fairly straightforward.

To set up a Windows Server 2003 to act as a VPN server

1. Run the Routing and Remote Access application.
2. Choose Action->New Routing and Remote Access Connection to start the wizard (see Figure 10.6).

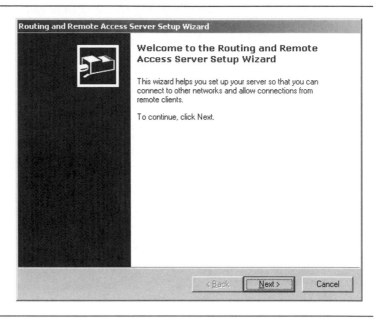

Figure 10.6 Running the Routing and Remote Access Server Setup Wizard

3. Choose the type of server you want to configure, in this case, a VPN (see Figure 10.7).

    Note: Notice that you can set up a standard VPN (the top radio button) or a VPN that is compatible with NAT (the third radio button from the top).

4. Choose the type of connections that you want to allow (either VPN, remote access, or both), as in Figure 10.8
5. Close the wizard. Windows asks if you want to start the new service.

Once you have started the VPN server software, setup is complete.

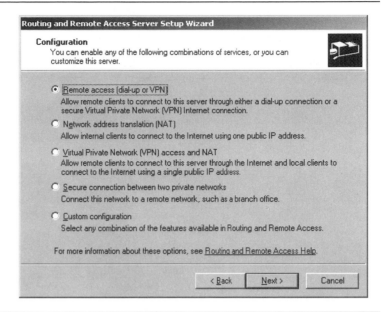

Figure 10.7 Choosing the type of service to configure

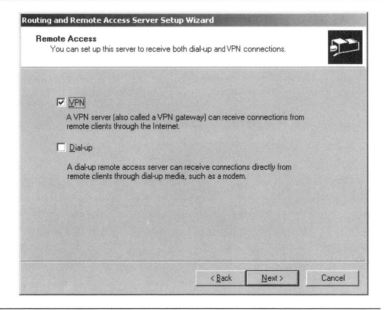

Figure 10.8 Choosing connection types

What do you get with a Windows Server 2003 VPN server? You get support for up to 128 PPTP users. You can monitor the connections from Routing and Remote Access. In Figure 10.9, for example, you can see part of the list of available VPN connections, each of which is known as a *miniport*.

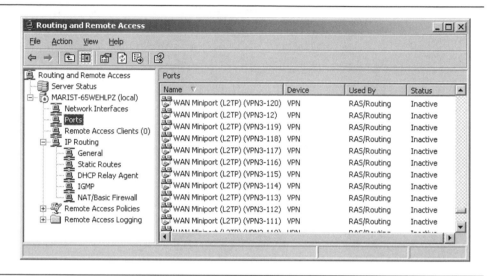

Figure 10.9 Windows Server 2003 VPN connection miniports

Each server that you run appears in the Routing and Remote Access window (see Figure 10.10). Other information in the application includes access to logs of remote connections and descriptions of currently connected clients (user name, duration of connection, and number of ports used).

> *Note: The VPN logs include information about accesses to the file system as well as selected applications, such as database management systems.*

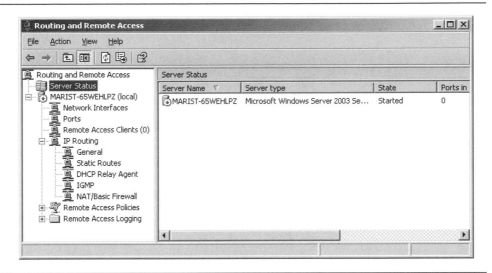

Figure 10.10 Server information in the administration window

Setting up a Windows VPN Client Connection

An end user (or the end user's IT department) sets up a VPN connection very much like any other network connection, using the Network Connection control panel tool:

1. Go to My Computer->Control Panel->Administrative Tools.
2. Double-click on the New Network Connection icon to launch the Network Connection Wizard (see Figure 10.11). Click the Next button.
3. Click the "Connect to private network through the Internet" radio button and then click Next (see Figure 10.12).
4. If the VPN requires a connection to an ISP, choose the "Automatically dial this connection" radio button and choose a prefigured connection from the pop-up menu. If the VPN will be using a direct connection to the Internet (for example, some type of broadband connection), then click the "Do not dial the initial connection" radio button (see Figure 10.13). Click the Next button.
5. Enter the domain name or IP address of the destination computer (see Figure 10.14). Click the Next button.

Figure 10.11 Running the Network Connection Wizard

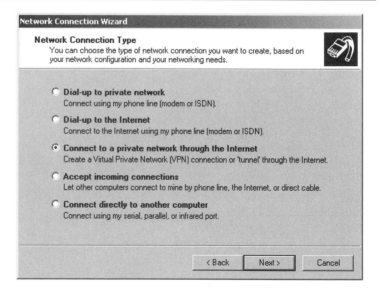

Figure 10.12 Choosing a type of network connection

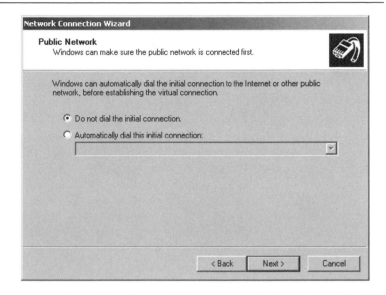

Figure 10.13 Choosing an initial connection

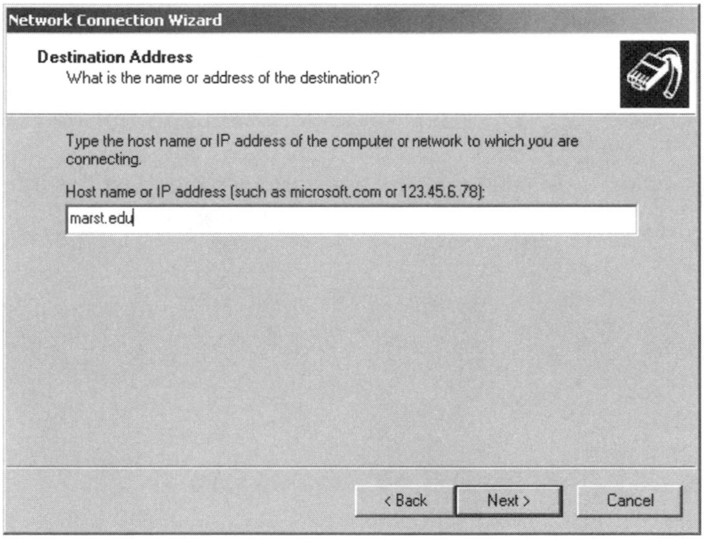

Figure 10.14 Identifying the VPN destination

6. If the connection is to be shared by multiple users, click the "For all users" radio button. Otherwise, click the "Only for myself" radio button, as in Figure 10.15. Click Next.

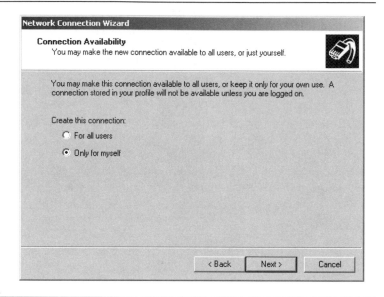

Figure 10.15 Choosing user accessibility for the new VPN connection

7. Enter a name for the connection and click Finish (see Figure 10.16).

At this point, the end user machine has information to contact a remote host, but doesn't know what type of VPN to establish. The user can set the VPN protocol from the Connect dialog box:

1. Double-click on the VPN connection icon that was created by the Network Connection Wizard to display the Connect dialog box (see Figure 10.17).
2. Click the Properties button to open the connection's properties sheet.
3. Click the Networking tab.
4. Select Internet Protocol in the Components list in the middle of the dialog box.
5. Choose the VPN protocol from the Type of VPN Server pop-up menu (see Figure 10.18).
6. Click OK to save the settings.

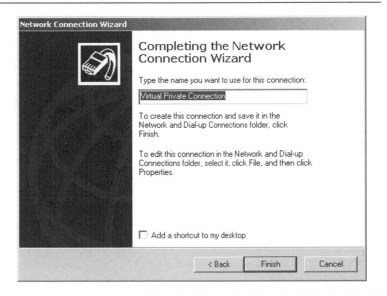

Figure 10.16 Finishing the VPN connection setup

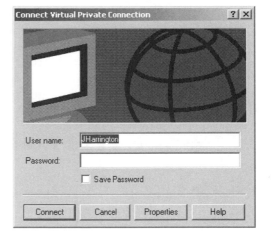

Figure 10.17 Connecting to a VPN

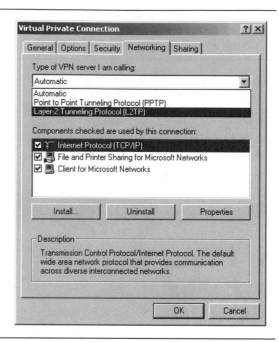

Figure 10.18 Setting the VPN protocol

When the user is ready to actually make the VPN connection, all he or she needs to do is open the Connect dialog box, enter a password, and click the Connect button. What the user sees once the connection is established depends, of course, on the type of network on the other end and the type of resources to which the user has access.

10.4.2 Macintosh OS X VPN Support

The Macintosh operating system (Mac OS X) provides both client and server support for PPTP and L2TP VPNs. Mac OS X Server (versions 10.3 and beyond) can handle OS X, Windows, and Linux clients using either of the two VPN technologies.

The Mac OS X Server Interface

Like Windows server software, OS X Server provides GUI setup for a VPN server (see Figure 10.19). As just mentioned, it handles Mac OS X, Windows and Linux clients using PPTP and/or L2TP over IPSec.

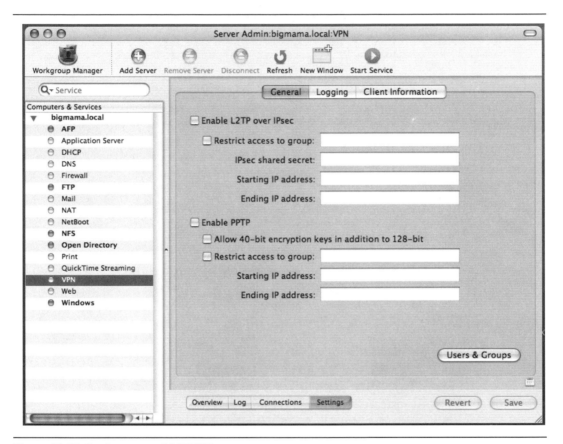

Figure 10.19 Setting up an OS X VPN

Should you choose to use OS X as a VPN server, you will get

- ◆ User authentication using MS-CHAP and IPSec (see Figure 10.20).
- ◆ Complete logging services (see Figure 10.21).
- ◆ Real-time information about connected clients (see Figure 10.22).

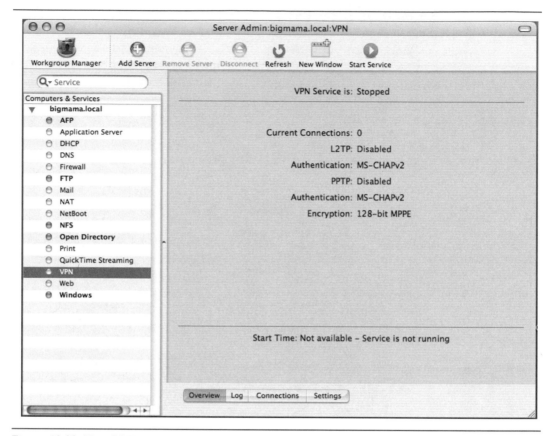

Figure 10.20 Mac OS X user authentication services

Setting Up a Mac OS X Client Connection

To set up the Mac OS X VPN client, a user works with the Internet Connect Application:

1. Launch Applications->Internet Connect.
2. Choose File->New VPN Connection.
3. Choose the type of VPN and click Continue (see Figure 10.23).
4. Enter the server address (domain name or IP address), the account name, and password (see Figure 10.24).

Figure 10.21 Configuring Mac OS X VPN logging

At this point, the connection is ready to use. The user can click Connect to begin using the VPN. However, the user can also create a client configuration from the Network preferences panel:

1. Open the System Preferences application.
2. Click on the Network icon to display the Network panel (see Figure 10.25).
3. If necessary, choose the Location for which the VPN configuration was created from the Location pop-up menu.
4. Highlight the VPN connection and click Connect.
5. Enter the connection information (see Figure 10.26) and click OK to begin the connection process.

Figure 10.22 Mac OS X Server VPN client information window

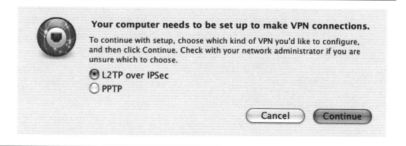

Figure 10.23 Choosing the type of VPN connection

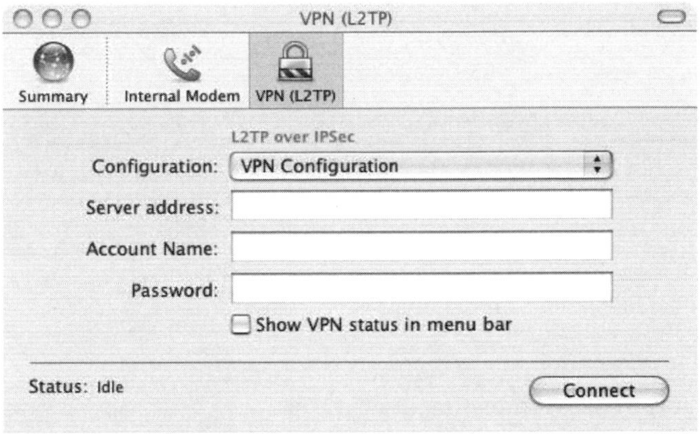

Figure 10.24 Specifying VPN connection information

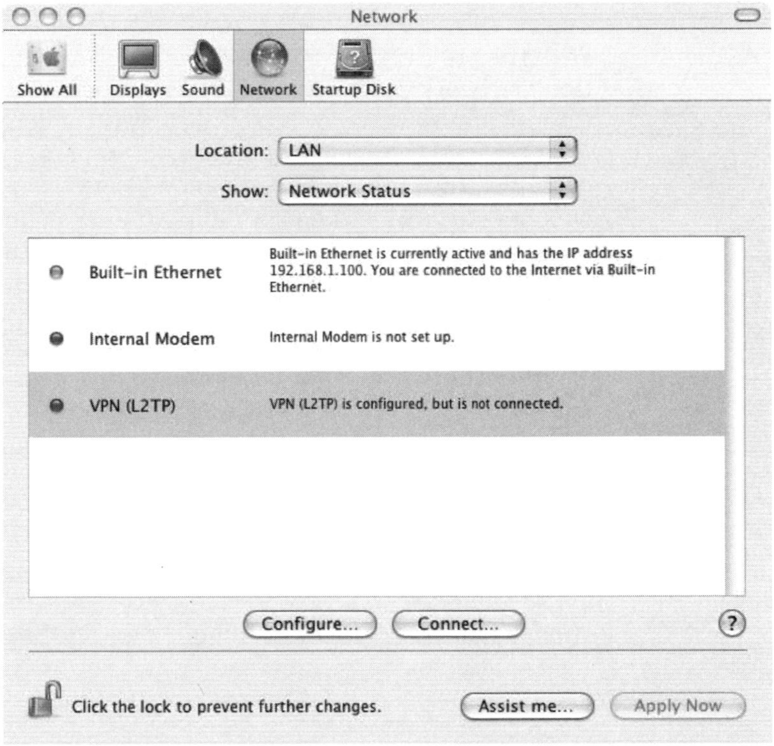

Figure 10.25 Choosing the network interface

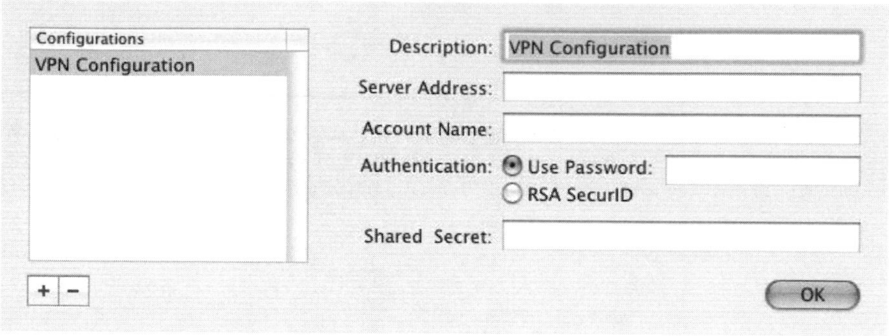

Figure 10.26 Connecting using a VPN

10.5 Summary

With the proliferation of mobile workers, remote access to an organization's network has become an essential part of data communications. In this chapter we have looked at the ways in which users access a network remotely and the security vulnerabilities presented by such access. For example, the traditional command line program used for remote access—`telnet`—sends its authentication information in the clear, making it easy for a system cracker to hijack the remote session or to initiate a man-in-the-middle attack. The alternative to `telnet` and the "r" remote access commands is to use `ssh`, the secure shell.

Another alternative for providing remote access is to use remote access software that gives remote users control over a computer on the local network. Users can use software on the computer and/or transfer files. Such software provides its own access controls that determine exactly what actions a remote user can perform.

To give remote users secure access to network resources over the Internet, you can set up a VPN. VPNs encrypt network traffic over an internet and may also provide user authentication and message integrity services.

Chapter 11: Wireless Security

In This Chapter

- ◆ Wireless standards
- ◆ Wireless network vulnerabilities
- ◆ Techniques for securing a wireless network

11.0 Introduction

As New York City was gearing up for the Republican National Convention at the end of August, 2004, people from Newbery Networks, Inc. performed a sample "war drive" around the site of the convention. (A war drive is an attempt to find unsecured wireless networks that a client computer can join without the knowledge of the operators of the network.) They took some wireless computing equipment and attempted to find wireless access points and to determine whether the networks they found were secure. The results were frightening.

The war drive found 7,000 wireless devices, 1,123 of which were within blocks of Madison Square Garden. They also discovered a network named "Wireless for Kerry"!

Of the 7,000 devices, 2,161 access points and 821 client machines were broadcasting unique SSIDs. Those 821 client machines therefore were looking for specific access points. A hacker could easily change the SSID on his or her access point to trick a client into connecting to it.

As a final test, the researchers set up a wireless honeypot, which appeared to be a Linksys access point. They discovered that a wireless device attempted to connect to it every 90 seconds.

> Note: For more details on this war drive, see Computerworld, September 6, 2004.

Wireless networks are very appealing: They're easy to install and allow users to connect from any location within range of an access point. Despite their flexibility, they are serious security risks if not handled carefully. In this chapter, we'll look at the provisions for security included in the wireless 802.11 standard, the risks inherent in that standard, and ways in which you can combat the problems.

Anecdote: Before we get into the meat of this chapter, another story about wireless insecurity is in order, given that wireless networks are so popular with home users. An IT professional was asked by someone at work how he connected to the Internet at home. "I don't know," he answered. "Maybe cable; maybe DSL. I just turn on my laptop and connect to one of my neighbor's wireless networks. I haven't needed my own Internet hookup." Uh oh.

Warning: It's easy to become distracted by the security problems that are unique to wireless networks. However, don't forget that the problems of wireless networks are *in addition* to all the other security vulnerabilities that we've discussed in this book. If you are responsible for networking in an organization with extremely sensitive data, you may want to think twice (and then think again) about the wisdom of installing a wireless network.

11.1 Wireless Standards

There are two basic types of wireless networking in use today. The first, the 802.11 group, is used to create networks that replace wired networks, connecting computers. The second, known as Bluetooth, was designed originally to connect wireless peripherals to a computer. However, Bluetooth can also be used to share files between devices over a very short distance.

11.1.1 802.11 Wireless Standards

Most of today's wireless networks are based on one of the 802.11 standards, which are summarized in Table 11.1. At the time this book was written, 802.11i, with its improved security features, had just been approved as a standard; products should be available at the time you are reading this book or very shortly thereafter.

Note: The 802.11x standards are known familiarly as Wi-Fi, short for Wireless Fidelity.

Standard	Characteristics	Comments
802.11a	Signals in 5 GHz radio band. 54 Mbps maximum throughput. Bandwidth shared by all users. Speed decreases with distance from access point.	Not widely used.
802.11b	Signals in 2.4 GHz radio band. 11 Mpbs maximum throughput. Speed decreases with distance from access point. Speed decreases as number of users goes up.	Security provided by WEP. Widely used.
802.11d	Supplement to 802.11b to support frequencies permitted by non-North American countries	
802.11e	Supplement to 802.11a, b, and g to add Quality of Service (QOS) support.	
802.11f	Intended to allow access points from different vendors to work with each other.	
802.11g	Signals in the 2.4 GHz radio band. 54 Mbps maximum throughput.	Major standard used in place of 802.11b. Provides backward compatibility with 802.11b devices but then slows down to 802.11b speed.
802.11h	Supplement to 802.11g to support European frequency regulations.	
802.11i	Supplement to 802.11a, b, and g that provides better security.	Adds strong encryption for security.

Table 11.1   The 802.11x standards

Standard	Characteristics	Comments
802.11n	New set of Physical and MAC layer protocols to provide speeds up to 100 Mbps.	At the time this book was published, 802.11n was still under development and not an accepted standard. However, a few "pre802.11n" devices were available.

Table 11.1 (continued) The 802.11x standards

Most of today's wireless networks are based on the 802.11b or 802.11g standards. Access points that support the faster 802.11g usually can also handle 802.11b. However, when 802.11b devices use an 802.11g access point, they force all traffic through the access point to slow to 802.11b speed.

11.1.2 Bluetooth

Bluetooth is a wireless technology designed to function over a short distance. As such, it is not intended to compete with 802.11, but to complement it. Bluetooth networks are generally not permanent, but *ad hoc*. In other words, they are established when needed and disassembled after a relatively short use. Bluetooth-enabled devices include keyboards and mice as well as handheld equipment such as cell phones and PDAs.

There is a single Bluetooth specification that includes Physical, Data Link, and Application layer protocols. Bluetooth's Physical layer requirements are summarized in Table 11.2.

> *Note: Short-distance networks created with Bluetooth are known as piconets. Piconets have a master-slave architecture, with the master device determining and controlling the frequency hopping characteristics of the network.*

Vendors that want to produce Bluetooth devices become members of the Bluetooth Special Interest Group. They can then submit their products for compatibility testing to the Bluetooth Qualification Program. The licensing for the Bluetooth standard—and permission to label a product as "Bluetooth"—requires certification by the Qualification Program.

Specification	Comments
Radio frequency	Band: Unlicensed ISM (Industrial, Scientific, and Medical) band Frequency: 2400–2483.5 MHz
Modulation	Gaussian frequency shift keying (GFSK)
Frequency Hopping Spread Spectrum	Hops at up to 1600 hops/sec Uses 79 channels with 1 MHz separation
Transmission power	Class 3: 1 mW (0dBm); range approximately 10 m Class 2: 2.5 mW (4dBm); range approximately 20 m Class 1: 100 mW (20dBm); range approximately 100 m
Link data rate	Maximum baseband data rate of 723.2 kb/s
Speech coding	64kb/s Continuously Variable Slope Delta Modification

Table 11.2   Bluetooth Physical layer specifications

11.1.3 The Forthcoming 802.16

The 802.11 standards cover wireless networks over relatively limited distances. A complementary set of standards—802.16, or *WiMAX*—are under development to provide wireless networks with a radius of as much as 50 km. The standards' major features include

- ♦ The ability to connect WiFi hotspots to the Internet.

- ♦ Shared data rates of up to 70 Mbps. (Theoretically, this can provide as many as 60 businesses with T1-level performance or more than 1,000 homes with 1 Mbps DSL connectivity.)

- ♦ Connection without line of sight to a base station.

- ♦ Interconnection with DSL, which will provide the last mile of connectivity to the home.

At the time this book was written, experimental WiMAX installations could be found in Seattle as well as two cities in China. More deployments and products were expected in 2005.

11.2 Wireless Network Vulnerabilities

Wireless networks are notorious for their security vulnerabilities. As you will see shortly, there are holes in 802.11b and 802.11g big enough to drive a cement truck through!

11.2.1 Signal Bleed and Insertion Attacks

The characteristic of radio frequency networks that makes them attractive in the first place—the ability of the signal to travel through walls—also makes them vulnerable to piggybacking by unauthorized users. The signal can bleed outside the area controlled by the organization running the network and unless secured, any users with compatible client equipment can insert themselves into the network and use it (an *insertion attack*). The unauthorized client may simply gain free Internet access or may be after something more sinister, such as access to corporate resources.

As well as war driving, miscreants looking for free Internet access have been known to walk (or even fly) to scan for unsecured, bleeding networks. They will then mark on the sidewalk (*war chalking*) to let others know that network access is available at that spot.

An aside: Warchalkers have used a set of symbols derived from hobo marks. The basic marks, as suggested by *http://www.blackgeltjones.com/warchalking/index2.html*, are:

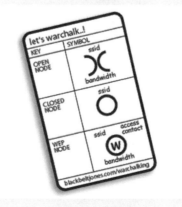

Unauthorized users using your wireless Internet connection instead of paying for their own connection steal bandwidth from authorized users, but cause few other problems. However, the problem is much more serious if a system cracker attaches an unauthorized access point to the network. Unauthorized access points can divert legitimate traffic, making it easy for system crackers to collect sensitive information, in particular, user names and passwords.

11.2.2 Signal Bleed and Interception Attacks

Wireless signal bleed makes it easy for a system cracker to receive the network signal (an *interception attack*) without disturbing network traffic. This is very similar to running a packet sniffing program on a wired network. However, to use a wireless sniffer, the system cracker must be physically near the network.

11.2.3 SSID Vulnerabilities

Service Set IDs (SSIDs) are identification words or phrases that access points broadcast to identify themselves. The problem is that the default SSIDs for access points from major manufacturers are well known (see Table 11.3). Even if a network administrator changes the SSID from the default, every client will use the same SSID to connect to the access point.

Vendor	SSID
Addtron	WLAN
Cisco	tsunami
Compaq	Compaq
Intel	intel
Linksys	linksys
Lucent	RoamAbout Default Network Name
3Com	101
Others	Default SSID
	Wireless

Table 11.3 Well-known SSIDs

Reality Check: You can change the SSID on an access point frequently, but like any shared password, the chances of it becoming known increase exponentially with the number of people who know it, especially if one of those "in the know" happens to be a former employee with a grudge. Attempts to secure something by keeping a shared "password" secure are doomed to failure.

With standards prior to 802.11i, SSIDs are not encrypted. Because they are transmitted in the clear, a system cracker can intercept one in a broadcast packet, even if it has been changed from the default. It is also fairly easy for a system cracker to try a brute force attack in an attempt to crack a changed SSID.

Probably the simplest way to avoid many SSID problems is to turn off the broadcasting of the SSIDs by access points. This essentially hides the wireless network from any client device that doesn't know the SSID of the access point to which it wants to connect.

11.2.4 Denial of Service Attacks

Wireless networks are very vulnerable to denial of service attacks. A system cracker can

- ◆ Perform any DoS attack to which wired networks are vulnerable.
- ◆ Jam the network's radio signal.
- ◆ Flood the network with illegitimate packets.

To prevent DoS attacks, you must prevent the system cracker from gaining access to the wireless network.

11.2.5 Battery Exhaustion Attacks

Bluetooth devices are subject to a type of attack that typically doesn't bother 802.11x equipped computers: *battery exhaustion attacks*. Most Bluetooth devices go into a power saving mode when not in use. If an attacker can prevent the device from doing so, then the device will drain its battery and become unavailable to its user.

11.3 Wireless Security Provisions

Although wireless networks are notoriously unsecure, the standards prior to 802.11i aren't necessarily bereft of security provisions. The problem is that the early security provisions aren't particularly effective. Bluetooth, which is designed for ad hoc networks, presents different challenges and solutions.

11.3.1 802.11x Security

The 802.11b standard introduced *Wired Equivalency Privacy* (WEP), which provides for encryption of data traffic and for the assurance of message integrity (i.e., that the message isn't changed during transmission).

WEP

WEP uses an encryption method called RC4. By encrypting the message payload it ensures message privacy; by adding what is known as a *checksum* it ensures message integrity. There is nothing intrinsically wrong with the RC4 algorithm, but WEP uses it poorly. As a result, WEP presents some significant weaknesses:

♦ The RC4 algorithm relies on a secret cryptographic key. However, in many cases all wireless access points and clients use the same key.

♦ The cryptographic key used by WEP is only 40 bits in length and rarely changes. WEP also uses a 24-bit IV (*initialization vector*), which changes every transmission. Even if a network changes the IV for each conversation, a moderately busy network will end up recycling and reusing IVs about every five hours. Whenever keys are reused (or not changed, in the case of the encryption key), a system cracker has the opportunity to collect multiple packets using the same key, making extracting the message content from the packet much easier.

♦ WEP encrypts only data. It doesn't encrypt the initialization of a connection, including client authorization information. The IV is also sent in the clear with every packet.

◆ Access points ship with WEP turned off. Network administrators need to turn it on to get any benefit at all.

◆ WEP can be difficult to configure because the key must be entered identically into every system. Therefore, many users don't bother to turn it on.

More on WEP: As mentioned earlier, WEP uses an encryption key that may be used by multiple clients and that doesn't change frequently. Here is how it works: The key and the IV are used as input to the RC4 algorithm to generate a pseudorandom stream, which is used as the key stream for the stream cypher (*Vernam cypher*) for the data. The problem is that the same input to the RC4 algorithm produces the same Vernam cypher key stream. Therefore, as the IVs are reused and combined with the unchanging encryption key, all a cracker needs to do is obtain an unencrypted message and its encrypted version. It isn't too hard to deduce the key stream and then use it to decrypt all messages using the same IV. Even without an unencrypted message, a cracker can perform a logical XOR operation on two messages encrypted with the same IV to produce a weakly encrypted message that is easier to crack.

Note: The RC4 algorithm and checksums are discussed in depth in Chapter 12.

802.11i Security and WPA

The 802.11i standard is not a physical layer standard, such as a, b, and g, but instead was designed to provide security for existing wireless technologies. However, because it took so long to develop 802.11i, an alternative security solution, which is compatible with 802.11i—*WiFi Protected Access* (WPA)—also emerged.

WPA.   WPA replaces WEP with stronger encryption, including a 48-bit IV. It also can operate in two modes. The first requires preshared keys—such as passwords—between an access point and a client. The second mode allows the use of external authentication services, such as RADIUS.

WPA's encryption uses the *Temporal Key Integrity Protocol* (TKIP). Its major provisions include a method for changing the encryption key with each packet sent during a communications session, making it much more difficult for a system cracker to decipher a message, even if he or she should intercept all packets from a single session.

WPA includes secure user authentication, something missing from WEP. As noted earlier, the WPA provisions allow access points to use a authentication server (for example, RADIUS) and also allow clients to authenticate access points. This can significantly reduce the chances that clients will connect to an unauthorized access point that has been inserted into a wireless network. If a network is too small to support an external authorization server, then WPA operates in its preshared key mode.

WPA can be added to most access points and client adapters that support WEP through a software upgrade.

802.11i on Top of WPA.

802.11i includes the WPA encryption methods, but in addition provides *Robust Security Network* (RSN), a procedure that allows access points and clients to determine which type of encryption will be used during a communications session. The beauty of this approach is that encryption methods can be updated as new algorithms are developed.

802.11i also mandates the use of *Advanced Encryption Standard* (AES) to provide even stronger encryption. Unfortunately, AES can't be added to existing access points with simply a software upgrade, as can WPA; it requires changes to the hardware, although most wireless equipment manufactured after 2002 is compatible with 802.11i.

> *Note: The U.S. government has endorsed AES as its primary encryption method, replacing the original Data Encryption Standard (DES). AES and DES are covered in more depth in Chapter 12.*

> *Note: 802.11i is known familiarly as WPA2.*

801.11 Authentication

Wireless standards provide protocols for authenticating wireless clients to access points. In addition to what is included in 802.11, there are some widely used proprietary protocols.

EAP.   The original 802.11 standard includes the *Extensible Authentication Protocol* (EAP) for authenticating wireless clients. This protocol was originally designed for PPP authentication but adapts well to wireless use because the process of adding a client to a wireless network is similar to dialing in to a network: The communicating devices must establish a connection and then authenticate the remote user.

EAP handles authentication after the communication channel has been established. Once the channel is in place, authentication takes place in the following way:

1. The authenticator—in the case of a wireless network, the access point—sends one or more authentication request packets to the device that is requesting authentication. The request packets may use one-time passwords, CHAP authentication, and so on. Each request packet uses a Type field to indicate the type of authentication requested.
2. The device requesting authentication responds to each request packet.
3. The authenticator evaluates each response packet.
4. The authenticator signals the result of the authentication process by sending a Success or Failure packet to the device requesting authentication.

The problem with EAP is that the standard does not include any provision for encrypting the authentication information.

Cisco's LEAP/PEAP Authentication.   As mentioned earlier, some wireless equipment manufacturers have developed proprietary protocols for authenticating wireless clients. One of the most widely used protocols—*Lightweight Extensible Authentication Protocol* (LEAP)—and its successor—*Protected Extensible Authentication Protocol* (PEAP)—were developed by Cisco for use on its Aironet wireless access points. (Microsoft and RSA Security were also involved in the development of PEAP.)

LEAP added the delivery of a one-time session encryption key to the EAP authentication mechanism. The intent was to make WEP stronger by supplying a different encryption key for each connection to the network.

PEAP, the version in use today, encrypts the authentication exchange using *Transport Layer Security (*TLS), which sets up an encrypted tunnel between two hosts. Once the encrypted tunnel is established, PEAP can use a variety of existing authentication methods such as one-time passwords and MS-CHAP. PEAP can also exchange authentication information with RADIUS servers.

Note: PEAP is supported only for Windows 2000, XP, and CE.

11.3.2 Bluetooth Security

Bluetooth's security is provided by the Data Link layer, which uses four pieces of information:

- ◆ Bluetooth address (BD_ADDR), a 48-bit address unique to each Bluetooth device
- ◆ Private authentication key, a 128–bit random number used in the authentication process
- ◆ Private encryption key, an 8–128 bit encryption key
- ◆ Random number (RAND), a 128-bit random or pseudo-random number generated by the device that changes frequently

Each device also has a PIN (personal identification number) that may need to be entered by users, either when the device is attempting to make a connection or when it is attempting to use a specific application.

The security of any given communication uses one of three modes:

- ◆ Mode 1: nonsecure (no encryption)
- ◆ Mode 2: service-level security (Security begins after the communication channel is created; all traffic addressed to specific devices is encrypted, but broadcast traffic is not encrypted.)
- ◆ Mode 3: link-level security (Security begins before the communication is created; all traffic is encrypted.)

Assuming that Bluetooth devices are communicating in either Mode 2 or Mode 3, then the security is handled by the *link key*, a 128-bit random number. It may be a session key (used just for the current communications session) or a semipermanent key (used repeatedly to authenticate the same devices). Bluetooth may also employ temporary keys, which are generated for one-to-many transmissions.

Assuming that two devices have not communicated in the past, a session begins with the creation of an initialization key, which is derived from the PIN, Bluetooth address of the device initiating the session, and the 128-bit random number. This key is used for the generation and exchange of the link key and is discarded once the link key is in place.

The link key is then combined with a 96-bit Ciphering Offset Number and the 128-bit random number to create the encryption key. Each time the Bluetooth devices enter Mode 2 or Mode 3 security, the devices generate a new encryption key. The encryption key is used to encrypt packet payloads.

The Bluetooth security provisions have several limitations:

♦ The encryption key varies in length from 8 to 128 bits. Even a 128-bit key isn't particularly invulnerable given today's computing power.

♦ Having to enter PINs into all communicating devices is inconvenient at best, especially since the PIN may need to be entered twice into each device.

♦ When working in Mode 2, the information used to generate the initialization key is sent through the air, in the clear, making the initialization key inherently insecure.

♦ No encryption can protect a Bluetooth device from a battery exhaustion attack.

11.4 Hands On: Securing Your 802.11x Wireless Network

If what you have read in this chapter makes you think that it's totally impossible to have a secure wireless network, don't panic. There are things you can do, using available technology, to mitigate much of the risk. For the most part, you need to change default settings on your access points, because they ship with their security features disabled.

If you have 802.11b equipment, do the following:

♦ To limit signal bleed, use directional antennas on access points. Whenever possible, turn down the signal strength on access points.

♦ Use WEP. Yes, it does send initialization information in the clear, but it can at least protect your data to some extent. It's certainly better than no encryption at all.

♦ Look at where your access points are located. If possible, place them toward the inside of the building rather than near windows or exterior walls. This will help cut down on the amount of the signal that escapes your premises.

♦ Change the default SSID of your access points. Keep in mind that an SSID is a value that client devices will use to authorize themselves to the access point, and therefore the SSID should adhere to the rules for strong passwords.

♦ Configure your access points so that they accept only the SSID that you create. By default, many access points will accept any SSID.

♦ If your access point supports MAC address filtering, turn it on. This allows you to register the MAC addresses of client devices with the access point. The access point will then accept only those clients whose MAC addresses it recognizes.

Regardless of the type of wireless network you have, there are additional techniques that can help you keep it secure:

♦ Audit the network regularly for unauthorized access points. Keep in mind that external system crackers aren't the only ones who might install access points of which you aren't aware. A department that wants extra mobility might purchase an access point and install it to extend the range of the existing network, for example.

♦ DHCP is convenient, but it also makes it easy for an unauthorized client device to obtain an IP address. If you turn off

DHCP and assign static IP addresses to client devices, it becomes much harder for a war driver to piggyback off your network.

♦ Consider creating a honeypot access point, or multiple honeypot access points, to confuse potential system crackers. Allow the honeypots to bleed outside the building so that they will be the first thing that system crackers encounter.

Note: If you want to experiment with 53,000 honeypots, try the open source software-only version of FakeAP, found at http://www.blackalchemy.to/Projects/fakeap/fake-ap.html.

♦ Create a DMZ for wireless devices, isolating access points (and their wireless clients) from the wired internal network, such as the architecture in Figure 11.1. Place the access points behind an exterior firewall. Place a second firewall between the access points and the internal wired network. This will allow the wireless clients to access the Internet with relative freedom, but restrict what they can do with the internal network. In fact, to access the internal network, wireless clients will need to use a VPN. You can also place additional checks for external attacks (for example, an IDS) in the DMZ, giving you a chance to catch such attacks before they reach the internal network. But most importantly, anyone piggybacking off the wireless signal will gain access to the network's WAN connection, but not to the internal network, further protecting it from cracking attempts.

11.5 Summary

This chapter covers the additional security risks introduced with a wireless network. The same signals that travel through walls to make it easy to set up a wireless network also make it easy for the signal to pass through exterior walls so that anyone with compatible equipment can insert a device into the network stream.

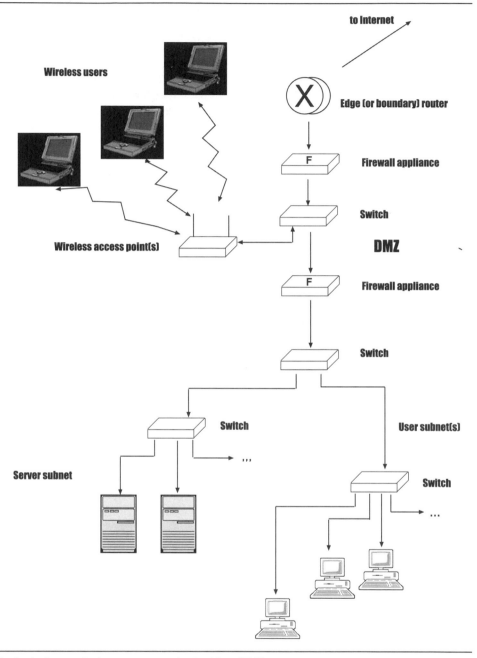

Figure 11.1   Isolating a wireless access point inside a DMZ

The additional security risks presented by wireless networks include:

- ◆ Insertion attacks, in which a system cracker inserts an access point or client into a network for the purpose of inserting unauthorized packets into the data stream.

- ◆ Interception attacks, in which a system cracker intercepts message traffic. The sniffed packets then can be subjected to analysis that will break weak encryption keys.

Wireless networks are governed by the 802.11x family of standards. The hardware standards—a, b, and g—include WEP encryption for security. However, WEP does not support user authentication and uses a short encryption key that can be easily cracked. The 802.11i protocol was ratified in 2004 to extend the physical standards by adding strong encryption and user authentication, both using an external authentication server and a preshared key. It includes WPA, which was used as an interim security standard while 802.11i was being ratified, and AES, both strong encryption methods.

Chapter 12: Encryption

In This Chapter

- ◆ Pros and cons of data encryption
- ◆ Single key encryption
- ◆ Two-key encryption
- ◆ Combining single and two-key encryption
- ◆ Message integrity
- ◆ Digital certificates
- ◆ PKI

12.0 Introduction

Encryption is a method of changing a message so that its content isn't intelligible to a casual viewer. Using something that only the sender and receiver know, the message is turned from readable to nonsense before it is sent and restored to readable form when it is received. Encryption is the primary technique for protecting the content of a data communications message while it is traveling outside the local network on which it originated. Encryption can also be used to protect data stored on a hard disk.

In this chapter we'll begin by looking and the pros and cons of encryption and then turn to encryption methods. We'll also look at techniques that aren't precisely encryption, but ensure message integrity (ensure that a message hasn't been modified during transmission) and at techniques for ensuring message authenticity (that a message actually came from the source from which it appears to have come). Finally, we'll look at *public key infrastructure* (PKI), the technology resources needed to manage an encryption program.

12.1 To Encrypt or Not to Encrypt

Right now, encryption is the best technique we have for ensuring the privacy of a message when it is outside our local network. However, it's not a perfect answer:

- ◆ Encrypting and decrypting messages consumes a lot of computing power, slowing down data communications.

- ◆ Negotiating the type of encryption to be used during a communications session lengthens the time needed to set up the session.

- ◆ Using encryption and digital certificates for authentication requires the development and maintenance of a PKI, which can be costly for a small organization.

Note: Many small organizations can use the open-source PGP (Pretty Good Privacy) to provide encryption support on a limited scale, without needing to maintain a full PKI

*infrastructure. PGP works well in small implementations,
but doesn't scale well.*

♦ You can't process data in encrypted form; it must be decrypted. If you use encryption to protect data stored on your servers, for example, it must be decrypted every time a user needs to search for or display data. This can significantly increase processing time.

♦ The secret keys for many well-known encryption algorithms can be cracked by today's high-end computers. Therefore, no encryption method should be considered totally uncrackable, especially when the problem is distributed among Internet users whose computers run a brute force attack during idle periods.

That being said, encryption and accompanying techniques are still the best we have for securing messages when they leave our networks and for protecting data stored on local hard drives. Like viruses and virus detection software developers, there is an ever escalating war between the developers of cryptographic schemes and those who crack them. The crackers figure out an efficient way to break a code and the developers make the code harder to crack.

12.2 Single Key Encryption Schemes

The algorithmically simplest type of encryption uses a single shared key to encrypt and decrypt a message. Because there is only one key, it must be known to both the sender and receiver. The result is encryption that is conceptually simple, but possibly difficult to manage.

> *Note: Because the key used by both sender and receiver is the same, single key encryption keys are also commonly known as symmetric keys.*

12.2.1 Substitution Cyphers

Single key encryption methods are essentially *substitution cyphers*, where one character is substituted for another based on a transformation that occurs when a key is applied to the original message; the same key and process is used to decrypt the message. When one character is substituted for another, we call it a *stream cypher*; when a longer key is applied to a group of characters, we call it a *block cypher*. Most of the substitution cyphers in use today are block cyphers because they are more secure than stream cyphers.

As a primitive example, let's encrypt the following phrase (the *plaintext*):

ENCRYPTION IS FUN

The algorithm we'll use is as follows:

1. Pick an encryption key. For our example, we'll use CODE.
2. Assign a numeric value to each character in the *alphabet*. In this case, the alphabet is all uppercase characters and the space. The numbers we'll use represent a character's ordinal position in alphabetical order; the space will be 0. (See Table 12.1.)

Letter	Code	Letter	Code
space	0	M	13
A	1	N	14
B	2	O	15
C	3	P	16
D	4	Q	17
E	5	R	18
F	6	S	19
G	7	T	20
H	8	U	21
I	9	V	22
J	10	W	23
K	11	X	24
L	12	Y	25
		Z	26

Table 12.1 Encoding scheme for the sample substitution cypher

3. Place the key directly underneath each character in the text. Repeat the key as necessary.

```
ENCRYPTION IS FUN
CODECODECODECODEC
```

4. Replace each character by its number.

```
05 14 03 18 25 16 20 09 15 14 00 09 19 00 06 21 14
03 15 04 05 03 15 04 05 03 15 04 05 03 15 04 05 03
```

5. Add the value of each letter in the message to the value of its corresponding letter in the key. Divide by the number of characters in the alphabet—in this example, 27—and keep the remainder. (This is modulo division.)

```
08 02 07 23 01 04 24 14 18 02 04 14 22 15 10 26 17
```

6. Substitute the character that corresponds to the remainder to generate the final encrypted message (the *cyphertext*).

```
HBGWADXNRBDNVOJZQ
```

The cyphertext is then transmitted. As you can see, the cyphertext looks like unintelligible nonsense. However, a short key that is repeated often is actually quite easy to crack. There are two things you can do to make the cypher more secure: Use a longer key and change the key each time it is applied.

In real-world single-key encryption schemes, the keys are made up of a random string of bits. Strong encryption uses 128-bit keys; shorter keys can be broken fairly easily by existing software.

The most secure single key encryption algorithms use a starting key (often called an *initialization vector*) that is changed each time the key is repeated. We could, for example, rotate the letters in the key. The encryption of the sample string we have been using would then become:

```
ENCRYPTION IS FUN
CODEODECDECOECODC
```

```
05 14 03 18 25 16 20 09 15 14 00 09 19 00 06 21 14
03 15 04 05 15 04 05 03 04 05 03 15 05 03 15 04 03
```

```
08 02 07 23 13 20 25 12 19 19 03 24 24 03 21 25 17
```

```
HBGWMTYLSSCXXCUYQ
```

This cyphertext will be more difficult to crack because a system cracker must not only discover the key, but also the algorithm used to transform the key.

12.2.2 Single-Key Encryption Algorithms

There are several single-key encryption methods that are, or have been, widely accepted and used by the data communications community. They differ from the simple example you just saw primarily in the way keys are generated. Most use key transformations to increase the difficulty of cracking the encryption.

Data Encryption Standard (DES)

The *Data Encryption Standard* (DES) was the U.S. government's first successful attempt at standardizing the encryption used to communicate with government agencies. It was formally adopted as a *Federal Information Processing Standard* (FIPS) in 1976. However, its short key length has made it relatively easy to crack with today's computing power (less than 24 hours), and although you may find it still in use commercially, it has been replaced for government use by AES (discussed in a following section).

DES works much like the second version of the sample substitution cypher presented earlier in this chapter. It takes a fixed-length key and applies it to plaintext to produce cyphertext. Each time the key is used, it is changed (a "permutation").

The DES key is 64 bits in length, although only 56 bits actually are used in the encryption; the remainder are parity bits used for error checking. The plaintext is modified in 64-bit chunks. Each time a key is used, it is exclusive-ORd (XORd) with the plaintext. (See the truth table in Table 12.2.)

Encrypting a single 64-bit block of plaintext with DES is not as simple as our example, however. It involves 16 rounds of plaintext transformations, including breaking the plaintext into two 32-bit chunks that are swapped repeatedly during the rounds. Each round also expands the 32-bit block to 48 bits, which are then XORd with a 48-bit subkey. The subkey has been generated by a "key schedule," an algorithm that creates

XOR	0	1
0	0	1
1	1	0

Table 12.2 The XOR logical operation truth table

the 48-bit subkeys based on the original 56-bit key. After XORing with the subkey, the 48-bit plaintext block is divided into 6-bit chunks (S-boxes), which then output 4-bit blocks, reducing the overall plaintext block back to its original 32-bits. (The security of DES rests with the transformation that occurs in the S-blocks.)

Decryption is similar to encryption with the exception that the key transformations must be generated and applied in the reverse order.

Because of its computational complexity, DES was often implemented in hardware.

Triple DES

The vulnerabilities in DES became very well known. Therefore, cryptographers developed an interim version, for use until another encryption method was adopted, called *Triple DES*. Triple DES uses a 192-bit key, three times the length of the 64-bit DES key. The algorithm repeats the DES encryption process three times, each time using a different 64 bits of the 192-bit key.

Because Triple DES is essentially DES performed three times, it is more than three times harder to crack. It is also three times slower to implement and therefore was never considered as a permanent encryption standard.

Advanced Encryption Standard (AES)

The *Advanced Encryption Standard* (AES) was developed in 1998 by Vincent Rijmen and Joan Daemen from their proprietary encryption scheme named Rijndael. (AES uses the same algorithms as Rijndael, but requires fixed key and plaintext block sizes; Rijndael can handle keys and block sizes in varying multiples of 32 bits between 128 and 256 bits.)

AES is similar to DES in that it uses key transformations for security. However, its keys are longer—128, 192, or 256 bits—and it works on 128-bit blocks of plaintext. It also uses S-boxes to output chunks of cyphertext through 10, 12, or 14 rounds of key transformations. (The number of rounds corresponds to the length of the key.)

> *Note: AES was adopted by the U.S. government as a replacement for DES in 2004. It is certified for use in encrypting top secret information and all classifications below that.*

As of the time this book was written, AES had not been broken.

Reality Check What would it take to break one of today's block substitution cyphers? A brute force attack to break a 100-bit key would be tough even for NSA. Brute force key breaking requires twice the effort for every additional bit in the key. For example, if it takes a day to break a 56-bit DES key with today's computing power, it would take about three years to break a 66-bit key, or 3000 years to break a 76-bit key. Why, then, use longer keys? Because computers are becoming exponentially more powerful, and the time may come when it *is* practical to break longer keys in a reasonable amount of time.

RC4

RC4—the type of encryption used by SSL, WEP, and WPA—is a symmetric key method that was developed by Ron Rivest in 1987. Because RC4 was developed by an employee of a commercial firm, the algorithm was considered proprietary. However, in 1994 the details appeared first on an Internet mailing list and were then posted to an Internet newsgroup. Currently there are proprietary implementations of RC4 as well as unauthorized—but legal—implementations developed from the publicly released information.

> *Note: Ron Rivest was working for RSA Security when he developed the RC4 algorithm. The founders of RSA, currently a major security company, are responsible for the development of public key encryption, the two-key encryption method described later in this chapter.*

Encryption with RC4 begins by initializing a random number generator with the secret key using the algorithm in Figure 12.1. (The code in this example is C or C++ (and quite close to Java), with some liberties taken to imply library functions that swap array values and perform the XOR operation.) The key can be 64, 128, or 256 bytes. (Longer keys make the encryption more difficult to crack, but also increase the computations required to encrypt and decrypt, slowing down processing.)

```
#define KEY_LEN 256
int s[256];
short key[KEY_LEN]; // the secret key
int j = 0;
for (int i = 0; i <= 255; i++)
    s[i] = i;
for (int i = 0; i <= 255; i++)
{
    j = (j + s[i] + key[i % KEY_LEN]) % 256;
    swap (s[i], s[j])
}
```

Figure 12.1 Initializing the RC4 random number generator

The encryption process uses the XOR logical operation: Each byte in the plaintext is XORd with a byte from the array generated during the initialization step, as in Figure 12.2. Decryption uses exactly the same algorithm.

```
void encrypt (short [] plaintext)
{
    int i = 0, j = 0, k;
    for (idx = 0; idx <= sizeof (plaintext); idx++)
    {
        i = ++i % 256;
        j = ++j % 256;
        swap (s[i], s[j]);
        k = s[(s[i] + s[j]) % 256);
        plaintext[idx] = k xor plaintext[idx];
    }
}
```

Figure 12.2 Encrypting plaintext using RC4

RC4 is fast enough and simple enough to be implemented in software, one of the reasons why it is used so widely.

12.2.3 Key Management Problems

The biggest problem with a single-key encryption scheme is that the secret key needs to be shared. Given that each party involved in the communication needs to know the key, what do you do when you have a large number of correspondents? If you use the same encryption key for all communication partners, then the chances that the key will remain secure are greatly diminished. However, if you have a different key for each party, then how do you keep track of all those keys?

Given that the security of a single-key encryption system rests on the inability of a system cracker to discern the starting key, key management becomes a major issue when you are administering a single-key system. How can you securely exchange keys? If you use the same key for more than one message, how can you ensure its security? The development of a solution has taken an interesting route: Initially, a two-key encryption scheme was proposed as an alternative to the single-key. As you will see in the next two sections of this chapter, performance problems with the two-key encryption have led to the solution in use today, which combines both single- and two-key methods.

Reality Check: During the 1980s, there was a move afoot by the U.S. Congress to get government involved in key management. The bill—which never made it out of Congress—specified that all organizations exchanging encrypted messages with the U.S. government should use an encryption method known as Clipper. The encryption keys would then be stored ("escrowed") by an agency hired by the government. If there was some need to instantly decrypt a message, a government agency could get a court order to retrieve the keys from escrow. This bill frightened many organizations; posters and ads saying "Sink the Clipper Chip" appeared. Most businesses were quite relieved when the bill died in Congress. When DES was approved as an encryption standard, it did *not* include a key escrow provision.

12.3 Two-Key Encryption Schemes

The serious key management issues surrounding symmetric key encryption methods prompted the development of an encryption method that didn't require the presharing of a secret key. Three researchers—Ronald

L. Rivest, Adi Shamir, and Leonard Adleman—proposed *public key encryption* (PKE) in 1977.

Note: The developers of public key encryption are the source of the acronym RSA, the name of their company that currently acts as one of the major issuers of digital certificates.

Note: PKE is sometimes also called asymmetric key encryption to differentiate it from symmetric key encryption.

The basic idea behind PKE is that you have different encryption and decryption keys. You publish the encryption key freely so that anyone can encrypt messages to send to you. However, your secret decryption key is the only key that can decrypt the message.

12.3.1 The Mathematics of Public Key Encryption

Public key encryption is mathematically fairly simple. Before you encrypt anything, you must produce your keys:

1. Take two very large prime numbers, p and q, and multiply them together, generating the quantity r. This will be the first part of the public encryption key.

   Note: For the example in this book, we're going to be using very small numbers. In practice, however, p and q are numbers on the order of 1024 bits, and their product is therefore quite large.

```
p = 3
q = 11
r = 3 * 11 = 33
```

2. Choose another number, e, that is "relatively prime" to (in other words, has no common factors with) $(p-1)(q-1)$, is greater than 1, and is less than $p * q$. Generally, any prime number larger than p and q will do the trick. This will become the other part of the public encryption key.

```
e = 13
```

3.   Compute the secret decryption key so that it is the multiplicative inverse of e. In other words, so that it satisfies the equation:

```
(d * e) % (p-1)(q-1) = 1
```

In our particular example, the computation would be

```
d * 13 % (2)(10) = 1
d = 7
```

4.   Publish r and e as the public key; keep d secret.

To encrypt, use the formula

```
C = T ^ e % r
```

where T is the plaintext character or bit-string to be encrypted and C is the cyphertext result.

For example, if we want to encrypt 16, then the math would be:

```
C = 16 ^ 13 % 33
C = 4503599627370496 % 33
C = 4
```

To decrypt the cyphertext, the formula is the same, but uses the decryption key:

```
T = C ^ d % r
```

In our example, it would be

```
T = 4 ^ 7 % 33
T = 16384 % 33
T = 16
```

Notice how large the numbers get to be in this simple example, especially when performing the exponentiation. Imagine that you are using real bytes (for example, ASCII codes); the numbers become astronomical. The result is that PKE takes a lot of computing power and is quite slow to perform.

How secure is PKE? Relatively secure. Its secrecy resides in the inability of today's computers to factor r into p and q in a reasonable amount of time. How big is a public key? As an example, take a look at Figure 12.3, a public key generated by PGP. This is an ASCII text version of the numeric key. In other words, each byte in the key is represented by a character. The actual key length in bits therefore is the number of characters multiplied by eight.

```
-----BEGIN PGP PUBLIC KEY BLOCK-----
Version: PGP 8.1 - not licensed for commercial use: www.pgp.com

mQGiBEHZUgARBADATTEOIoKHYgBhkWjIKtlKYOO2QuetgV3tf5FgOduGXDTRZaFj
1dHswjW3M2y1YMTGQxWbGcrFgGEufX2xe4BL247Yb15NO9e3V8Caz4eJKGenehxE
IMqdhVA6TzOHuFjbChTVNYX6Io7Z1s1EdWwpXusjbze1trQlmgOYdF2Z9QCg/OFg
XHEg8cgWKuOOX4Yu+nAOaXUD/A1NwTFjEeMrzrALumk1bcs5OEdyUw/2YrJnOZf9
TtlpWADpFpo7YeBwCc1Qdxa7iV271rfjA6UyXylrVZMn5C38fourNW/rsbOWx7XZ
1NO44kXdOGggsuM8VZ+fOWJFkiU3wsZCcgokRAaFV7wbucxJHnPAzNPBllI9dPiV
9PE3BACJYtTvPTwQrWaYZ433DjGEJoUbqsXOKEaGcVxZL3YJ76ez8U7jO3xa1/A1
7LGW///qHPs43oplD3C91mSZACzOYDkTgFh1NdJa4a/Yoq1P5rSGHJ+N1YLibzcC
KY3UPeclM5CFNcjlKRNjnifP3NSabSR91e/COLV4OzzoErVv8rQnSmFuIEwuIEhh
cnJpbmdOb24gPGljb21wdXRlQG1hcmlzdC5lZU+iQBdBBARAgAdBQJB2VIABwsJ
CAcDAgoCGQQEFGwMAAAAFHgEAAAAACgkQRHhEIW/F7boaFQCfbUY6fdsJT3Q8X1vA
1SFLKF4y6rOAnOZ+Tt+6os5W7MgwGu2OxCm78NsJuQINBEHZUgAQCAD2Qle3CH8I
F3KiutapQvMF6PlTETlPtvFuuUs4INoBp1ajFOmPQFXzOAfGyOOplK33TGSGSfgM
g71l6RfUodNQ+PVZX9x2Uk89PY3bzpnhV5JZzf24rnRPxfx2vIPFRzBhznzJZv8V
+bv9kV7HAarTW56NoKVyOtQa8L9GAFgr5fSI/VhOSdvNILSd5JEHNmszbDgNRROP
fIizHHxbLY7288kjwEPwpVsYjY67VYy4XTjTNP18F1dDoxOYbN4zISy1Kv884bEp
QBgRjXyEpwpy1obEAxnIByl6ypUM2Zafq9AKUJsCRtMIPWakXUGfnHy9iUsiGSa6
q6Jew1XpMgs7AAICB/95ypZFNCpLcXqPijsXkTLtZF+u+g2OyazeN+BSt131XegI
LdVDgzi9pcXZWVxz5aaElG/OTUOYevzKB9WK6I3hVjpU+sFyrBirlct/2qnG5HJu
UEftJgCWjNOOTRuSWMMcpRJoQvbqLfaokwpqCPyISRiJBlUB+SP3v8GPZ51caIuo
rfb/54m1tgjxS1hsT+e3slAhIWzemWBtcrhqOmCgNwdqm4mOgI/rXeO8R/KFd83K
uylK4mjySXfVUW+at41eM79OUTL92ZRRDEZKI17vWMu7D3P3nGhTu+c5CqlDdPLX
2opXjted/2Cz1xAmUQ3ibyx8TSpC3/m4u5CjT9lGiQBMBBgRAgAMBQJB2VIABRsM
AAAAAoJEER4RCFvxe265qoAoI/8oEWcuDOSrQaos+XWioyruaQBAKDwlmgjqUYl
3hjWsO3wK/2vL8cWLw==
=p8kw
-----END PGP PUBLIC KEY BLOCK-----
```

Figure 12.3   A public key generated by PGP

Note: For more information on PGP, see the Hands-On section of this chapter, beginning on page 301.

Because of the long keys, the time it takes to perform encryption and decryption has meant that PKE isn't suitable for encrypting large amounts of traffic. The workable solution has been to combine single- and two-key encryption.

12.4 Combining Single- and Two-Key Encryption

Most encrypted transmissions today use a combination of single- and two-key encryption. The process works as follows:

1. The sender and receiver negotiate encryption methods.
2. Each generates a private symmetric encryption key (a *session key*). This key will be used to encrypt and decrypt messages for the current communications session only.
3. The sender and receiver encrypt the session key using PKE and send the session keys to each other.
4. The remainder of messages in the session are encrypted using the symmetric key.

This combination of the two types of encryption provides solutions to most of the problems we've noted earlier in this chapter. PKE, which is generally considered to be the most secure and is the slowest encryption method, is used to encrypt only a small amount of data. The session keys are therefore exchanged securely, alleviating key management issues. Because the symmetric keys are used only for a single session, it is highly unlikely that a system cracker would have time to intercept enough packets to determine the key before the session ended.

12.5 Ensuring Message Integrity

Encryption ensures message privacy, preventing unauthorized people from viewing the content of a message. It does not, however, ensure *message integrity*, preventing someone from changing the message while it is in transit.

One widely used solution is to create a *message digest*, or *digital signature*, a compressed transformation of the message that has the property that a small change in the input (the message) produces a large change in the output (the message digest). The message digest is computed as the message is assembled for transmission and attached to the message itself. The recipient then recomputes the message digest and compares it to what was received. If the two digests don't match, then the message was altered during transmission.

Reality Check: Even if the sent and received message digests don't match, it doesn't necessarily mean that someone tampered with the message. It could very well be that the message was damaged in transmit and some bits were altered. The message digest, therefore, serves as an error checking mechanism as well as ensuring message integrity.

Most message digests are created using a process called *hashing*, which takes an input string and puts it through a predefined transformation. The output is a shorter string of some fixed length. In the case of message digests, the output of the most widely used algorithms is between 128 and 160 bits.

For example, if we take the string

```
Here is a test string that is longer than the output string and we
    can see the result of an MD5 hash.
```

and use the MD5 algorithm to create a digest, the result—expressed as a hexadecimal value—is

```
99b7db6c4d4f16214caabf5c2ce42277
```

Now, let's change one character in the input string, replacing the "s" in "test" with an "n":

```
Here is a tent string that is longer than the output string and we
    can see the result of an MD5 hash.
```

As you can see, the resulting message digest is quite different:

```
7bf3c56f2032908b107316a82b801a7f
```

> *Note: The original proposal for the MD5 message digest algorithm indicates that only once in $2 \wedge 64$ digest computations would it be likely that two different messages would produce the same message digest (a "collision"). However, on average you would need to generate $2 \wedge 127$ hashes before a collision would occur.*

Good hashing algorithms are *one-way*, in the sense that you can't reconstruct the message from the hashed output. Having the message digest doesn't allow a system cracker to determine the message in a packet. The most common way to use message digests in a cracking attempt is a brute force attack that runs millions of potential messages through the algorithm to find matching digests. When the digests match, then the system cracker has determined the message.

12.5.1 Message Digest Algorithms

The algorithms for message digests are well-known, much like cryptography algorithms. The most commonly used today include:

- ◆ MD5: MD5 was developed in 1991 by Ronald Rivest as a successor to MD4 and MD2. It produces a 128-bit output string that is generally considered quite secure. Research by RSA indicates that it would take a computer designed specifically to crack MD5 24 days to generate a collision.

- ◆ SHA-1: SHA-1 is an alternative to MD5 that was developed by NIST. It produces a 160-bit output string. Because it has a longer output string, it is considered more resilient to brute-force cracking attempts than MD5.

- ◆ HMAC: HMAC is an extension to both MD5 and SHA-1 that adds a password, further increasing the security of both algorithms.

12.5.2 Checksums

Another way to ensure message integrity is to use a *checksum*, a simpler form of a message digest. Because they are not as secure as message digests, checksums are most commonly used to indicate accidental modifications to data during transmission, rather than malicious modifications.

CRC Checksums

The most commonly used checksum algorithm is a *cyclical redundancy check* (CRC). As you can see in Figure 12.4, the algorithm performs modulo 2 division by shifting the input string to the left.

```
unsigned long doCRC (long inputString[], int polyFunction)
{
    unsigned long workingStorage = 0;
    for (int i = 1; i <= len (inputString); i++)
    {
        //--isolate leftmost bit of workingStorage
        //Logically AND with 2 ^ 31 (the value 2147483648)
        //to clear out other bits
        //Then shift to leave only leftmost bit

        unsigned short theBit = (workingStorage & 2147483648) >> 31;

        if (theBitit xor inputString[i] == 1)
            workingStorage = (workingStorage << 1) xor polyFunction);
        else
            workingStorage = workingStorage << 1;
    }
}
```

Figure 12.4 Generating a cyclical redundancy check

The polyFunction variable in Figure 12.4 is the value of a polynomial expression that varies depending on the type of CRC being performed. You can find the polynomials in Table 12.3.

Type of CRC	Polynomial Expression
CRC-8	$x^8 + x^2 + x + 1$
CRC-32	0x04C11DB7
CRC-CCITT	$x^{16} + x^{12} + x^5 + 1$
IBM-CRC-16	$x^{16} + x^{15} + x^2 + 1$
802.3 Frames	$x^{32} + x^{26} + x^{23} + x^{22} + x^{16} + x^{12} + x^{11} + x^{10} + x^8 + x^7 + x^5 + x^4 + x^2 + x + 1$

Table 12.3 Polynomial expression used in major types of CRC computations

TCP Checksums

TCP uses a checksum to verify the accurate transmission of a segment. When the destination host's recomputation of a checksum does not match what accompanies the segment, the segment is discarded and no acknowledgement segment is sent. This lack of an acknowledgement, of course, is what triggers the retransmission of the segment.

Unlike CRC checksums, the TCP checksum isn't computed using just the message. Instead, TCP first creates a *pseudo header* that is used specifically for the checksum calculation; it is *not* transmitted with the segment. (You can find the composition of the pseudo header in Table 12.4.)

TCP then places the pseudo header in front of the regular TCP header and calculates the checksum using the both the pseudo header and the entire TCP segment.

Data	Length in Bytes	Content
Source address	4	IP address of source host
Destination address	4	IP address of destination host
Reserved	1	0
Protocol	1	The protocol generating the segment (TCP)
Length	2	The length of the segment

Table 12.4 Fields in a TCP pseudo header

Note: The TCP checksum ends up as a field in the TCP header. This creates a wee bit of a problem when using that header in calculating the checksum. What to do? Use all 0s for the computation.

The beauty of the pseudo header approach is that it protects more than just the integrity of the data portion of the segment; it also catches changes in the fields in the pseudo header. In addition, because the pseudo header is constructed of data in the segment, the pseudo header doesn't need to be sent along with the segment.

12.6 Message Authentication and Digital Certificates

The final piece of the message security puzzle is authentication: Ensuring that the message actually comes from the source from which it appears to come. There are two major methods of authenticating a sender. The first involves using public key encryption without the use of a third-party *certification authority* (CA); the second uses digital certificates, which come from a CA.

12.6.1 Authenticating with PKE Alone

The fact that the encryption and decryption keys used in public key encryption are multiplicative inverses of one another makes it easy to use them to authenticate a message. Here's how it's typically done:

1. Generate a message digest.
2. Encrypt the digest using your decryption key, something only you know.
3. Send the encrypted digest with the message.
4. The recipient decrypts the digest with your public encryption key. If it decrypts successfully, then the recipient knows that it could have come only from you, since no one else could have produced something that could be *decrypted* with your public key.

12.6.2 Authenticating with Digital Certificates

If you need to perform message authentication with a destination with which you don't correspond regularly, then you may not have the destination's public key. The distribution of that key may be handled by a third party, the CA. Assuming that the third party is trusted, then this ensures that the public key definitely belongs to the intended communications partner and that it isn't a spoof provided by a system cracker.

Digital certificates are electronic messages that are issued by a CA, a company that has been paid to verify a client's public key and send it along with authentication information when requested by a potential electronic correspondent. Prior to using a digital certificate, a sender must first obtain the digital certificate service from a CA. The certificate, which typically contains the data in Table 12.5 (assuming that it adheres to the standard known as X.509), is then stored with a communications application, such as a Web server. The certificate is signed (encrypted) using the CA's private key.

Field	Comments
Version	The certificate version
Serial number	A unique identifier for the certificate
Algorithm ID	The algorithm used to generate the certificate
Issuer	The CA
Validity	The range of dates over which the certificate is valid
Subject	The owner of the certificate
Public key information	The public key algorithm and the owner's public key
Issuer unique identifier	CA's identifier
Subject unique identifier	Owner's identifier
Extensions	

Table 12.5 The structure of an X.509 digital certificate

The encrypted certificate is sent to any potential correspondent software at the beginning of a communications session (the "verifier"). The verifier must then decide whether to trust the CA. Assuming the CA is trusted, the verifier uses the CA's public key to decrypt the certificate. (The CA's public key should be readily available, such as on the CA's Web site or sent with the digital certificate). A successful decryption of the digital certificate means that the certificate was indeed issued by the CA and that the credentials contained in the certificate are valid. The verifier can then trust the owner of the certificate.

If the verifier doesn't trust the CA, then the CA must send along a digital certificate of its own, which in turn may come from a CA that the verifier trusts. If it doesn't, then the second CA must include its digital certificate, and so on. The result is a hierarchy of certificates. Eventually, there will be a root to the hierarchy, a CA that the verifier does indeed trust.

One of the things that makes trusting a digital certificate difficult is that certificates expire. How does a verifier know that a certificate is still valid? CAs maintain lists of revoked certificates. However, a verifier must contact the CA to check whether a certificate is on the list. Not only does this consume additional time during the communications session, but the lists aren't necessarily always up to date. It is therefore up to the verifier to decide what to do when the date range in the certificate has expired and the certificate is not on the revoked list. In most cases, the verifier must discard an out-of-date certificate. There is no simple way to determine whether the certificate has been renewed.

12.7 Composition and Purpose of PKI

Large organizations will need to maintain many digital certificates, at least one for each application that is engaging in secure communications. To help manage the certificates, organizations develop *public key infrastructures* (PKIs). A PKI will handle

- ◆ Issuing digital certificates to users
- ◆ PKE, including key management
- ◆ Relationships with third party CAs
- ◆ Renewing and revoking certificates

PKI is a software product that an organization purchases so that it can issue its own certificates. There are two types of PKI that the software can manage. The first, *closed PKI*, is designed for a small, known set of correspondents. For example, you might use closed PKI to secure communications with suppliers. Closed PKI is a stand-alone solution in that it doesn't require the continued services of the PKI software vendor. It does, however, require proprietary software and end-user training.

The second type of PKI, *open PKI*, is more flexible. It allows the organization to issue its own certificates and takes advantage of certificate support built into existing applications. However, open PKI requires continuing management services from the PKI software vendor. In most cases, the organization issues its own certificates to users while the vendor handles generating certificates, validation, renewal, and revocation. The vendor may also provide user authentication services.

12.8 Hands On

In this final Hands On section, we'll take a look at where you can get some of the software discussed in this chapter. In particular, we'll cover a pair of the largest third-party CAs in the world along with two encryption software packages that have freeware (and open source) versions along with the more capable commercial versions.

12.8.1 Third-Party Certificate Authorities

There are a number of commercial CAs that you can use to obtain digital certificates. In this section we'll look at some of the major, trusted firms.

VeriSign

When it comes to the Internet, few companies could be considered as pivotal as VeriSign: It administers two of the Internet's 13 backbone DNS servers. But that's not where it generates its revenue. VeriSign is in the business of providing a wide range of services—security, payment processing, communications, directory services, Web site hosting, e-mail—to the Internet community.

VeriSign is one of the most trusted CAs in the world. In addition to issuing certificates, it maintains a network of CAs that it has certified as trustworthy.

VeriSign sells its own PKI software that organizations can use to generate digital certificates. The product is a typical open PKI solution, in which organizations gain the ability to issue their own certificates, yet use VeriSign resources for validation, renewal, and revocation of certificates.

Note: VeriSign can be found at http://www.verisign.com.

RSA

RSA is the commercial home for the developers of public key encryption. Currently, it provides a wide range of security services for businesses, including acting as the root signer of digital certificates. Because

RSA's founders have solid credentials in the security community, certificates validated by RSA are almost always trusted.

Along with acting as a trusted root signer, RSA supports organizations that want to issue their own CAs under their own brand names. Like VeriSign, it sells PKI software that supports local issuing of digital certificates, yet uses the vendor's resources for certificate management.

Note: RSA can be found at http://www.rsasecurity.com.

12.8.2 Encryption Software

So you want to encrypt your data. Where in the world do you get encryption software? For small-scale implementations, there is freeware; medium to enterprise-level implementations can use the commercial version of the freeware products or purchase other proprietary software. In keeping with the goal of this book to acquaint you with open source and free software wherever possible, this section introduces two of the most commonly used encryption products that have free or open source versions available.

PGP

PGP, or *Pretty Good Privacy*, began life as a program to encrypt individual e-mails. It now also protects data stored on hard drives. The commercial versions run on Windows and Mac OS X and support a wide variety of encryption protocols, including symmetric key algorithms in Table 12.6 and the public key algorithms in Table 12.7. In addition, PGP creates message digests using the hashing algorithms in Table 12.8.

There is a freeware version of PGP that can be used by individuals at home for personal activities, by students, and by not-for-profit institutions. PGP provides PKE and digital signatures for files and e-mail; the freeware version does not include the disk-based encryption.

Installing the Software.   Setting up and using PGP is relatively straightforward, and works more or less identically under Windows and Mac OS X.

1. Run the installer, accepting whatever license agreement is appropriate.

Algorithm
AES
CAST
TripleDES
IDEA[a]
Twofish

Table 12.6 Symmetric key algorithms supported by PGP

> a. IDEA is a proprietary encryption algorithm and its inclusion in PGP places some restrictions on how the freeware version can be used.

Algorithm
Diffie-Hellman
DSS
RSA (up to 4096-bit keys)

Table 12.7 Public key algorithms supported by PGP

Algorithm
SHA-1
MD5
RIPEMD-160

Table 12.8 Hashing algorithms supported by PGP

2. PGP manages groups of public keys called keyrings. When installing for the first time, you will need to set up a new keyring (Figure 12.5).
3. For the PC, choose which components of PGP you want to install (see Figure 12.6). (Mac OS X manages everything through a single, integrated application rather than several stand-alone applications, so all components are installed by default.)

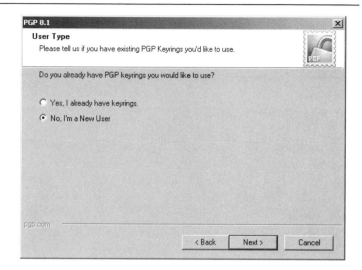

Figure 12.5   Installing PGP as a new user

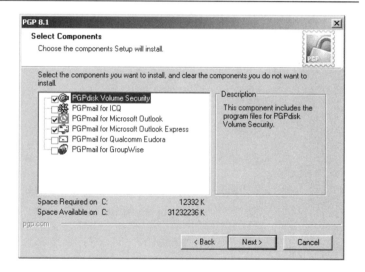

Figure 12.6   Choosing PGP components for the PC

4. Choose the location for the software (see Figure 12.7). The installer copies the required software to your hard disk.

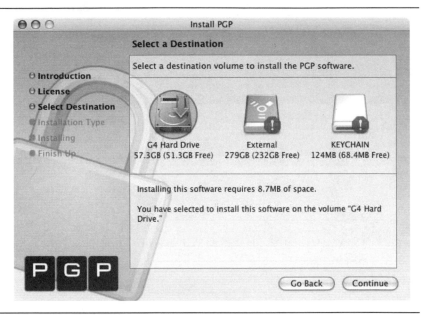

Figure 12.7   Choosing the location to install PGP

Creating a Key.   The first time you run PGP, you will be required to create a public key/private key pair. If you are using Mac OS X, launch the PGP application. If you are using Windows, run PGPKey:

1. The Key Generation Wizard appears for Windows users (see Figure 12.8); Mac OS X users get the New Key Assistant (see Figure 12.9).
2. Enter your name and e-mail address (see Figure 12.10).
3. Enter a passphrase to secure access to the key (see Figure 12.11). Notice that the longer the passphrase, the more secure PGP considers it to be.
4. PGP generates the key (see Figure 12.12).
5. The process finishes with instructions for submitting the key to a keyserver (see Figure 12.13).

Now that you have a public/private key pair, you will need to share your public key with other users so they can encrypt messages to send to

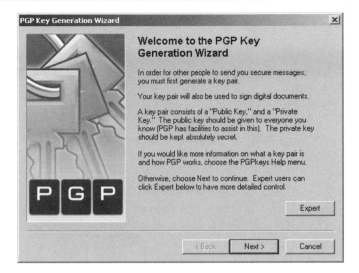

Figure 12.8   Starting the Windows Key Generation Wizard

Figure 12.9   The Mac OS X New Key Assistant

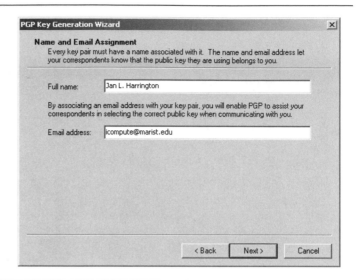

Figure 12.10   Supplying a name and e-mail address for a new key

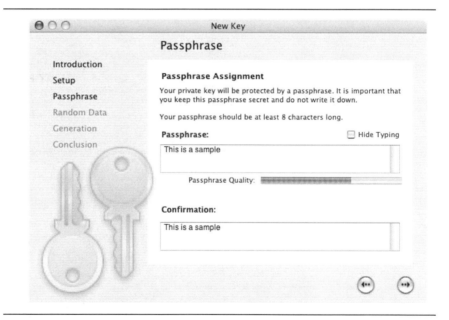

Figure 12.11   Entering a passphrase to secure a key

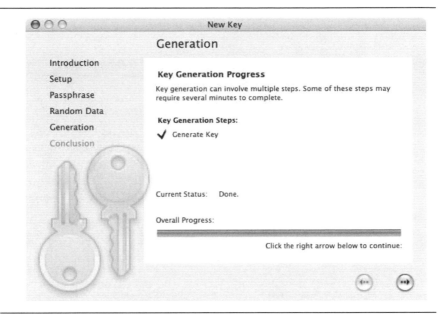

Figure 12.12   Generating the new key

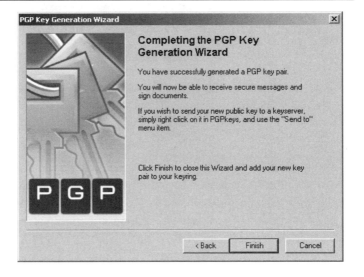

Figure 12.13   Completing the key generation process

you. You can do this by submitting your public key to a keyserver, such as the one maintained by PGP (*keyserver.pgp.com*).

Submitting Your Key to a Keyserver. To submit your key to a keyserver:

1. Select the key in the PGPkeys window.
2. Click the Send to Server icon in the toolbar or choose Server->Send To->*name of server*. PGP sends the key to the selected server and lets you know that the submission was successful.
3. Within a few minutes, you will receive an e-mail asking you to verify the key submission (see Figure 12.14). Click on the link in the e-mail.

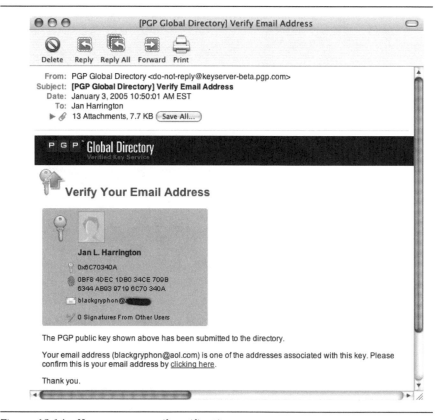

Figure 12.14   Keyserver e-mail verification message

4. A verification Web page appears in your default browser. Assuming that you did intend to send the key to the keyserver, click the Accept button (see Figure 12.15).

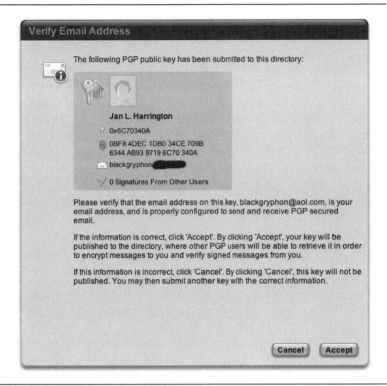

Figure 12.15   Verifying a key submission

5. When the confirmation Web page appears, click the arrow to download the verification key (see Figure 12.16).

6. PGPkeys decrypts the verification key (see Figure 12.17) and then displays a window for importing the verification key into your keyring (see Figure 12.18).

7. Select the verification key and click OK. PGPkeys will move the verification key into your keyring.

At this point, you can use the verification key to sign other keys and mark them as trusted. To do so, you click in the PGPkeys Validity column for a key (or digital signature) that is not marked as Trusted. As you can

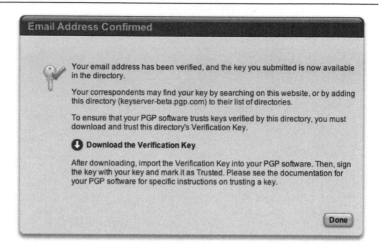

Figure 12.16   Downloading the verification key

Figure 12.17   Decrypting the verification key

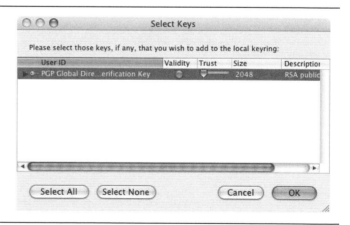

Figure 12.18   Choosing to add a verification key to a keyring

see in Figure 12.19, you can then set the options for how the key will be validated.

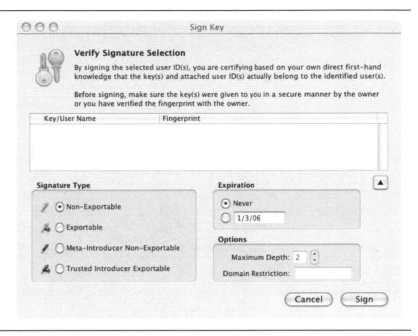

Figure 12.19   Verifying a digital signature

Finding Public Keys.   If you are going to encrypt messages to send to someone else, you need the intended recipient's public key. One way to get it is to search a keyserver for a key using the PGPkeys application's Search facility. To find someone's key:

1.   Run PGPkeys (Windows, as in Figure 12.20) or the PGP application (Mac OS X, as in Figure 12.21).
2.   Choose Search from the Server menu.
3.   Enter the search criteria (see Figure 12.22).
4.   Click the Search button. PGP searches the keyserver database and returns any matching public keys found (see Figure 12.23).

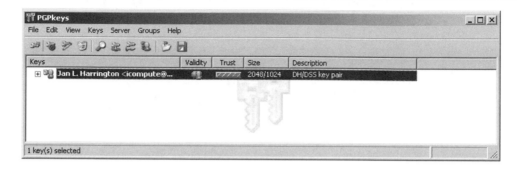

Figure 12.20   The Windows PGPkeys application

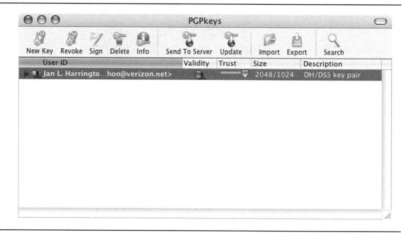

Figure 12.21   The Mac OS X PGPkeys window

5. Assuming that the key you want appears in the search result, drag
    the key into the PGPkeys window. The key will then be available to
    use for encrypting messages to the key's owner.

Encrypting Messages.   Once you have keys established and
made available to others, you can use them to encrypt e-mail and files.
The commercial version of the software contains plug-ins for popular
mail clients. However, if you are using the freeware version, then you
must perform the encryption manually.

> *Note: The commercial version of PGP will also encrypt
> files stored on disk.*

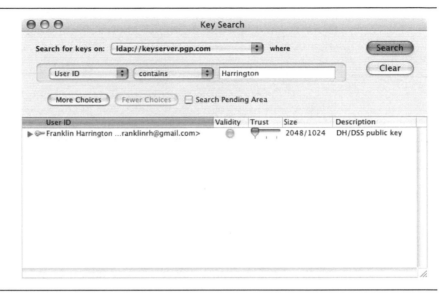

Figure 12.22   Entering search criteria for finding a public key

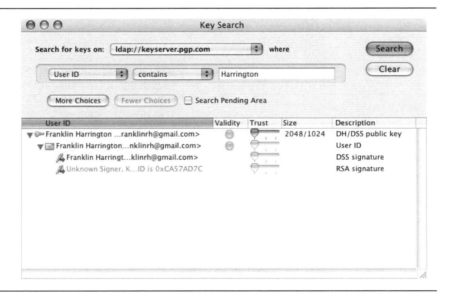

Figure 12.23   The result of a public key search

If you are using the commercial version and an e-mail client for which there is a plug-in (for example, Microsoft Outlook or Mac OS X Mail), then encrypting e-mail is relatively straightforward:

1. Compose the e-mail in the normal way.
2. Find the button or command that triggers encryption. (This varies depending on the e-mail client. For example, if you are using a Microsoft e-mail client such as Outlook or Entourage, you will find a PGP script in the Scripts menu.)
3. Send the message in the normal way.

What occurs next depends on whether PGP can find the message recipient's public key in your PGP keyring. If the public key is present, PGP uses the key automatically without further intervention on your part. However, if it can't find the public key, then a list of known PGP recipients appears (see Figure 12.24). You can then choose the recipient from the list. Keep in mind that you must have a public key for a recipient stored in your keyring before PGP can encrypt a message intended for that recipient. If the person you want isn't in the recipients list, PGP will search for a public key for that recipient and add his or her public key to your keyring.

If you are using the freeware version of PGP or an e-mail client for which a plug-in isn't available, then the encryption process is a bit more involved. For Windows, you use the PGPtray application:

1. Compose the e-mail in the normal way.
2. Click on the PGPtray icon and choose either Encrypt, Sign, or Encrypt & Sign from the Current Window menu. PGP displays a list of recipients for whom you have a public key.
3. Choose the recipient of the e-mail and click OK. You'll see the encrypted text in the body of the e-mail message, replacing the plaintext. It will look something like Figure 12.25.
4. Send the message in the normal way.

If you are using Mac OS X

1. Compose the e-mail in the normal way.
2. Select the text to be encrypted and copy it to the clipboard.
3. Switch to the PGP application.

Figure 12.24   Choosing a PGP recipient

```
-----BEGIN PGP MESSAGE-----
Version: PGP 8.1 - not licensed for commercial use: www.pgp.com

qANQR1DBwU4DIIi6YTOfzdkQCADqmXTrlVThLu/zRU0B2OrHOP4kJg61UNdZ30dw
5VASemJkA1wJqLQ4JXE/S7d81lMPOAMA/gUnf2MpVqD7gcJMVRrzZAJ9tMGeGRYE
/zRvwFAKikEZ18qeXHtAVo82Ph8QziKdsUTYBTEqy1Iy9P+fXjXkByBE4BaNFzgk
8lIOCi+vqIO8RLvjLUYHm+ZWEBjMn4udZHO4XruVvcGdD3XNN2fvvlb25jGsACft
sD8JoApUponWiyxgm6h1Y50JQzzrgxOFAuMox2+Eu+09/WxISn50O+ZIfGTFJNAu
OhCmiJed94cCOzNOCxkRE//N7LZCcy6vNoZKC2DXGoKeavVfB/96Y3DuZ/IQPdxC
FXxI2nBl60VjtoxGgAphzL2BjOzfJfBv2xOo6IAKqrPv1AsZGoaboKSvS5JJXp9K
yaAOqrXtOXeukbMrtEO62zsfx3ON84V97NOKTa/f15DeJicWIKSVcYhdp84ElpVs
ZodIjM9aGKZvmNI4QKI8asf4+J75FOcFhk2lPdxBrh363z03TSzj7dsOCCjTZ/pS
+vL+IYDdh/ntbREOrD4SogfZvVUQhbzV4eVFK57Ph7NJY2lpKd5Yjm2Qpgu1zbBK
gOxEuCYR+pUpa1aRwUZX+BRsA5XFhJ+iMnXYMqQINk4I5wHSiv6gUezvsNNwTFRj
CBC5xn2tOjOBnULmAmvElgTgIy3w2cB4Nmh1/JSN3Kk/Z7AODa94GlLwnDgIWHkC
xySZAVO7jqyk8pToZ9FNKpj6rAan
=df9J
-----END PGP MESSAGE-----
```

Figure 12.25   The ASCII version of an encrypted e-mail

4. Choose Mail->*clipboard option*, where the clipboard option is Encrypt Clipboard, Sign Clipboard, or Encrypt & Sign Clipboard.
5. Return to the e-mail client application.
6. Paste the encrypted contents of the clipboard back into the body of
   the e-mail, replacing the selected plaintext.
7. Send the e-mail in the normal way.

> *Note: For more information on PGP or to download the
> freeware version, see http://www.pgp.com.*

GPG

GPG (*GnuPG*) was developed in 1999 to provide a completely free replacement for PGP. It runs on a variety of UNIX platforms—in particular,
FreeBSD, OpenBSD, and NetBSD—as well as Windows and Mac OS X.

GPG supports all of the encryption algorithms supported by GPG, with
the exception of proprietary algorithms such as IDEA. It can also decrypt PGP 5, 6, and 7 messages.

> *Note: For more information on GPG or to download it, see
> http://www.gnupg.org.*

12.9 Summary

This chapter presents use of encryption to ensure the privacy of a message while it is in transit over a network or stored on a hard disk. It also
considers the use of message digests to ensure message integrity and
digital certifications for message authentication.

There are two major encryption methods in use today. The first uses a
single shared key to encrypt and decrypt messages. The second is a
two-key system in which one key is public and the other private. Either
key can be used to encrypt a message; only the other key can decrypt it.

Because of performance problems with two-key encryption and key
management problems with single-key systems, the two are often combined. Single keys are generated for each communication session and
secured during their exchange by two-key encryption.

Message digests are a compressed version of the message. When a message is received, the recipient recomputes the digest. If the recipient's recomputation matches what arrived with the message, then the recipient can be relatively certain that the message was not damaged or tampered with during transmission.

Digital certificates provide secure ways of exchanging the public portion of a two-key encryption system as well as verifying the identity of the sender of the message. The verification is provided by a trusted source, often a third-party certificate authority.

Appendix A: The TCP/IP Protocol Stack

In This Appendix

- ◆ The operating of a protocol stack
- ◆ The Application layer
- ◆ The Transport layer
- ◆ The Internet layer
- ◆ The Logical Link Control layer
- ◆ The MAC layer
- ◆ The Physical layer

A.0 Introduction

If you had taken a college-level data communications course in the early 1990s, you would have learned that a theoretical set of protocols developed by the International Standards Organization (ISO) would govern the language used for network message exchange for the foreseeable future. At that time, we were still unaware of the overwhelming impact the Internet would have on networking. The ISO's protocol stack—the Open Systems Interconnect (OSI) stack—has been largely overwhelmed by TCP/IP, the collection of protocols used by the Internet.

The only OSI protocols that are in wide use today are those in the lowest two levels in the protocol stack, where they have been merged into the TCP/IP protocol stack. Almost all network communications today are based on that combined set of protocols.

The purpose of this appendix is to provide an overview of the structure of the TCP/IP protocol stack and the major protocols at each layer. Details on the operation of those protocols most relevant to security issues can be found throughout the body of this book.

A.1 The Operation of a Protocol Stack

The protocols in a protocol stack are organized so that protocols that provide similar functions are grouped into a single layer. The original TCP/IP provided five layers (see Figure A.1). However, as mentioned in the introduction to this appendix, the lower two layers have incorporated protocols that were originally part of the OSI protocol stack. Notice in Figure A.2 that the TCP/IP Network layer has been split into a Logical Link Control layer and a Media Access Control (MAC) layer.

The actual exchange of bits occurs only at the Physical layer. The remaining layers are software protocols. Conceptually, each layer communicates with the matching layer on the machine with which it is exchanging messages, as in Figure A.3. However, because bits flow between machines only at the Physical layer, the actual communication is down one protocol stack, across the Physical layer, and up the receiving protocol stack (see Figure A.4).

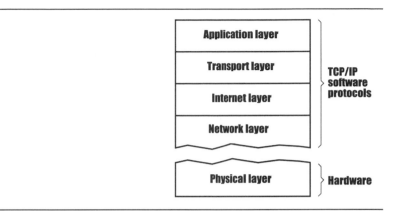

Figure A.1 The original TCP/IP protocol stack

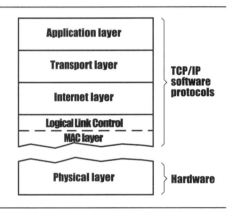

Figure A.2 The TCP/IP protocol stack incorporating OSI layers

The top three layers in the TCP/IP protocol stack are independent on the hardware a network is using. The remaining layers, however, are hardware-dependent, often meaning that there will be multiple sets of protocol specifications corresponding to different types of hardware.

As a message moves down the protocol stack on the sending machine, it is *encapsulated*: Each software layer below the Application layer adds a header (and possibly a trailer) to the message before passing it down. On the receiving end, each layer strips off the header (and trailer, if present) before passing the message up to the next layer. By the time the message reaches the Application layer on the destination machine, it has been restored to is original state.

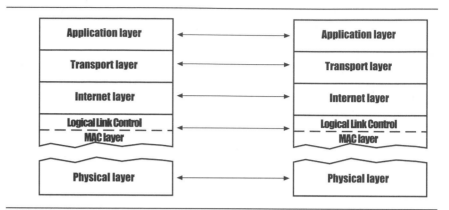

Figure A.3 Logical protocol communication

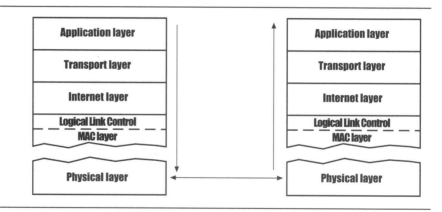

Figure A.4 The actual path for protocol communication

A.2 The Application Layer

The Application layer handles the interaction with the end user. All messages originate there. Commonly, the Application layer sends a string of text down to the Transport layer, which begins the encapsulation process.

Frequently used Application layer protocols are summarized in Table A.1. In most cases, the specifications for a protocol include the syntax and commands to be used when formulating the message. For example, to retrieve a Web page, a Web browser formats a GET command, which includes the URL of the page to be retrieved.

Acronym	Name	Purpose
HTTP	Hypertext Transport Protocol	Manage the interaction between Web clients (browsers) and Web servers
SMTP	Simple Mail Transport Protocol	Transfer e-mail messages between client (e-mail client software) and e-mail server
MIME	Multipurpose Internet Mail Extensions	Provide format conversation for e-mail extensions so they can travel over a TCP/IP network
POP3	Post Office Protocol	Handle e-mail transfer
DNS	Domain Name Server	Manage the mapping of domain names to IP addresses
	telnet	Remote system login
FTP	File Transfer Protocol	Transfer files
NNTP	Network News Transfer Protocol	Exchange Internet news articles between servers
NNRP	Network News Reading Protocol	Manage the interaction between a news client (a news reader) and a newsgroup server

Table A.1 Frequently used TCP/IP application layer protocols

Users rarely interact with the Application layer protocol directly. Instead, applications present a more user-friendly interface to the user and then formulate the communications command out of sight of the user.

A.3 The Transport Layer

The Transport layer contains two protocols: TCP (Transmission Control Protocol) and UDP (User Datagram Protocol). They are fundamentally different in the way in which they operate. TCP provides a virtual connection between the communicating Transport layers and is suitable for long messages; UDP does not provide a virtual connection and is most commonly used for short messages.

A.3.1 TCP

Because TCP sets up a logical connection between two communicating hosts and provides error detection and correction, it is said to be *reliable*. The beauty of having TCP handle the error correction is that lower level protocols need to worry only about error detection.

When TCP receives a message from the Application layer, it attaches a header to the message, creating a *segment*. You can find the structure of a segment in Figure A.5. The application layer message appears in the Data field; the rest of the segment is the header. The header fields are summarized in Table A.2.

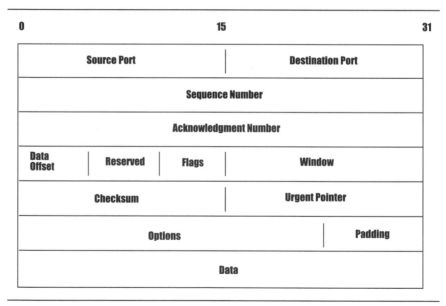

Figure A.5 The structure of a TCP segment

Field	Size	Contents
Source Port	16 bits	The TCP software port originating the message (for example, port 80 for the Web).
Destination Port	16 bits	The TCP software port to which the message is being sent.
Sequence Number	32 bits	A number indicating the segment's position in the set of segments that comprise the entire message. TCP counts the number of octets[a] in the data field of the entire message and assigns each segment a sequence number that represents the number of the first data octet in that sequence. The recipient uses the sequence numbers to reassemble a message into the correct order, even if the segments are received out of order.
Acknowledgment Number	32 bits	A number acknowledging the receipt of a segment. It is set to the number of the next octet the recipient expects to receive.
Data Offset	4 bits	The number of 32-bit units in the segment, indicating where the Data field begins.
Reserved	6 bits	Not used currently. Set to zero.
Flags (Control Bits)	6 bits	URG: Read Urgent Pointer field ACK: Read Acknowledgment field PSH: Push function RST: Connection reset SYN: Synchronize FIN: Last segment in the set
Window	16 bits	
Checksum	16 bits	A message digest (see Chapter 12 for details)
Urgent Pointer	16 points	An offset into the Data field indicating where urgent data begin. Read only if the URG flag is set.

Table A.2   Fields in a TCP header

Field	Size	Contents
Options	variable (multiple of 8 bits)	A collection of information about the segment, including the maximum segment size.
Padding	variable	Extra space added to ensure that the Data field begins on a 32-bit boundary

Table A.2 (continued) Fields in a TCP header

a. An *octet* is a byte.

TCP manages its error correction in the following way:

1.   Establish a virtual connection using the three-way handshake. (See Chapter 6 for details.)
2.   Establish an initial sequence number. It may be 0 or, more commonly, a random number.
3.   Send the first segment.
4.   When the segment is received, the recipient counts the number of octets in the Data field and adds 1. This will be the value of the next sequence number.
5.   Place the computed next sequence number in the Acknowledgment field of a segment and send it back to the sender.
6.   If the source does not receive the acknowledgment segment in a preset amount of time, retransmit the segment.

Because each segment received must be acknowledged, TCP is a *verbose protocol*. It also is not a particularly fast protocol.

A.3.2 UDP

UDP does not provide error correction and is therefore a *best effort,* or *unreliable,* protocol. UPD *datagrams* are transmitted without the provision for an acknowledgement. Because there is no virtual connection between sender and receiver, UDP is also said to be *connectionless*.

Although it might seem that UDP's unreliability might make it unsuitable for much use, it is actually able to carry a number of Application layer protocol messages. (TCP carries about 80 percent of Internet traffic;

UDP carries the rest.) The most common Application layer protocols carried by UDP datagrams can be found in Table A.3.

Acronym	Name	Comments
NFS	Network File System	Handles interactions with a remote server
proprietary		Streaming audio and video
proprietary		IP telephony
SNMP	Simple Network Management Protocol	Network management
RIP	Routing Information Protocol	Updates the routing tables in routers
DNS	Domain Name Server	Maps IP addresses to domain names

Table A.3 Application layer protocols carried by UDP datagrams

A.4 The Internet Layer

Like the Transport layer, the Internet layer has only two protocols: IP (Internet Protocol) and ICMP (Internet Control Message Protocol). The latter is used to carry IP control messages. It is IP, however, that forms the backbone of the TCP/IP protocol stack because every data-carrying message passes through it.

IP is connectionless, and therefore unreliable. (Remember that it doesn't need to do error correction because TCP is taking care of that.) IP does do error detection, however. It uses a checksum to verify that a message was received without alteration. If it determines that the message was altered, it discards the message. Because the Transport layer on the receiving machine will never receive the message, the Transport layer on the sending machine won't receive an acknowledgment for the packet, triggering a retransmission.

IP receives a segment from the Transport layer. It adds its own header and footer, creating a *packet*, which it then sends to the Data Link Layer.

IP also handles *fragmentation*, the splitting and reassembly of packets based on the largest packet size a network can handle. In addition, IP takes care of packet routing.

> *Note: Most routers don't have an entire TCP/IP protocol stack, but only the bottom layers, stopping with the Internet layer. They don't need the Transport and Application layers because they can route packets using IP.*

An IP packet encapsulates an entire Transport layer segment, placing the segment (including the Transport layer header) into its Data field, as in Figure A.6. The uses of the fields in the header are summarized in Table A.4.

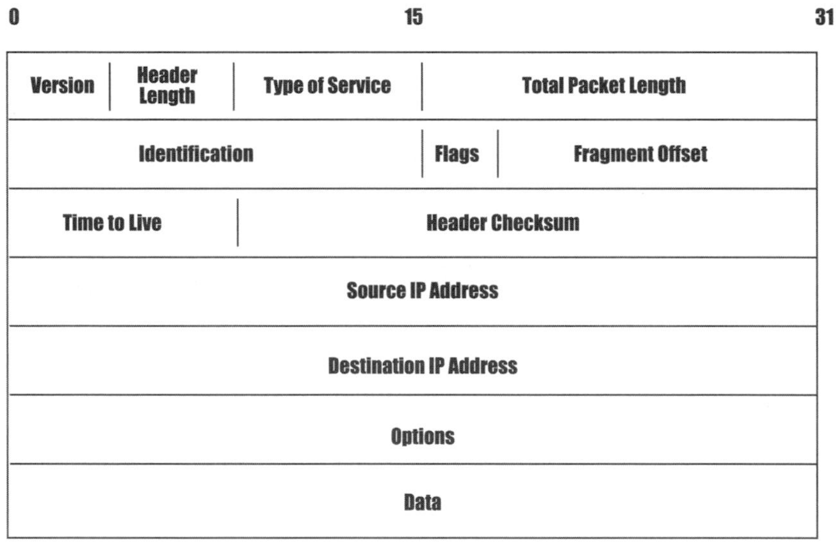

0		15		31
Version	Header Length	Type of Service	Total Packet Length	
Identification			Flags	Fragment Offset
Time to Live		Header Checksum		
Source IP Address				
Destination IP Address				
Options				
Data				

Figure A.6 The structure of an IP packet

Many of the fields in the IP header deal with fragmentation, which occurs because different types of networks have different limits on the size of packets they can carry. When a router receives a packet that is too large for the network over which it must send a packet, it extracts the data portion of the original packet and breaks it into chunks. Then it adds a complete IP header to each chunk, creating a message fragment. A packet may be fragmented many times before it reaches its destination.

Field	Size	Contents
Version	4 bits	The IP version (4 or 6).
IP Header Length	4 bits	The number of 32-bit words in the header.
Type of Service	8 bits	The type of service requested. This field currently is very rarely used.
Total Packet Length	16 bits	Number of octets in the entire packet (header and data).
Identification	16 bits	If the packet is part of a set of fragments, a value that, when combined with the source IP address, uniquely identifies this fragment.
Flags	3 bits	Flags that provide fragmentation information. If the third bit is set, there are additional fragments for the packet. If the second bit is set, the packet is not to be fragmented.
Fragment Offset	13 bits	The position of this fragment in the original packet, indicated by the number of octets it begins from the start of the original packet.
Time to Live	8 bits	The maximum number of router hops allowed for the packet. The purpose of this value is to keep a packet from circulating forever around the network. Each router decrements this value by one.
Protocol	8 bits	The type of Transport layer protocol segment being carried by the packet.
Source IP Address	32 bits	The IP address of the originator of the message.
Destination IP address	32 bits	The IP address of the message's intended recipient.
Options	Multiple of 32 bits	Used occasionally today, but usually left empty because many routers drop datagrams with nonempty options.

Table A.4 The header fields in an IP packet

However, the fragments are not reassembled into the message until all fragments have been received by the destination machine. This is because all fragments may not travel by the same route to reach their destination. In addition, differences in the speed of network links may cause the fragments to arrive out of order.

A.5 The Logical Link Control Layer

The Logical Link Control (LLC) layer provides the major interface between the hardware below and the software layers above. Because it sits between the protocols in the MAC layer that regulate access to transmission media and the rest of the protocol stack, the LLC layer lets the upper layers communicate with any form of transmission media in the same way.

The LLC layer receives an IP packet from the Internet layer and formats it into *frames*, the units that will be sent across the physical media. The organization of a frame, however, depends on the type of MAC protocol that will be used. This means that the LLC is hardware-dependent, unlike the upper layers in the protocol stack.

LLC layer protocols include specifications for the frames of many types of physical networks, including Ethernet, Token Ring (rarely used today because it has become nearly impossible to find parts to maintain the hardware), and FDDI (Fiber Distributed Data Interface). LLC also includes WAN protocols such as ATM, Frame Relay, SONET, X.25, and PPP (Point-to-Point protocol, used for communication between dial-up modems).

A.6 The MAC Layer

Regardless of the type of media used in a network—copper wire, fiber optics, or radio waves—the physical network is a shared highway. Something must regulate which host on a network can transmit at any given time so that multiple transmissions don't corrupt one another. That is the job of the Media Access Control, or MAC, layer.

The most widely used MAC protocol today is Ethernet, which employs *Carrier Sense Multiple Access/Collision Detection* (CSMA/CD) to regulate access to wire. Assuming that host A wants to send a message to host B, CSMA/CD works in the following way:

1. Host A checks the network media to see if it is in use. When in use, the media has a carrier signal that a host can detect.

2. If the bus is in use, host A waits a random amount of time and then returns to Step 1. Otherwise, it places its frame onto the wire.

3. Host A listens to the network media while it is transmitting. If another host has transmitted at exactly the same time, a *collision* will have occurred and both frames will be corrupted. Host A will transmit a jamming signal to alert all other hosts that a collision has occurred. The other hosts detect the "jabber."

4. If a collision has occurred, host A waits a random amount of time and returns to Step 1.

5. The frame travels to the network's hub or switch. If the network has a hub, then the frame is broadcast out all the hub's ports. All attached devices read the destination address of the frame and all, except host B, discard the frame. If the network has a switch, then the switch either routes the frame out the appropriate port so that it can reach its destination or, if the switch doesn't know where the destination is located, broadcasts the frame out all ports except the incoming port.

> *Note: The word "wire" can be a bit funny when used to describe network media. To many data communications people, "wire" is any media, even if it refers to optical media or a wireless data path.*

Reality Check: The Token Ring MAC protocol avoids collisions by requiring a host to have possession of the network's single token to transmit. Although a well-performing protocol, Token Ring is essentially dead today. If you have a wired LAN, then you can use Ethernet, or Ethernet, or Ethernet, and if you don't like those choices, you can have Ethernet instead. This is just another instance where the best technology doesn't necessarily win in the marketplace. Like Beta video tapes, Token Ring is a better performer than its competition. For example, Ethernets tend to bog down when loaded to more than 80 percent of available bandwidth where Token Ring networks tend to function much better under heavy loads. But Token Ring was very expensive compared to Ethernet: A Token Ring adapter card for a PC cost around $300 at the same time that an Ethernet card cost $15.

Most wireless LANs use a slight variation of CSMA/CD to regulate media access: CSMA/CA, where the CA stands for Collision Avoidance. The major difference between CSMA/CD and CSMA/CA is that CSMA/CA does not check for collisions after a frame is transmitted. (It is virtually impossible to detect collisions on a wireless network, at least in any efficient fashion.) Instead, each time a host needs to wait for the media to become idle, the wait time increases, up to a maximum that usually varies with the network load.

A.7 The Physical Layer

At the bottom of the TCP/IP protocol stack lies the Physical layer, the only layer that specifies hardware. It consists of protocols that lay out the types of hardware over which network signals will travel.

There are literally hundreds of Physical layer protocols. Those that you will encounter most frequently include the Ethernet protocols:

- ◆ 10BASE-T: Largely outdated, 10BASE-T describes the transmission of data at up to 10 Mbs over copper wire (usually Cat 5 cabling).

- ◆ 100BASE-T: Supporting speeds of up to 100 Mbs over Cat 5 cabling, 100BASE-T is also known as Fast Ethernet. It is the common standard used in most networks today for connecting end user equipment and slow network-attached peripherals (for example, printers) to switches or other interconnection devices.

♦ 100BASE-FX: Specifies the operation of Fast Ethernet using fiber optic cabling.

♦ 1000BASE-X: Gigabit Ethernet (up to 1 Gbs) runs primarily over fiber optic cable and is used most commonly to connect servers and server farms to interconnection hardware. In most cases, end user equipment isn't fast enough to take advantage of Gigabit Ethernet speeds and therefore putting it on the desktop would be an unnecessary expense. Gigabit Ethernet can also now run over copper wire for short distances.

Standards for 10 Gb Ethernet were ratified in 2002. Although some equipment is available for creating networks utilizing this speed, it is significantly more expensive than even Gigabit Ethernet and therefore has yet to be widely deployed.

> *Note: There are two older Ethernet standards—10BASE5 for thick coax cabling and 10BASE2 for thin coax cabling—that are virtually extinct. However, there is a slim chance that you might encounter a legacy network using coaxial cables.*

Appendix B: TCP and UDP Ports

In This Appendix

◆ A table of well-known ports
◆ A selection of a few widely used registered ports

B.0 Well-Known Ports

Software ports are used by TCP/IP to associate segments with application programs running on a host that receives a message. The *well-known ports* are those used primarily by communications processes and other privileged applications, and have numbers between 0 and 1023.

> *Note: Application developers can register ports for their programs with IANA. Registered ports are in the range of 1024 through 49151. Ports between 49152 and 65536 are dynamic and/or private.*

The following table contains a selection of well-known ports that you may want your firewall to block. In almost all cases, both TCP and UDP have the same port number assignments. Registered Ports

Port	Protocol or Application
1	TCP Port Service Multiplier (TCPMUX)
5	Remote Job Entry (RJE)
7	ECHO
17	Quote of the Day
18	Message Send Protocol (MSP)
20	FTP (default data port)
21	FTP (control port)
22	SSH Remote Login Protocol
23	Telnet
24	Any private mail system
25	SMTP
29	MSG ICP
35	Any private print server
37	Time
38	Remote Access Protocol
39	Remote Location Protocol

Table B.1   Well-known TCP and UDP ports

Port	Protocol or Application
41	Graphics
42	Host Name Server
43	WhoIs
44	Message Processing Module (MPM) Flags Protocol
49	Login Host Protocol (Login)
53	DNS
57	Any private terminal access
58	XNS Mail
59	Any private file service
65	Terminal Access Control Access Control System (TACACS) Database Service
66	Oracle SQL*NET
67, 68	Bootstrap Protocol Server
69	Trivial File Transfer Protocol
70	Gopher
71, 72, 73, 74	Remote Job Service
75	Any private dial out service
77	Any private RJE service
79	Finger
80	HTTP
80	Nimda[a]
84	Common Trace Facility
85	MIT ML Device
86	Micro Focus COBOL
87	Any private terminal link
88	Kerberos
92	Network Printing Protocol
93	Device Control Protocol

Table B.1 (continued) Well-known TCP and UDP ports

Port	Protocol or Application
103	X,400 Standard
107	Remote Telnet Service
109	Post Office Protocol (POP2)
110	Post Office Protocol (POP3)
115	Simple File Transfer Protocol
117	UUCP Path Service
118	SQL Services
119	Network News Transfer Protocol (NNTP)
123	Network Time Protocol
129	Password Generator Protocol
137	NETBIOS Name Service
138	NETBIOS Datagram Service
139	NETBIOS Session Service
143	Internet Message Access Protocol (IMAP4)
150	SQL*NET
152	Background File Transfer Protocol
153	SGMP
156	SQL Server
158	PCMail Server
161	SNMP
162	SNMP TRAP
197	Directory Location Service (DLS)
201–208	AppleTalk
209	Quick Mail Transfer Protocol
213	IPX
389	Lightweight Directory Access Protocol (LDAP)
395	Novell Netware over IP
402	Genie Protocol

Table B.1 (continued) Well-known TCP and UDP ports

Port	Protocol or Application
407	Timbuktu
443	HTTPS
444	Simple Network Paging Protocol
445	Microsoft-DS
445	Sasser[b]
458	Apple QuickTime
512	biff
513	login (remote login using telnet)
514	who
515	shell
546	DHCP Client
547	DHCP Server
563	SNEWS
569	MSN
591	FileMaker 6.0 Web Sharing
592	Eudora
666	Doom
729–731	IBM NetView
749, 750	Kerberos
989, 990	FTP data over TLS/SSL
991	Netnews Administration Services
992	telnet over TLS/SSL
993	imap4 over TLS/SSL
994	irc over TLS/SSL
995	pop3 over TLS/SSL

Table B.1 (continued) Well-known TCP and UDP ports

a. This worm uses the same port as HTTP, which is, of course, an unauthorized use of the port.
b. Another piece of malware using a port without authorization.

In this section you will find a table containing a selection of widely used or important registered ports. Note those that represent malware are not registered, but are nonetheless using ports in the registered ports range. Also notice that the heaviest port users are network games!

Port	Name
1027	ICQ
1080	SOCKS
1214	Kazaa
1337	WASTE (Encrypted file sharing program)
1524	Trinoo (TCP)
2555	RTSP Streaming Media Proxy
3001	Remote Control Service
3128	HTTP (Used by web caches)
3150	DeepThroat
3306	MySQL
3380	SOCKS Proxy Server
3381	Telnet Proxy Server
3382	WWW Proxy Server
3383	FTP Proxy Server
3384	POP3 Proxy Server
3385	SMTP Server
3521	Netrek
5000	Universal Plug and Play
5190–5194	AOL and AOL Instant Messenger
5432	Postgres
5800	VNC (Remote desktop protocol for use over HTTP)
5900	VNC (Remote desktop protocol)
5999	EverQuest (UDP)
6000	X11

Table B.2   Selected registered TCP ports

6667	IRC	
7000	EverQuest (TCP)	
8000	iRDMI	
8080	HTTP (Alternative port often used when a second Web server is running on the same machine as a Web server using port 80.)	
8998	Sobig.F	
26000	Quake	
27444	Trinoo (UDP)	
27500	Quake World	
27665	Trinoo (TCP)	
27910	Quake II	
27960	Quake III	
31335	Trinoo (UDP)	
31337	Back Orifice	
34555	Trinoo (UDP)	
35555	Trinoo (UDP)	

Table B.2 (continued) Selected registered TCP ports

B.1 Port List References

There are several places to find complete lists of port assignments:

♦ Complete list of assigned ports:
   http://www.iana.org/assignments/port-numbers

♦ Ports used by Trojan horses:
   http://www.simovits.com/trojans/trojans.html

♦ Searchable database of assigned ports:
   http://ports.tantalo.net/

Appendix C: Security Update Sites

In This Appendix

◆ Web sites to visit to keep up to date on security matters

C.0 Professional Security Update Sites

There are two major Web sites that monitor system cracker activity across the Internet:

- *http://www.cert.org*: CERT (located in the Carnegie Mellon Software Engineering Institute) is a federally funded security research and development center. The CERT site posts security alerts, papers on the result of security research, and security tips for end users. Documents on the site identify threats, describe how they work, and suggest remedies. CERT also offers professional training courses.

- *http://isc.sans.org*: SANS is a training institute that also monitors Internet security threats. Its Internet Storm Center site also presents an analysis of various threats over the recent past.

Other professional sites include:

- *http://www.auscert.org.au/render.html?cid=1*: The Australian Computer Emergency Response Team.

- *http://ciac.llnl.gov/cgi-bin/index/bulletins*: Computer Incident Advisory Capability (CIAC) from the U.S. Department of Energy.

- *http://www.secureroot.com/*: A wide variety of links to descriptions of types of attacks, current security advisories, forums, exploits categories by platform, and so on.

- *http://www.antiphishing.org*: The site of the Anti-Phishing Working Group, an organization the monitors phishing attempts and provides advice on how to avoid being trapped by them.

C.1 Other Sites of Interest

- *http://www.staysafeonline.info/*: The National Cyber Security Alliance provides security tips for small business and home end users. The information there may be useful as part of a user education program.

♦ *http://securityresponse.symantec.com/*: Symantec, a developer of security software, provides updates on the most recent viruses to emerge. The page also includes links to other security advisories, as well as freely available malware removal tools.

♦ *http://us.mcafee.com/virusInfo/default.asp?cid=10371*: McAfee, another developer of security software, also provides information on current virus threats and provides removal tools.

♦ *http://www.sophos.com*: Sophos is another security software developer whose Web site contains information about the latest virus threats.

♦ *http://www.antionline.com/*: AntiOnline is a place to meet others concerned with computer security. Answers to security questions on message boards are rated.

♦ *http://csrc.nist.gov/*: The Computer Security Resource Center (CSRC) of the National Institute of Standards and Technology (NIST) provides information on standards, testing, research, and so on.

♦ *http://www.microsoft.com/athome/security/protect/ default.aspx*: Microsoft's Protect Your PC site.

♦ *http://www.infosyssec.com/*: InfoSysSec is a portal to a wide variety of security resources.

347

Advanced Encryption Standard (AES): A symmetric key encryption method that supports up to 256-bit keys.

Audit policy: A feature of the Windows operating system that allows a user to filter which system events are recorded in the system logs.

Authentication: Verifying that the sender of a message is who he or she claims to be.

Authentication header: An IPSec protocol that takes care of verifying the identify of a message sender.

Best effort protocol: A data communications protocol that does not provide error correction.

Blind TCP spoofing: An attack in which the system cracker intercepts the SYN/ACK message from a destination host during the establishment of a TCP connection. The cracker then sends its own SYN/ACK to the origination host and from then on continues to impersonate the destination.

Block substitution cypher: A substitution cypher that applies a multiple character key to multiple characters of a message at one time.

Brute force: Attacks on a computer system that involve repeatedly trying to access the computer through entry points, such as trying groups of dial-up numbers, user names, and passwords in the hopes that something will work.

Buffer: A portion of main memory set aside to hold an input value.

Buffer overflow: An attack that takes advantage of a programming error. It allows a system cracker to insert his or her own program code and execute any program on the compromised computer.

Callback: A technique for securing dial-up network access in which the remote modem dials the network modem, establishes the user's identify, and then signs up. The network modem then calls the remote computer at a number previously stored on the network.

Carrier sense multiple access/collision detection (CSMA/CD): The MAC layer protocol used by Ethernet to control which host has access to the transmission media at any given time.

Certificate of authority (CA): The certification by a third-party agency that a computer is a trusted host.

Certification authority (CA): A trusted company that issues certificates of authority.

Challenge handshake authentication protocol (CHAP): An authentication protocol designed for dial-in access.

Checksum: A value appended to a message to ensure message integrity. A checksum is computed from the contents of a message. It is recomputed from the message at the message's destination and compared to the value that accompanied the message. If the checksums match, message integrity is ensured.

Connection-oriented protocol: A data communications protocol, such as TCP, that creates a virtual circuit for the duration of a message exchange.

Connectionless protocol: A data communications protocol, such as UDP, that does not create a virtual circuit. Message units are independent rather than part of a large message.

Cracker: In the hacker community, someone who attempts to gain unauthorized access to computer resources.

Cyclical redundancy check (CRC): A type of checksum used to ensure message integrity.

Daemon: A background process that typically performs operating system services. Some daemons may, however, be launched by software installed by system crackers and therefore may be running without the knowledge of the computer user.

Data encryption standard (DES): A symmetric key encryption algorithm using 64-bit keys once endorsed by the U.S. government as a standard. Because DES keys are so easy to crack, it has been replaced by AES.

Datagram: The message until prepared by UDP by encapsulating an Application layer protocol.

Denial of service (DoS): An attack that attempts to prevent legitimate users from accessing a computing resource. It may overwhelm a network by consuming most of the available bandwidth or it may attack a server by overwhelming it with processes or causing it to crash.

Digital signature: A compressed transformation of a message such that a small change in the message causes a large change in the digital signature; a message digest.

Disk mirroring: Keeping an automatic backup hard drive that is written to at the same time as the primary hard drive. Disk mirroring is most typically performed by RAID hardware and/or software.

Distributed DoS: A distributed denial of service attack; a DoS attack launched from more than one source computer.

DMZ: A part of a network that isolates a machine exposed to an internet (specifically, the Internet) from the internal network.

DNS spoofing: An attack that redirects users to a Web site other than the one to which a domain name is actually registered.

Encapsulating Security Payload (ESP): An IPSec protocol that provides encryption for the data field of an IP packet.

Encapsulation: The process of taking a message unit and placing a header (and possible trailer) around it, putting the original message unit unchanged into the data field of the new unit. Encapsulation is used at all layers of the TCP/IP protocol stack except the Physical layer.

Encryption: Changing data so that it is unintelligible to casual observation.

Extensible Authentication Protocol (EAP): An 802.11 protocol that governs the authentication of wireless clients to base stations.

Firewall: Software that can be configured to block external traffic from entering a local network. Firewalls may filter packets by the port to which they are addressed or by providing proxies for specific applications.

Firewall appliance: A stand-alone piece of hardware running firewall software.

Fragmentation: Breaking a frame into smaller pieces so that it can travel over a network that has a smaller maximum frame size than the network over which the frame traveled most recently.

Frame: The message unit created by Logical Link Control layer protocols by encapsulating IP packets.

Generic routing encapsulation (GRE): The process used by PPTP to secure a PPP frame.

GnuGP (GPG): An open source encryption method that includes no proprietary encryption algorithms.

Hacker: In the hacker community, someone who can write an ingenious bit of software. In the general population, someone who attempts to gain unauthorized access to computer resources.

Hashing: A process by which a message is compressed. Because the same algorithm is used to produce the hash each time, the same message will generate the same hash whenever it is processed by the algorithm.

Honeypot: A trap set for a potential system cracker. It looks like a real host to attract the cracker but contains no sensitive data. The idea is to get the cracker to spend time with the honeypot, leaving real network resources untouched.

Initialization vector: For single (symmetric) key algorithms that include changing the key each time it is used, the initial key that begins the encryption process.

Insertion attack: An attack on a wireless network in which an authorized piece of hardware is inserted into the network.

Interception attack: An attack on a wireless network in which a system cracker intercepts traffic on the network.

Intrusion detection system (IDS): Software that monitors network traffic and alerts network administrators when an unauthorized attempt to gain access to network resources is detected.

Intrusion prevention system (IPS): Software that monitors network traffic and attempts to identify cracking attacks before they penetrate the network's outer defenses.

IPSec: A protocol added to TCP/IP to handle data security, particularly for VPNs and SSL.

IPSec NAT traversal (NAT-T): A method of network address translation that is compatible with L2TP VPNs.

IP source routing: Routing of a message performed on the computer originating the message rather than by routers along the path traveled by the message.

IP spoofing: A type of attack in which the cracker makes a packet appear to come from a trusted host to convince a recipient to download malware or visit a spoofed Web site.

Layer 2 tunneling protocol (L2TP): A VPN technology that can work over WANs that use protocol stacks other than TCP/IP.

Lightweight Extensible Authentication Protocol (LEAP): A proprietary wireless authentication protocol developed by Cisco that has been superseded by PEAP.

Loadable kernel module (LKM): A compiled UNIX module that can be loaded into RAM while the OS is running to extend the functionality of the OS.

Log analyzer: Software that analyzes and presents the contents of computer system logs.

Macro virus: A virus that is embedded in macros written for Microsoft Office appications.

Malicious cache poisoning: A type of DNS spoofing attack that involves modification of the data in the cache of a domain name server.

Malware: Malicious software such as viruses, worms, and Trojan horses.

Man in the middle: A type of attack in which the system cracker intercepts the packets in a communication, terminates the session with the server, and impersonates the server to continue communication with the client.

Message digest: A hash of all or part of a message from which the message cannot be reconstructed. Used to ensure message integrity, the digest is appended to the message when sent and recomputed from the message when received. If the two hashes match, then message integrity is ensured.

Message integrity: Ensuring that the contents of a message are not changed while the message is in transit over a network.

MS-CHAP: The Microsoft version of CHAP.

Network address translation (NAT): Translating an incoming IP address—one that is exposed to the Internet—and translating it to a local IP address that is hidden from the Internet. NAT is most commonly performed by routers.

Network mapping: The process of discovering the IP addresses that are actually functioning on a network.

Network security: Protecting data that are stored on or that travel over a network against both accidental and intentional unauthorized disclosure or modification.

One-way hash: The output of a hashing algorithm from which the original message cannot be regenerated.

Open port: A port for which packets will be accepted.

Packet: The message unit created by IP when it encapsulates a TCP segment or UDP datagram.

Password hash: The encrypted form of a password, stored in the Registry of current Windows operating system versions and in all versions of UNIX. Password hashes are never decrypted. Instead, the password entered by a user is encrypted and compared to the stored password hash to determine whether a match exists.

Password list file: A file with a .pwl extension used in Windows 95 and 98 to store passwords.

Password synchronization: A technique for allowing users to log onto a network once and gain access to all network resources to which they are entitled.

Pingpong: An attack in which a system cracker spoofs the IP return address in a UDP datagram. The spoofed address is usually a host on the victim's network. The victim machine responds with a random string of characters, which then goes to the host on the same network. The two machines continue to send meaningless strings of characters back and forth.

Plaintext: The unencrypted version of a message.

Point-to-point protocol (PPP): The most common protocol used to govern traffic between two modems.

Point-to-point tunneling protocol (PPTP): A dial-up protocol used for VPNs.

Polymorphic: A virus that can change itself as it propagates so that each copy looks a bit different from all others.

Port: In TCP/IP terminology, a software identifier that corresponds to a specific application or protocol running on a host.

Pretty Good Privacy (PGP): An encryption method with a freeware version used to encrypt e-mail and data stored on hard disks.

Privacy: The need to restrict access to data.

Protected Extensible Authentication Protocol (PEAP): A proprietary wireless authentication protocol developed by Cisco, Microsoft, and RSA Security.

Proxy server: Software that uses network address translation (NAT) to hide local network addresses from the Internet.

Pseudo header: A header generated by TCP to use in computing a checksum for a TCP segment. The pseudo header is not transmitted with the segment.

Public key encryption (PKE): A two-key encryption algorithm in which one key is made public so messages can be encrypted and sent to the key's owner. The second key is kept secret and used to decrypt the message.

Public key infrastructure (PKI): The software and other technology resources needed to manage an encryption program.

Reimage: Restore a hard disk to a known state by replacing the entire contents of the disk with a clean copy held on a server somewhere else on the network.

Reliable protocol: A data communications protocol that provides error detection and correction.

Remote authentication dial-in user service (RADIUS): A stand-alone server that provides user authentication. Although originally intended only for dial-in users, it now can authenticate users accessing the network in any way.

Robust security network (RSN): A wireless security protocol included in the 802.11i standard that allows access points and clients to determine which type of encryption will be used during a communications session.

Root kit: A collection of programs that allow a system cracker to access a compromised computer at any desired time and gain root or administrator privileges.

Secure sockets layer (SSL): A protocol used primarily for the safe transmission of data from a Web page to a Web server, but also used in the implementation of VPNs.

Security: What you do to ensure the privacy of data.

Security audit: A process that determines how well a network is protected against a variety of threats.

Security policy: A document that lays out the philosophy and structure of an organization's security efforts.

Security association: An IPSec process through which a third-party agency certifies that a computer is a trusted host.

Segment: The message unit created by TCP when it encapsulates an Application layer message.

Service set ID (SSID): The identification word or phrase that wireless access points broadcast to identify themselves.

Shadow computer: A machine that is identical to a primary server that can become the primary server if the current primary goes down for any reason.

Shadow passwords: The UNIX technique of storing encrypted passwords in a secondary file, rather than in the world-readable */etc/passwd* file.

Shared secret: A password or passphrase known to the two parties engaged in a message exchange.

Single key encryption: Encryption methods that use a single key shared by both partners in a message exchange.

Single sign-on: Allowing a user to sign onto a network with one password that gives the user access to all system resources to which he or she has been given access.

Social engineering: Tricking someone with confidential information into releasing that information by convincing the victim that the information release is authorized or required in some way.

Spoofing: Actions that make an electronic transmission appear to originate from somewhere that it does not.

Spyware: Malware that collects private information with the knowledge or consent of the person whose information is being collected and uses the victim's own Internet bandwidth to transmit the information.

Stream substitution cypher: An encryption method in which one character is substituted for another.

Strong password: A password constructed in such a way that it is unlikely that a system cracker could break it.

Substitution cypher: An encryption method in which characters are substituted for other characters.

Symmetric key encryption: Encryption methods that use a single key shared by both partners in a message exchange.

SYN flood: An early form of DoS attack in which an attacker sends TCP connection requests to a server with invalid IP return addresses. The server sends the SYN/ACK messages and keeps the connection open, waiting for an ACK message that will never arrive.

Temporal key integrity protocol (TKIP): An encryption protocol that includes a method for changing the encryption key with each packet sent during a communications session.

Three-way handshake: The method by which TCP establishes a virtual connection between communicating systems. The first host sends a SYN message. The second responds with SYN and ACK messages. The first completes the handshaking by sending an ACK message.

Transport Layer Security (TLS): A protocol for creating a host-to-host encrypted tunnel for use during the authentication phase of a network connection. As a replacement for SSL, it can be used to secure an entire network session.

Transport mode: An IPSec mode in which data encryption is provided from one host to the other.

TripleDES: A version of DES that uses a 192-bit key that is actually three DES 64-bit keys. Although more secure that the original DES, it is not as secure as AES.

Trojan horse: A form of malware that resides quietly on a victim's hard disk until activated remotely by a system cracker.

Tunnel: A secure path between two network devices, commonly connected by the Internet. Tunnels are usually associated with VPNs and may run from one host to another, or may run from one server to another.

Tunnel mode: An IPSec mode in which a secure tunnel is provided from server to server, securing transmission over the Internet.

Unreliable protocol: A data communications protocol that may provide error detection but in any case does not provide error correction.

Verbose protocol: A protocol, such as TCP, that has a great deal of overhead and generates a lot of network traffic.

Virtual private network (VPN): Technology that allows remote users to use the Internet (or other internet) to connect to a local network securely, giving users the same access they would have if they were located on the network's premises.

Virus: A self-propagating piece of malware that runs as an executable program on a target machine.

War dialing: Using software to dial many telephone numbers in an attempt to find those that reach computer systems.

War driving: Driving through an area with wireless equipment looking for wireless networks to which an attacker can connect.

Well-known port: A TCP/UDP port number in the range 0 through 1023.

Wi-Fi Protected Access (WPA): A security protocol for wireless networks that emerged as a more secure alternative to WEP.

WiMAX: The new set of standards (802.16) being developed for large wireless networks, covering up to 50 km.

Wireless Fidelity (Wi-Fi): The standards that govern wireless networks.

Wired equivalency privacy (WEP): The security protocol that is part of the 802.11b wireless network standard. Its implementation is considered poor and not particularly effective.

Worm: A self-propagating piece of malware that uses up system resources but generally does not damage anything stored on the computer.

Zone transfer: The transfer of DNS information from a DNS server to another computer (not necessarily a DNS server).

Index

Photo Credits